BREAK GLASS

UNABRIDGED AND COMPLETE

In Case of Genocide Break Glass – How We End Genocidal Indifference.

By

RICHARD C. O'BRIEN

Edited by

Alice Peck

Contributions by: Sasha Taurke:
Father's Arrest in the Middle of the Night.

Special Thank You for Extended Quotation:
Danny Smith: *Wallenberg*
Christopher Browning: *Ordinary Men.*

Cover Design: Arif Laeeq. Photo Credit and Thank You:
armeniapedia.org, Nella Questione Armena, Padua, Italy 1962,
Saharatribune.com and Steve Halperson

BREAK GLASS

UNABRIDGED AND COMPLETE

In Case of Genocide Break Glass – How We End Genocidal Indifference.

By

RICHARD C. O'BRIEN

DEDICATION

I dedicate this book to the millions and millions of people who had their lives cruelly and unfairly taken from them and their families that suffered their loss.

I dedicate this work to the heroes who combat genocide, human rights violations, starvation, famine and those who are practitioners of conflict prevention, intervention and resolution, wherever you are, near and far.

I also, of course, dedicate this work to my parents John and Susan who taught me the lesson of exercising moral imperative through action, and my children, Annalise and John, who stole my heart.

Lastly, and not unimportantly, I dedicate this book to you, the reader. I hope this book inspires you to go out and do something meaningful and impactful. You are humanity's best hope. It is my hope that there are those among you who will start anew the next generation of genocide prevention, or famine prevention, or conflict prevention work. Godspeed.

- Richard O'Brien, At a
  Starbucks, DMV.
  August 2023.

Break Glass Contents: In Case of Genocide Break Glass - How We End Genocidal Indifference.

■■■

BOOK TWO: GENOCIDE PREVENTION MANUAL.

CHAPTER ONE:

"HELP US WE ARE BEING MASSACRED."

The following was the first action the Center for the Prevention of Genocide took during an ongoing massacre.

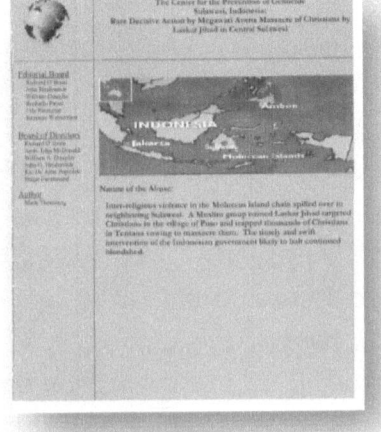

"Help Us We Are Being Massacred." - Sulawesi, Indonesia.

It was exactly 1:45 am when I noticed the newly arrived email; it caught my attention immediately with the title 'Help us we are being massacred.' As I quickly read the email, I realized that all of the theory behind our center was about to be put into

11

practice. The email told how at that moment on the opposite end of the world, villagers were running with children and belongings in hand from the smoldering ruins of the villages near Poso, on the Island of Sulawesi, Indonesia. 'Our coffee was from Sulawesi' I thought. Some of the villagers of Poso had not been as fortunate as those who were seeking to reach the protection of the larger township of Tentena. Swift on their trail, leaving bodies and devastation, raping and pillaging like a scene out of medieval times, were the Laskar Jihad warriors who had sworn revenge on the Christian population of Sulawesi in retribution for Christian attacks on Muslims the year before in the Moluccas Islands.

The email was from a priest I would get to know better before he was to die, as well as two other witnesses to the horror that was speeding through the tropical Indonesia jungle toward Tentena. They estimated the Laskar Jihad militia between nine hundred to several thousand attackers as they pursued unarmed Christians. When the fleeing Christians arrived in Tentena they found that the township was neither armed nor defendable – there were simply too few weapons. Compounding the horror in the jungle, Tentena was being surrounded and sealed off with yelled promises from the unseen militia voices that they were going to massacre all Christians before Christmas. It was now December the second, 1:50 am. I walked over to the glass framed sign hanging on the wall that read, "In Case of Genocide – Break Glass" and took it down.

As I read the instructions, I realized we created them for a full staff. Alone I settled in to use the phone and called one board member and one volunteer.

Mark Thornburg was a delightful and capable young man with a quick wit and a studied Carl Sagan delivery. His voice was sonorous, deep and deliberate as I woke him from his slumber.

"To what do I owe the pleasure of a call from the Center for the Prevention of Genocide in the middle of the night?" He intoned.

I told him about the massacre email. He cleared his head quickly and asked a few pertinent questions. I then identified our two main priorities. First, we needed to know whether anyone else had the story - any of the wire services or major publications. If so, that took the pressure off of us to confirm it and get it out to the media. Second, I explained, we needed to get neutral third party confirmation before we could publish any part of the story. Mark stretched at the other end of the phone and said,

"I'll begin working on the wire services and press reports and I'll let you know soon if anyone has it."

"That's why I pay you the big money." I said.

"In-deed. Georgetown out." Mark booted his computer and began working feverishly to pull up all wire services, AP, Reuters, UPI and press from the area.

I opened the desk drawer and pulled out our three phone cards. My first instinct was to call the US Embassy in Jakarta in the Capital of Indonesia to see if they had any word on the Sulawesi situation. The first card died before I could leave my first message.

13

I worked my way through the minutes on the second card through the Embassy operator trying several different

Embassy officials to no avail. Everyone in the embassy was apparently out to lunch or wasn't answering. The final phone card. After trying a few more extensions with no luck I turned to the U.S. Embassy operator.

"Operator, what's your name?"

"Mary, sir." She had the voice of a kindly grandmother.

"Okay Mary, I am going to have to rely on you."

"What do you mean sir?" she gently prodded

"Well, Mary this is going to be the most important phone call you're going to take this month. Right now there is a massacre being reported on the Island of Sulawesi. Now we don't know the sources who are giving us the information personally and don't know how credible they are so we can't release it to the press. But if we can get a credible person at the Embassy who can confirm the facts then we can release the information. By being able to do that, we can bring some attention to the area and maybe get the right people to intervene to help save those lives.

"Mary, we are just a small organization, and my phone card is literally ready to run out so we need to find someone fast. I need you to put your thinking cap on and think, who can you get a hold of that would be in a position to know whether this is happening."

"Oh, my, this is important, isn't it?" She sounded concerned.

"Oh, let me think, let me think." She said softly and paused.

"I have an idea. Would the Counselor General on the Island of Surabaya help? Surabaya is the Island next to Sulawesi."

"Mary he's perfect. If he doesn't know, no one with the embassy will."

She gave me his number and I thanked her. I immediately called Counselor General Robert Pollard on the island of Surabaya and his secretary answered promptly. He was out but would be back in five minutes. I had eight minutes left on the card. In five minutes sharp I called back. 'Oh yes, you just caught him, he was just leaving for his home.' Call him on the other line, she gave me that number – now with the connection fee I would have two or three minutes to confirm the facts with him.

"Yes, Robert Pollard here." His accent sounded more British than American. I introduced myself briefly and gave him the information we had and asked him what, specifically, could he confirm? He thought for a moment, then said,

"Well, yes, that's pretty much accurate. Your figures are a little off though. There aren't 90,000 Christians trapped there, only about 45,000. Yes, they are surrounded and unarmed. Yes, there was a massacre near Poso and other villages in the area and a responsible guesstimate of the

number of Laskar Jihad warriors is between nine-hundred and two thousand. But I must tell you we are swamped here because of the flow of people and information, lots of inquiries about the situation because of friends and relatives in jeopardy. So much so I have to leave the office to write up this report to get it back to the States."

I thanked him and the line went dead. The card had just run out. But we had our confirmation. By the skin on our teeth we had it! In a few minutes Mark was back on the phone with me. No one had news of the massacre or the trapped civilians. No wire services. No print media. No one. We were among the first in the world to know. Now, with our limited personnel and resources – who, in the world, do we tell?

* * *

John Heidenrich's voice cracked with sleep and he sounded irritable.

"Okay, okay, give me a second to think." He groused.

I repeated my question, slower.

"Who, with our limited means, should we give the information to? No one stateside is open for business; Europe wouldn't be open for a couple of hours. Our value now is based on getting the information to the right people, but who?"

"I've got it." He said, "The Australians! They have a strategic interest. They have even deployed troops to East Timor."

He was right, as he should be; John was the only member of our board of directors who had written an entire book on genocide prevention. He had also run a subcontracted early warning system for the State Department during its brief existence. The company he worked for, Open Source Solutions, won the contract by going up against some of the US government's best researchers. A well-known Cabinet secretary challenged Open Source Solutions to find all they could on the Internet on a particular country - Burundi. The Internet was Open Sources bread and butter search vehicle. If they produced better research than the government agency within 24 hours, they would be awarded the contract. They buried the government agency in research and were promptly awarded the subcontract for a little less than two years.

John's Russian-born wife was woken by the call so he begged off.

Mark and I began the arduous task of emailing and faxing every single major radio station, TV station and print media in Australia. We began with ABC radio of Australia. I faxed copy after copy of the press release to the scores of media outlets and he emailed them. The fax machine jammed several times before it would allow me to finish the job.

It was an hour later that Mark called me out of breath with the news. ABC Radio of Australia had broken the story using largely our text. Shortly after ABC Radio of Australia broke the story, the wire services around the world picked it up.

We had confirmed the information with a neutral third party. We had released it to the proper media outlet and the

17

wire picked it up. So far so good, but now for the hard part, we needed to find someone on Capitol Hill who would do something about it.

* * *

Mark and I, looking slightly haggard, greeted the first interns who arrived at the Center at 9:00am. We herded them into the boardroom to prep them for Capitol Hill. We set up

maps and made copies of the original report, press releases and the wire service reports. Over the next hour each of the volunteers was taught the facts and the background information. The materials were stacked in neat piles on the oversized thick wooden table and placed into packets for Capitol Hill. We painstakingly redacted the contact names and email addresses with black magic marker from each document. We drew up a plan to go to every office on the House side of the Capitol that sat on the Human Rights Caucus and the Appropriation Committee. We were to concentrate on the conservative members. We felt strongly that if the situation were to be resolved, a conservative Christian Coalition supported member of the U.S. House of Representatives, someone the President, George W. Bush, would listen to, and needed to be convinced of the urgency. They needed to feel outraged that Indonesia was about to receive a major military hardware aid package from the U.S. while Christians were being massacred there. That Representative needed to call the White House, possibly the President himself, who would then need to call President Megawati of Indonesia to voice the Administration's concerns about Christians being massacred and remind her of the impending aid. There was a massive

18

disbursement of military hardware about to occur within three months and the over one hundred million dollars' worth of aid might be in jeopardy, it could be argued, if Indonesia continued to allow its Christians to be massacred. The U.S was concurrently fighting another 'Jihad' in Afghanistan against the Taliban at the time. This was clearly something that could be leveraged to get a response to help the people trapped in Tentena. Could Indonesia's President Megawati be urged to deploy the military to stop the killing in Tentena?

I sat outside U.S. Congressman Ballenger's office for fifteen minutes when he walked in.

"Y' here for me?" Asked a sixty something unpresuming man.

"Yessir." Without hesitating.

"C'mon in."

His office was a standard Congressional Office with nicely upholstered chairs, a rich wooden coffee table, ornamental molding on the walls and an impressive looking, leather inlay mahogany desk. There was a framed photo of a factory on the wall next to his desk. He was friendly in a folksy Southern way. I gave him a compelling but brief history of the conflict and the immediate jeopardy these people were facing. I handed him the firsthand information and the Center's Moluccas report. A look of condescension came across his face. He lowered his voice in a conspiratorial tone.

"You know who loves this kinda stuff, Tom Lantos and Cynthia McKinney, those liberals just love this stuff." He pushed the report back across the table at me.

"I'll get you their chiefs of staffs names and numbers." He assured me. I knew that the opportunity to get this done was slipping through my hands. He was my tenth office and he was the perfect person to get this done. This was no time for fear or politeness. I had to hit him head on or lose him.

"Congressman Ballenger, with all due respect, I didn't come here to see Mr. Lantos or Ms. McKinney. I came here specifically to see you. You have a strong and devout Christian population in your district. Your district and the Christian Coalition, I'm sure care deeply about Christians being massacred and I know that they would be impressed that you cared enough to pick up the phone and get the ball moving with the administration." I stopped talking and looked at him. The time ticked away and he looked at me.

Slowly, with a slightly sardonic expression on his face, he reached for the report again.

"Now where exactly is this place again?"

* * *

At the end of two days' effort we had seen senior staff, human rights liaisons and members of Congress themselves in dozens of offices on the Human Rights Caucus. By the end of our second day our reason to advocate had ceased to exist.

President Megawati had sent the troops in to rescue the Christians. Within 48 hours of the first report of trouble on

Sulawesi, Indonesia dispatched 4,000 troops to Tentena to protect the Christians in danger. The troops arrived and quickly dispersed the members of Laskar Jihad with hardly a shot fired. The threat vanished into thin air. Within one year the head of Laskar Jihad would be behind bars and the history of massacre and counter massacre between the Muslim and Christian population was to cease.

We didn't know for sure if Congressman Ballenger made the call after giving us assurances, or if another one of the Congressional offices we contacted that day made the call, or if President Megawati decided to send troops on her own. We had confirmed it, put the word out to the press and pressured Congress to have the administration pressure President Megawati when no one else appeared to be working on it. It seemed to us that our first attempt into human rights early warning had yielded some impressive results. This was the first time in modern Indonesian history when the government had acted with decisive commitment to human rights by dispatching the troops. We were amazed.

For four years the Center for the Prevention of Genocide (C.P.G) provided timely early warning information from genocidal hotspots around the world for four years. It rang the warning bell regarding massacres in DR Congo, Uganda, Sudan, Colombia, India, Indonesia and many other places where there was imminent danger to unarmed civilian populations. In 2004, after four years, we closed our doors just after we began to issue warnings about a little known place called Darfur, Sudan.

The C.P.G's successful creation of an early warning system that told of these unfolding danger zones around the world underscores the fact that early warning systems work. If an understaffed and under-funded group could take this mission and have relative success, imagine what can be done at the national or international level. The UN currently has a 'Special Advisor' on genocide prevention, Adama Dieng. Three of his people work on early warning. He has quite a difficult mission in front of him. His office lacks funding, resources, personnel, a clear mission and a standing intervention force for deployment to where civilians are being massacred. There is nothing more important in the world than addressing this unfinished business.

Introduction

This world has seen genocide centuries and millennia before it was given a name. In ancient times, entire tribes and races were decimated by growing empires the world over. No continent was immune to these early acts of genocide – the killing of an ethnic, religious, racial or national group. Even famed figures like Caesar were known to their contemporaries for destroying entire tribes. The Middle-Ages were no exception as Mesoamerican tribes enslaved competing tribes and Genghis Khan famously declared against resisting towns that 'no one should be spared except children under the size of an ox-cart wheel.' But of all the Centuries, ancient and current, this past Century is one of the bloodiest of all time. There are many reasons for this – among them are the improvement of the technologies of war, the proliferation of weapons and nationalism. The obvious dangers of nationalism are well known – with total warfare and industrialized genocide at the top the list. On one hand, nationalism is a man-made phenomenon that we, as individuals, are usually proud of. It is an effective organizational tool for economic productivity and safety. We often consider our national affiliation as part of our identity as well as our ethnic, religious and tribal affiliations. We usually feel a particular bond with the people in our group to which 'we belong.' But there is a subtle danger of nationalism that enables and emboldens genocidaires the world over and is as dangerous as any weapon. The subtle danger is that, while it makes us closer to a comparatively small number of people, *it allows us to assign a lesser station of humanity to those who are not our nationality, ethnicity, race or religion.* It allows us to turn a blind eye to the suffering of others due to a lack of strategic interest, proximity to our group and a lack of connection, and thus it reduces the moral imperative to act. Potential genocidaires know the world community is unlikely to respond if those being targeted have nothing anyone wants. Ask yourself, if a criminal knows there will be no consequences for their actions, how can we reasonably expect his criminal conduct to desist?

It is also true that when impending, preventable disasters happen in places around the world to people who have no relation or connection to you or your self-interest, the likelihood of your intervention in their plight decreases geometrically. This phenomenon has been consistent for at least the past one hundred years.

This book focuses more on recent genocide-prevention action and a prescription to end genocide and less on the history of the past one-hundred years of genocide. No book can cover it all. There are stories, lives and heroism that will remain lost forever. This book begins with a look at genocide over the past century. It gives examples of the cruelty, the misery, the indifference and the heroism of the human condition. It is a clear call for investment in prevention strategies and the organizations that sponsor them. The lessons of early warning and response has eluded our policymakers as we veer from one preventable man-made catastrophe to another.

This book also contains a second book, a manual. These are the first-hand documents from the Center for the Prevention of Genocide. It outlines what to consider if you ever start a human rights NGO and how to go about it. It is thorough. It covers everything from how to advocate on the phone, to writing a press release, to building a communications network of hundreds of sources. It even includes personnel documents you will need if you ever get serious about starting an NGO. It is my greatest wish that at some point the Center be restarted and its life-saving mission continued. But whether it is genocide-prevention or some other worthy cause, the manual can be of use to you.

My personal interest in genocide grew into a thesis for college and a deeply held conviction that genocide is preventable. While the stories featured in these pages depict heroic efforts to save victims are inspiring, the other side of the story, the cruelty of man, made me conclude that institutionalized early warning and reaction were necessary to anticipate the latter. The heroism which occurs during genocide is the band aid, the temporary solution. The remedy that will cure this sick part of the human condition is early warning and response.

A powerful nation possesses sufficient strength to defend itself from threats of excessive external or internal nationalism. But in countries where groups are excluded from the protection of the state, these defenseless minorities are often at the mercy of forces armed with unlimited cruelty. When genocidal abuse occurs in these situations, it is essential that other nations step in for the sake of the at-risk humanity. This is an issue of the highest moral order. Failure to intervene in genocidal activities has allowed the massacre of families, villages and entire peoples, while those of us in the rest of the world sit as quiet observers and subtle, unwitting accomplices.

Because genocide usually occurs in places where few, if any, people and nations have an interest, a mechanism to prevent and intervene must be created. If we take into account that the human condition can be as vile and mean as it can be heroic and graceful, we must anticipate and resolve these

25

inevitabilities long before they occur. The current uncoordinated, ad-hoc strategy of the international community when faced with unfolding acts of genocide is not a substitute for early warning and early action. When the time for heroism is at hand and a person must risk his or her life to save others, by that time we, the world community, have failed to do our job.

This book provides examples of how the responses to genocide are varied and span the breadth of human compassion. The main body of the book chronicles recent examples of successful actions by the Center for the Prevention of Genocide and the international community to end genocide after it has already started. These chapters can be instructive for policy makers, governments and agencies in the creation of an early warning system to end genocide. The group of young human rights activists I was privileged to know, helped attempt to prevent genocide from 2000 – 2004 at the Center for the Prevention of Genocide (CPG), where I served as Director. Many of them have gone on to successful careers in the U.S. State Department, as Deputy U.S. Attorney Generals, Non-Profit executives and fundraisers and one even became a popular pop star in Russia. After the brief historical narrative, we pick up, chronologically, with the work and action from the founding of the CPG in 2000.

In Case of Genocide – Break Glass *Abridged* is *actual* book about the CPG, genocide prevention work and concludes by recommending sound strategies for ending genocide throughout the world. The theme of this entire work is that *genocide is preventable.* Absolutely and categorically, it can be eradicated from the human condition. Successful genocide prevention work has occurred in Eastern D.R. Congo, Sudan,

Indonesia and Gujarat, India and these examples can serve as templates for future successful prevention in the future. Moreover, I recommend a combination of institutionalized early warning and rapid response, multi-track diplomacy, democracy-building and EU lessons from Jean Monnet as a specific prescription for ending genocide in our lifetimes.

The Unabridged, longer version of this book is not the issue you are holding, That version includes an actual Genocide Prevention Manual and has crucial instructions and information for how to run a life-saving early warning system. Included are templates that we used at the CPG for: on-the-ground fact finding, report writing, and dissemination and advocacy to policymakers. The premise here is that almost anyone can undertake to gather this kind of information, confirm and publish it and put it into the right hands in an attempt to end the killing. By placing these tools in the reader's hands, the work of the former CPG staff and volunteers had the potential to keep saving lives.

The human condition is complex. Unfortunately, as much as heroism is part of human nature, so too is criminal or evil conduct, and so too is indifference. Take, for example, some of the fascist leaders during the Holocaust, who stepped in to prevent Jews from being sent to the concentration camps. These figures, who allied themselves with Hitler's Third Reich, and often committed numerous evil acts, sometimes intervened to stop the killing. The dictators' Mussolini of Italy and King Boris of Bulgaria were known to have slowed and stopped the deportation of Jews in their countries. Even in a place as synonymous with evil as the gas chambers of Auschwitz, when a sixteen year old girl survived the zyklon B poison and sat bewildered, naked and covered with a blanket in the SS

27

officer's kitchen, these same SS monsters, flitted around her providing soup and trying to figure out how to let her live. At some basic place in their humanity, beyond the dogma, and the routinization of the task, these men who had become monsters, briefly, became fathers and brothers again. How do we change from people with some sense of basic morality to indifferent bystanders or even, the criminals themselves? Time and again our species has shown an unbelievable propensity to kill unarmed minorities, usually women and children, for ethnic, national, religious, racial and ideological pretenses, while the rest of us usually did nothing. What makes people kill unarmed civilians, when every natural instinct should tell us it is wrong? And what makes most of us do nothing about it? Lastly and most importantly, what can be done to permanently end this conduct among our species?

* * *

A friend of mine, Aeon, observed that we are in the 21st Century using the 18th Century craft of diplomacy. There is truth in this. We have at our disposal the means for solving most conflict in the world, but we choose not to use them. Instead we rely on high tension, time-honored methods where national leaders meet and bargain for a perceived public advantage in their dispute. This antiquated method has mixed results. Today, there are other truly modern and very effective options; there are trained cadres of professionals who are engaged in diplomacy and conflict prevention at the first track (governmental), through to the twelve tracks of multi-track diplomacy. There is the School for Conflict Analysis and

Resolution at George Mason University, the Munk School at the University of Toronto, and the Institute for Multi-Track Diplomacy which are contributing to cutting edge strategies for peace and conflict resolution that can affect people around the world. The usefulness of these norms and strategies, which are only in their first and second generations of development, is rarely noticed. These conflict prevention practitioners are an unknown cadre, often braving places most of us would not dream to venture. They are the warriors for peace, and they are largely unknown. They are a fundamental element for good and they are just beginning to be used in U.S foreign and worldwide foreign policy. Their field of conflict-prevention needs to become the norm of how we solve the problems of the world.

While circling around the idea of the value we put on human life, and specifically how it relates to our foreign policies, I received an email from my friend Aeon which began with this sentence: 'Human Life is not the Bottom Line in the Decision-Making Process.' This was the idea I was circling. If you look at which issues that define and guide our actions in foreign policy, there is a long list that does not have protection of non-American life near the top. This is a fundamental flaw. There is no asset more valuable than human life; instinctively, when you look at your family, friends, colleagues and community you know this is true. But this self-evident moral truth, 'human life is the bottom line,' which is the bedrock of our shared values, is nowhere reflected in the of our foreign policy nor of most nations around the world.

* * *

While this book tells the hopeful stories of individuals, organizations and governments who rallied on behalf of endangered people and succeeded in protecting them, this is admittedly one of the least effective ways to end genocidal conduct. We cannot look to individuals to be the long-term solution for ending genocide. We need to create a permanent system that will automatically trigger reactions both suitable, and strong enough to end the killing, and defuse potential situations likely to evolve into killing. A complete system must be put in place that is more than an understaffed agency with a noble vision, a vague mandate and little on-the-ground influence. It should be a sound predictor that has United Nations authority to trigger a rapid-deploy force to halt massacres on the ground. In recent years we have seen exactly this kind of *ad hoc* rapid deploy force stop genocide in its tracks. The French forces that went into Eastern DR Congo in the summer of 2003 stopped the massacres in the Ituri province. The Indonesian government sent 4,000 troops to end the massacres on the island of Sulawesi in 2001 and there are several historical examples when force or aforethought instantly ended massacres. The credible threat of force can bring genocide to an end as well as a multitude of other preventative strategies. Few situations will require military intervention. Once an institutionalized military response precedent has been set, perpetrators will be less likely to follow through with genocidal acts. It is the same with any crime. Crime decreases when there are likely immediate consequences for criminals. The majority of situations that have the potential of genocide can be avoided by conflict prevention, economic pressure, diplomacy, political pressure, humanitarian aid and a range of other options that befit each situation. But a permanent and real military option, in the very specific instance of the initiation of genocide, with a standing military, budget and resources, will afford the international community a last resort and will help make other options more palatable for potential perpetrators. It will create a realistic disincentive to kill.

That was, after all, the lesson of Rwanda. No one had a strategic interest in the area which proved to be fatal for over 800,000 Rwandans. Better early warning and a standing rapid-deploy or other intervention mechanism did not (and still does not) exist and could have saved all of those lives. Even without the moral component of the argument, from a cost-benefit analysis, the cost of prevention in this instance would have been a fraction of the cost that was paid in repair, refugee camps, the spread of instability and of course, in lives.

Today, our local interest is not our *only* interest. The world interest is becoming part of our local interest, whether we like it or not, technology is making our world much smaller. Generations before us have responded to the call for action befitting their time. Leadership and morality are inconvenient burdens, but one that when we, as individuals, nations and the world community shirk it invariably leads to the loss of innocent lives and the diminution of our ethical credibility.

CHAPTER TWO: MY PERSONAL ARMENIA.

The Lesson of Musa Dagh.
My Personal Reasons for Writing this Book.
The Evidence: Handwritten Orders for Genocide.

"To serve Armenia is to serve civilization."[1]

Lord Gladstone

The Lesson of Musa Dagh.

[2] Musa Dagh Armenians escaping to a French freighter.

---

[1] Joseph Burtt, *The People of Ararat.* (London: Leonard and Virginia Woolf at the Hogarth Press, 1926), 9.
[2] Armeniapedia.org

In the spring of 1915, the first hint of trouble for Armenians in Turkey was when the Young Turk government sent a directive to the local authorities ordering all Armenian communities disarmed. The justification seemed plausible enough; the rifles handed out to communities several years earlier during a time of strife were no longer necessary now that the threat had passed. However, Turkey was entering the First World War and the justification raised some eyebrows. Nonetheless, the vast majority of Armenians obediently complied. For hundreds of years the Armenian population were second class citizens in the class system of the Ottoman Empire. Compliance and accommodation were a way of life since long before Roman times. The Armenian in town of Musa Dagh (Mount Moses), overlooking the Mediterranean coast, did not comply. A disturbing rumor had reached town and the local Armenian leaders chose to keep the weapons and buried the rifles in a church graveyard. A few days later the order was given for all Armenians of Musa Dagh to gather the belongings they could carry in preparation to be moved in a couple of days. The Armenian townspeople were split, some wanted to avoid trouble and decided to leave with the troops when they arrived, but others, the majority, decided to pack as much food, supplies and arms as possible, fortify themselves atop the great hill overlooking the town of Musa Dagh and hide. Almost all those who left peaceably were killed immediately after they were marched out of town, with the women and children being brutalized and raped. The majority who hid on the top of the hill were eventually discovered. When the Turkish troops came to kill them, they fought with surprising ability and vigor and beat back wave after wave of attacks. They used heavy rocks, the advantage of the terrain, rifles and anything they could think of to defend their families. A former soldier was in their midst and supervised their defense. After forty days, when supplies, ammunition and hope were running low, a passing French-flagged ship responded to their distress flag and the Armenians of Musa Dagh escaped to the ship under the cover of darkness. All survived except the soldier Gabriel Bagradian and his son Stephan. The 40 Days of Musa Dagh is not fiction; I have met Musa Dagh Armenians. The lesson of Musa Dagh is instructive; be prepared. When endangered, prepare to defend, flee or perish.

My Personal Reasons for Writing This Book.

I grew up hearing stories of the Armenian genocide. My mother would not talk about it. But my father, who was not Armenian, told me the stories of family who were killed or fled. That was the beginning of my journey to make sense of how a remarkable and peaceful people could be targeted for death. At family events, when I would look at my relatives, or even today as I look at my children, I could not and cannot comprehend why anyone would ever be offended by these beautiful people. There were two genocides of Armenians in 1894 and 1909 prior to the big genocide in 1915, which killed approximately one of every three Armenians. The earlier genocides occurred at the hands of the Ottoman Sultan Abdul Hamid and the 1915 genocide was ordered by the 'Young Turk' government.

The genocide began April 24th, 1915, with the arrest of the leadership of the Armenian community in Constantinople. The Young Turk government began to round up the Armenian intellectuals, leaders and clergy in Constantinople and sent them inland. Less public scrutiny and transparency always offers human nature the opportunity to do evil without consequences. The Turkish military began to go from town to town, ring the town bell, take the men off to do some work unarmed. The men would be massacred outside town and then the troops would return to do whatever they wished to the

women and children. The men and women were so unsuspecting of the troop's motives they went willingly to their own execution. Sometimes, the women and children would be marched into the Deir ez Zor desert and left to starve, which they did. The term 'starving Armenians' became a well-known phrase throughout the world during this crisis.

This was the Twentieth Century's first missed opportunity to develop a legal channel to restrict such activity. Humanity was indeed shocked by what had occurred. Even in the face of staggering First World War casualties, the world community recognized the particularly heinous nature of these massacres. This was wholesale slaughter rarely witnessed since the time of Genghis Khan.

My great-grandfather was killed in front of my great grandmother. He was chopped to pieces by heavy sword. My great grandmother then fled across the Dier ez Zor desert hiding in caves, the same caves that Syrians are hiding in today (2014). In one instance, my great grandmother told my father that when the Turkish troops were so close to a group of twenty hiding Armenians, a young mother held her newborn baby so tightly to muffle its cries, she accidentally smothered it to death.

Great grandma's friend Topal Serpic told how, driven by starvation, she marveled when she saw fruit atop a tree, until she noticed what was underneath it. Many severed head lay scattered around the base of the tree. Unable to climb the tree, with shaking hands, she stacked several of the severed Armenian heads in a staircase of heads that she carefully climbed. She steadied herself and carefully straightened and reached for the fruit. She slipped. The nightmare of being enveloped in a sea of heads was one that reoccurred throughout the rest of her life.

My grandfather, a young shepherd, was adopted by a Turkish family until arrangements could be made for him to immigrate to Canada. Grandma, his future wife, hid in Constantinople in a Muslim School that was a secret Christian abbey by night, until she too could flee to Canada. Eventually, those family members who survived gravitated toward Brantford, Ontario, where my mother was born in 1925. Our family was among the lucky ones, losing only great grandfather and several of his family, but the children survived.

Lord Gladstone spoke to the British Parliament about rescuing the Armenians in their desperate plight at the end of World War Two. He spoke of the need for civilization never to stand by and let that sort of massacre happen again. "To serve the cause of the Armenians is to serve the cause of civilization." It was an idealistic age; few would imagine that a century later civilization would continue to fail in that service of humanity.

The Evidence.

Perpetrators of genocides rarely leave a clear paper trail with descriptions, orders and correspondence as did the 'Young Turk' government did regarding the Armenian genocide. While first-hand reports exist in many languages, the clearest evidence is the documentation of the genocide by the 'Young Turk' leadership, itself. Included here are copies of the actual written orders for genocide signed by Ismail Enver. I found the following documents in the appendices of an Italian book on genocide published in 1962 in a library in Geneva. Having looked at every English and French book in the HEI University library on genocide, I turned to the German and Italian books.

Crouching down to read the titles from the bottom shelf, I noticed a distinctive-looking large old book in Italian. It had the words 'Nella Questione Armena.' Thinking there was only one question that warrants a book regarding Armenians, I flipped through the book scanning to see if anything looked interesting. What I found in the appendices of this book was astonishing.

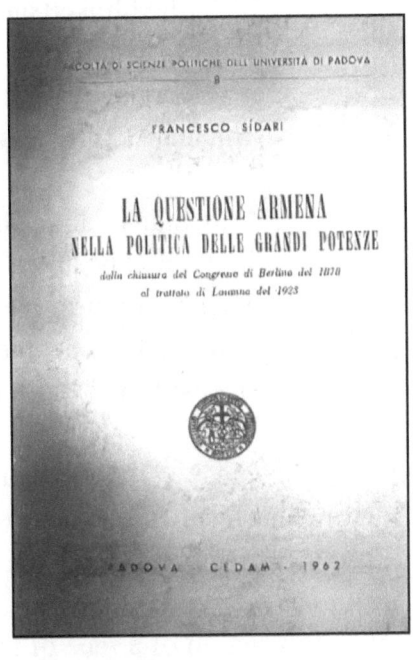

There, translated in Italian from the original handwritten Arabic, were what appeared to be documents dating back to the Armenian massacres, with the signatures of Enver Pasha and Talaat Bey, two of the architects of the genocide against the Armenians. I could make out that the letters were about the Armenians. Could it be that I was looking at one of the only surviving copies of the handwritten order for genocide, actually signed by the Young Turk leaders? Four months later, back at Georgetown

University, I had my answer. I had stopped by the Italian Department at Georgetown to seek help in translating the documents. A quiet woman, sitting at a desk in the department, agreed to help. Halfway through typing the translation, her fingers halted. She turned slowly to me:

"Do you know what this document is?"

"I am not sure. But I think I do." I said.

"It's" She blinked and looked at it again.

"It's the handwritten order for the extermination of Armenians." She was appalled with disbelief:

"Armenians and those who have an Armenian name…will be killed. Make sure the killings occur with no hesitation or mercy of children of one month of age through all old people ninety years of age does not take place within cities in the view of the population."

On this piece of paper was the handwritten order for the Armenian genocide. This piece of paper led to the deaths of some of my family and one million Armenians. It was very similar to a record I had read about Genghis Khan's orders for the destruction of a race of people who had resisted his forces. 'Let all of their people perish who are taller than an ox cartwheel.' Here was the ancient scourge of humanity in black and white writing, against my family.

**STATO MAGGIORE
DELL'OTTAVO CORPO D'ARMATA IMPERIALE**

Sezione 2529

ALLEGATO N. 1

Traduzione

RISERVATO   COPIA

2529.

Dal superiore Comando in capo in seconda è stato comunicato che senza ordine del Quartiere Generale non venga trasferito fuori dal paese alcun armeno, sia esso uomo o donna e di qualsiasi età.

Inoltre

2530.

1. Tra gli Armeni che dovranno essere trasferiti, le famiglie di coloro che siano sotto la tutela di militari o di impiegati statali rimarranno nei luoghi in cui già risiederano.

2. Qualora costoro restino superino nei paesi e villaggi in cui rimangono il numero di cinque case, a partire dalle famiglie di militari, verranno distribuiti in villaggi musulmani di loro scelta, nell'interno dei distretti (kazà) e sangiaccati, da cui dipendono, a patto però di non superare la suddetta densità, e cosendo osservata, nei limiti di cento, la proporzione del cinque per cento.

3. In tal modo in un villaggio musulmano di venti case potrà trovar posto solo una casa armena.

4. Nei paesi e villaggi di cento e più case potranno trovar posto non più di cinque case.

5. Disposizioni in questo senso sono state impartite dal Ministero degli Interni ai villaggi.

6. Le liste delle famiglie dei ribelli verranno compilate al più presto e consegnate ai funzionari locali.

7. Questi ordini del superiore Comando in capo in seconda sono stati riferiti letteralmente.

Se vi sono famiglie di soldati o impiegati che sino a ora sono state trasferite, verrà loro concesso di ritornare.

2 agosto 1331 (2 agosto 1915).

Al Comando Centrale.

Sono state riportate sopra letteralmente le copie di due ordini pervenuti al Comando in seconda della Quarta Armata. Si significa che si proceda a norma delle loro disposizioni.

8 agosto 1331 (8 agosto 1915).

Il Vice Comandante dell'Ottavo Corpo d'Armata

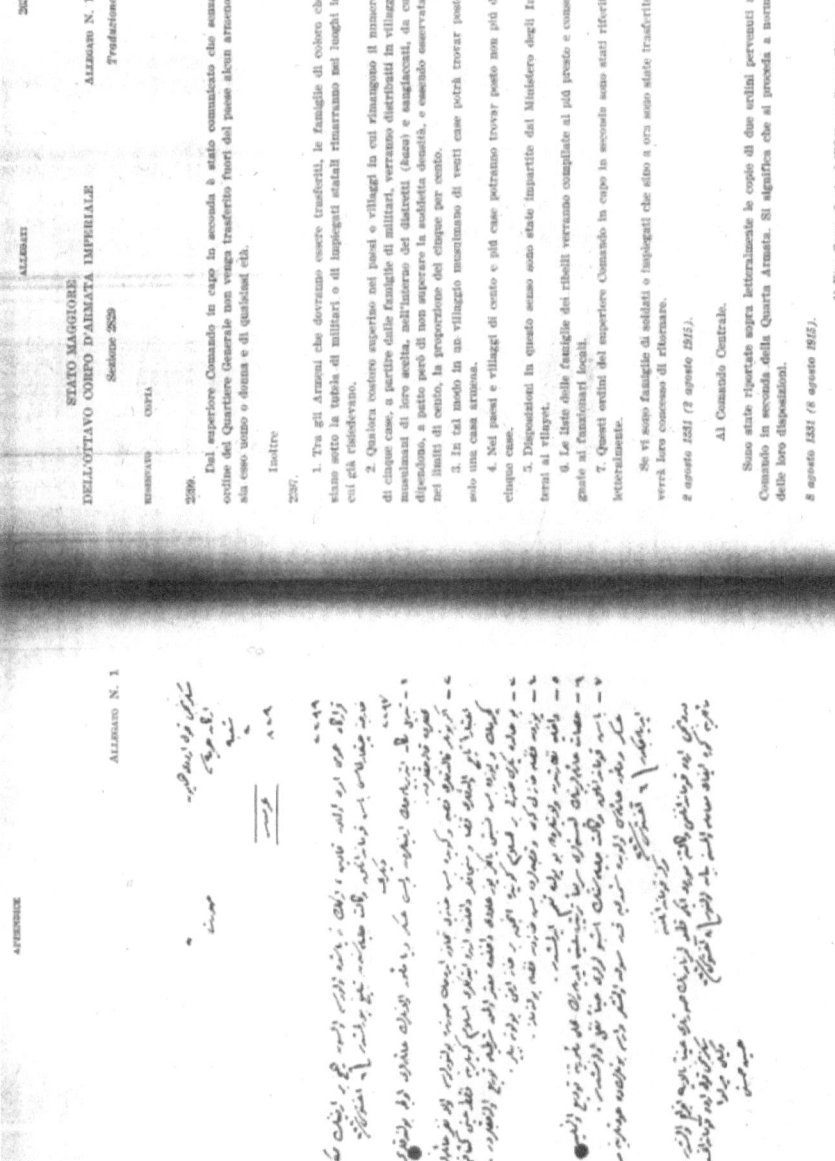

One of these documents is here translated.

Attachment
"The same documents of attachment no. 6 and 4.
In addition:

One line in Armenian: The secret of events of March 2, 1918
(Damascus). Telegraph to Damascus.

In Turkish:

Because of the present situation the total extinction of the
Armenian race has been decided (or deliberated) by High Decree.

1. We will act as follows toward the Armenians:
2. The Armenians and those who have an Armenian name
   who are among the inhabitants of the realm protected
   by God with the exception of children up to the age of
   five years of age will be killed, being the rebels who
   were taken out of towns and villages.
3. All the Armenian military who are currently employed
   in the Imperial Army will be separated from their units
   without provoking incidents and killed by gun in a
   concealed place without contact with the local
   population.
4. The Armenian officers that are in the army will be
   imprisoned in the general quarters of the units to
   which they belong until a new order is issued.
5. Since specific letters will circulate regarding the
   execution of these three articles after 48 hours since

---

[3] La Questione Armena Nella Politica delle Grandi Potenze by F. Sidari.
Padova: Scienze Polotiche dell'Universita, 1962. Appendix.

the date of their (the letters) arrival at the headquarters of each unit, no action is to be taken before except for necessary preparations.

Second in Command

Enver

The same document as attached no. 2.

In addition:

Copy of the telegram send by Talaat Pasha to Atif Bey, 'Vali' of Ankara:

Make Sure the killings with no hesitation and mercy of children one month of age through all old people of 90 years of age does not take place within cities in the presence (view) of the population."[4]

As someone who has grown up hearing accounts from family and has spent a portion of my adult life researching the Armenian genocide, I see no room for doubt of the veracity of the genocide. The signed orders, the first-hand accounts, in several languages, by hundreds of witnesses, and hundreds and hundreds of thousands of survivors leads me to believe that any objective scholar would confirm credibility of what common sense and evidence has clearly demonstrated. This unfortunate denial was and still is the accepted policy of the Turkish government. Though no perpetrators are alive today, and the Turkish government today bears little resemblance to the 'Young Turk' government a century ago, its continued denial

---

[4] Ibid., Appendix.

of the obvious, is more than hurtful, it makes modern Turkey subtly complicit with the actions of a previous government it would otherwise have little in common. Only in recent years have the first publications in Turkish appeared to begin to discuss the Armenian genocide in public. It is a matter of respect for the dead, setting the record straight and acknowledging the preciousness of the lives lost.

Far from distancing themselves from the genocide, the ruling 'Young Turk' troika confirmed that they were responsible for the Armenian Genocide in a conversation with the U.S Ambassador Morganthau to Turkey. Enver Pasha and Talaat Bey's assured the US Ambassador and German Embassy officials in Turkey that they were directly responsible for the killing.

In reply to the US Ambassador Morgenthau who was deploring the massacres against the Armenian and attributing them to irresponsible underlings in the distant provinces, Enver's reply was:

> "You are greatly mistaken. We have this country absolutely under our control. I have no desire to shift blame onto our underlings and I am entirely willing to accept the responsibility myself for everything that has taken place."

In a conversation with Mordtmann of the German Embassy in June of 1915 Talaat said:

> "Turkey is taking advantage of the war in order to thoroughly liquidate internal foes, (i.e. the indigenous Christians), without thereby being disturbed by foreign intervention."

After the German Ambassador persistently brought up the Armenian question in 1918, Talaat said with a smile:

"What on earth do you want? The question is settled. There are no more Armenians."[5]

There was no shame on the part of the perpetrators. They justified the horror that had occurred throughout Turkey as a useful tool to solidify their nation and religion.

As with all known genocides, Turkey had bystanders who were indifferent, or took part in the criminal activity or heroic. A number of Turkish individuals and families helped hide, smuggle and even adopt some of their Armenian neighbor's children. Many survivors' accounts bear witness to this credit to human nature. Some took orphaned Armenian children into their homes. Others nourished fleeing Armenians and helped them on their way. But large portions of the Turkish population were presented with a *fait accompli*. One day they had Armenian neighbors and the next day they were gone; they were being marched out of town with some of their belongings. While some Turkish or Kurdish neighbors benefited from the abandoned Armenian homes and belongings, others sought to help their neighbors and friends.

The secrecy of the plan was essential, otherwise the remaining Armenian population would have panicked at the oncoming massacres and armed themselves. This secrecy was crucial during the Holocaust as well. In the towns of Sivas, Van and others, resistance was organized to no avail, except for Musa Dagh, where most of the population escaped to a French

---

[5] Vahakn, Dadrian, *Genocide: A Critical Bibliographical Review*
http://www.cilicia.com/armo10a.html

freight ship through a combination of tenacity, foresight and incredible luck.[6] Musa Dagh had an escape route that other Armenian cities and neighborhoods did not.

Far from being indifferent to the plight of the Armenians, the Allied European powers and some of Turkey's German allies, denounced the Turkish genocidal activities. The world was shocked and began clamoring for something to be done about it. What exactly could be done about it was difficult to envision until the Ottoman/Turkish forces were defeated. The time for preventative action had passed years before.

Once the massacres had ended, the allies and international organizations sent aid to the Armenians. The issue of how this utterly devastated nation could be protected so it could rebuild was thoroughly discussed. The ideas ranged from the concept of a French protectorate, to an American protectorate, to the independence of traditional Armenia as outlined in the Treaty of Sevres. No action to protect the Armenians occurred, however, because within a short period of time the re-formed Turkish forces swept the allies and the new fledgling independent Armenian state from Anatolia. The Allies, weary of war, relented to the domestic opposition to prolonged foreign entanglement and ultimately the *de facto* ground situation became permanent. The issue of independence for Armenia was dropped shortly after a joint Turkish-Soviet invasion partitioned the nation in 1921.

There were no trials of the people responsible for the genocide. Herein lies the final enduring lessons of the Armenian tragedy. There was no punishment for the

---

[6] Franz Werfel, *The Forty Days of Musa Dagh.* (New York: Carol and Graf Publishing, 1991).

perpetrators, no apology or acknowledgement by the new Turkish government for the actions of the 'Young Turk' government. The apology or acknowledgement is an important step in the victim community's ability to heal and move on from genocide. The lack of accountability and acknowledgement may be part of the reason why a sense of despair and mourning was reflected in ethos of many of the older Armenians who seemed to permanently wear black as if reflexive of that state of mourning. More importantly for the world, no protections were created to safeguard against similar activity in the future.

The Armenian genocide became the blueprint for many genocides to come, with the key steps being:

- Vilify and disarm the minority
- Remove them to remote locations and as quickly and secretly as possible
- Kill them.

Without early warning and response capacity to anticipate and defuse future genocide and massacres, mankind was, and remains, destined to repeat itself.

In Turkey today, it is only beginning to be possible to talk about the Armenian Genocide, but it is still quite dangerous and controversial to do so. The only thing that ties the present government to the 'Young Turks', ironically, is their denial of the 'Young Turk' acts – their continuation of this denial is what makes them subtly complicit. In a letter in August 2013 to the Washington Post, the Turkish Foreign Minister rightly decried the genocide occurring in Syria. It has occurred near Homs, in the countryside, in cities and in the Deir ez Zor desert. The Deir ez Zor, the same desert to which my great-grandmother fled, where her friend Topal Serpic climbed a mountain of severed heads, where a generation of Armenian women and children were left without food and water to die. The desert has remained the same, and so has the crime.

CHAPTER THREE: 20TH CENTURY GENOCIDE.

UKRAINE HOLODOMOR (1932-1933).

"On the battlefield men die quickly, they fight back,
they are sustained by fellowship and a sense of duty.
Here I saw people dying in solitude by slow degrees."

> - Victor Kravchenko, a
> former communist
> activist on the Ukraine
> starvation of the
> Holodomor.

The use of starvation as a tactic to depopulate an area would not end with my ancestors the Armenians. In less than fifteen years, between five to ten million Ukrainian farmers would be intentionally starved to death. The perpetrator was Soviet leader Joseph Stalin and his policies designed to end a nascent independence movement and force the collectivization of farms.

Ethnic and religious massacre and genocide had existed for millenniums. The targeting of a specific nationality is only a few hundred years old because of the newness of the modern phenomenon of the nation-state. But ideological genocide and ideological mass atrocities are phenomenon borne of the 20th Century.

In 1932, Joseph Stalin was ending his first brutal, but successful, five-year plan. His massive program of rapid industrialization was fortified with a ruthlessness that the Czars had rarely approached. Calling in sick and arriving late to work were often considered indications of counter revolutionary thought and were punishable by exile to Siberian work camps. While iron ore and steel production had doubled in four years, the collectivization of privately-owned farms was slower to take shape. Stalin had decided to double his industrial efforts and attempt to finish the collectivization of all privately-owned farms in his second five-year plan. Old opposition forces began to take root in Ukraine where the kulak farmers sought to protect their farms and way of life. This resistance to collectivism and the independence movement were cause for immediate concern to the acutely paranoid Stalin.

The last civil war between 'red' and 'white' Russians was still a recent memory and the thought of starting another civil war, on national fault lines as well as ideological ones, did not appeal to Stalin. Instead, he sent Soviet soldiers into Ukraine - not to invade, but to seize all grain, harvests and livestock from the farms throughout this fertile region. Then a nation starved to death. The most conservative estimates place the number of Ukrainians who perished at between 5-6 million. Stalin himself and others close to the Soviet leadership estimated the number to be ten million killed. Entire villages starved out of existence. Entire regions were devastated as if by a bomb that left the landscape devoid of most human life but the buildings still standing.

This strategy was not new. From ancient times through the Middle Ages, armies sieged and starved towns and kingdoms into submission. It was only fifty-five years before the Holodomor (Ukraine starvation) that United States President Rutherford B. Hayes used starvation as a weapon against the Sioux Confederacy in 1877. Hayes could not envision remobilizing the Union forces when the nation was trying to put the bloodshed of the civil war behind it. An inexpensive and simple solution was to send soldiers and contractors into the American plains to annihilate the Buffalo. Without their dietary staple of Buffalo, the Sioux Confederation tribes starved. Some migrated to Canada, and others surrendered to be confined to reservations.

The use of starvation as a tool of war has been repeated since the Sioux, the Armenians, and the Ukrainians, throughout the Twentieth Century to include the Ibo of Nigeria, and in more history the non-Party members in North Korea and Zimbabwe, the Nuba of Sudan, and recently in al Shabaab-controlled areas of Somalia. Starvation has been used as a military or political tool and a method of genocide in each decade of the past one hundred years. Famine when used by regimes and militias as a tool of warfare against civilians renders the perpetrators as guilty of genocide as those perpetrated it with gas, machetes or guns.

Though the UN Genocide Convention definition of genocide does not specifically include ideological groups as potential victims, the Ukrainian Famine of 1932-33 was indisputably genocide. It was orchestrated against the Ukrainian nationalist movement and directed by Stalin. Crops seized from the farmers were used for internal Soviet redistribution and for sale outside of the Soviet Union. Storage granaries in Ukraine were emptied and millions of Ukrainians perished.

Ukrainians fled the famine when they could. Many attempted to flee to the Caucuses but were usually caught and returned to Ukraine to starve. Soon the railroads and other transportation authorities made escape almost impossible

"...in connection with mass exodus of peasants beyond the borders of Ukraine... the Commissar of Railways and...transport divisions to immediately inform all railway stations about the suspension of ticket sales for destinations beyond Ukraine's borders to villagers who have not secured permission to leave from their (district)."[7]

The children were perhaps the greatest victims of all. They easily succumbed to illnesses and starvation. Royal Consul Gradenigo of Italy described the horror that awaited children and adults who became too weak or ill.

"A week ago a special service was created to catch unsupervised children. There are also children brought here and left by parents who went back to their villages to die. They hope that someone in the city will provide shelter and take care of them. Lately, these children could be seen crawling and crying on the sidewalks. One newborn was sucking milk from the breast of its gray-faced, dead mother.

The swollen are shuttled on freight trains to rural areas 50 to 60 kilometers outside the city where nobody can see them die. The railcars are filled up and bolted shut. I learned these details from the health workers and can

---

[7] Resolution of the CC CPU Politburo executing January 22 Order from USSR SNK and CC AUCP(b). January 23, 1933. Pp. 86-87.

thus guarantee the reliability of this information."[8] Report from the Consul of Italy.

These scenes rival the gruesomeness of any genocides – the horrible fate of millions of children and the lack of human dignity shown to hundreds of thousands of victims in various acts of defilement, are among the basest activities in human experience. The diplomat concluded with his belief that the Ukraine would be 'Russified' and lose its Ukrainian character.[9]" How prescient; this is certainly proving to be true in the South and East Ukraine and has contributed to instability in the early years of modern Ukraine's fledgling democracy.

---

[8] Report from the Consul of Italy in Kharkiv to the Minister of Foreign Affairs of Italy on "Famine and the Ukrainian Situation." May 31, 1933. Pp. 107 – 109.

[9] Ibid.

The Soviet Union Purges (1934 – 1939).

"How can I know you so long after sad separation,
Where's your voice, glance, and face upon which I so
strongly depend? Where's the dear hand that touched
me with caring and loving sensation? Tell me, how can
I know you so long after sad separation, after tears
without end."

Maria Taurke

Poem to her husband who never returned.

In the 1930s, the world witnessed some of the worst
ideologically based mass atrocities at the hands of the Soviet
Union's dictator Joseph Stalin. He victimized his own people in
the Soviet Union in the name of counter revolutionary purges.
The 'great purge' destroyed lives, families and communities
and left scars that are still felt today. Some scholars do not
include 'ideologically-based' massacres as genocide – I do. My
friend, Sasha, has a powerful presence and is a decorated
American Colonel. Sasha's father was dragged away in the
middle of the night and executed for a crime that didn't exist.

"Father's Arrest in the Middle of the Night.

By Erwin Alexander ("Sasha") Taurke

For ten years, Mother and Father had consciously
decided not to have children. Conditions just were not right –
too much hunger, too much insecurity, too many purges – who
in their right minds would want to bring children into this kind

of world? Finally, in the early nineteen thirties, it seemed to Mother and Father that the cycle was broken. The terror had receded. The population was urged to live without fear and produce again. And Mother and Father decided to try for a child, and on the fourth of May 1934, the overjoyed couple received a baby boy.

The photo album shows typical family bliss: the boy at one month; the boy at a month and a half, the boy at two months; the boy at three and at six months, and a year, and a year and a half, and two. The boy is being carried proudly by Father on shoulders, is shown in Mother's arms, is lying naked on the beach, is with relatives on an outing; the boy at two and a half. Then the photographs stop for a long period of time, and when they appear again, the father is no longer there.

Father was arrested in the early fall of 1937 in the typical fashion - at night past the midnight hours, with a loud, peremptory banging on the door and a shouting "open immediately or the door goes." Frightened but curious corridor neighbors (who are also curiously thankful that it isn't them) peek out of their doors in blankets and nightclothes. A squad of huge, booted men marches in. While the leader barks: "You are under arrest, get dressed and come with us," the others begin to ransack the room, searching for whatever incriminating evidence they can find, or manufacture. The frightened family is only given minutes to say good-bye to each other before the arrested member is marched off.

Father leaned over my little bed. Half-wakened by the noise, I stirred and then, through my sleep, recited my favorite poem, from my most favorite bedtime book about a little engine that could, and traveling far away but coming back:

Firemen are at the engine;
Steam is rising from the engine.
Fare you well! We're on our way.
We'll be back some other day.

At any rate, that's what I remember vaguely from my childhood, because I stopped liking the story.

Tears falling on my cover do not help. Father is led away. This is the last time that my mother sees my father ever again.

Father had several sessions with his interrogator throughout the last weeks of his freedom. He would come home, shaken and pale, crawl under the blankets, and whisper to Mother what he had endured. Of course he was not supposed to talk, since he was sworn to secrecy after each interrogation session. Mother said that Father was asked several times to betray someone else and to become a secret collaborator, but he refused. Perhaps this was the ultimate reason for his final arrest and his subsequent fate.

Once a person is in the clutches of the secret police system, he disappears as if into a black hole. All contact with him is refused. No news of his condition is ever given. No reason for an arrest is offered. Desperate family members go to the secret police office, only to be told, again and again, to come back later. And you are spoken to only if there is an offering presented to the official. With mother, this lasted for about six months. Finally, in the middle of winter, she got word that my father, in accordance with Article 58 of the criminal code, was sentenced to 10 years of hard labor "under conditions of severe isolation."

"Severe isolation" meant that for the duration of the sentence there would be no news of the prisoner. No letters are allowed. No packages can be sent. No visits are possible. The person may die, and their loved one may not know for years what happened. It's just yet another nice twist of totalitarian justice. However, even in the harshest totalitarian system, there are always ways to find out what happened, despite the best efforts of the regime. Shortly after getting the official information about him, Mother received a so-called blood notice that Father was shot. Blood notices are little pieces of clothing, sometimes a flat stone, sometimes a piece of wood, upon which, scratched by a nail or written in blood, is a short message about a prisoner. When prisoners are sentenced to hard labor, they are transported to their assigned labor camps under guard in cattle cars with barbed wire on openings. After writing the message on a torn bit of his clothing, or some other material, the prisoner then pushes the message out of the boxcar through cracks in the slats onto the tracks. After the train leaves, villagers from around the area gather and check the tracks for messages, and then try to get the messages to relatives, because they hope that they themselves will get messages about their own loved ones when and if their time comes.

The message read: "Karl Taurke. Kiev. Shot"

Immediately after my father was sentenced, Mother was declared to be the "wife of the enemy of the people" and issued a so-called "Wolf's Pass." Under a "Wolf Pass," the person has to report every week to a police station to obtain a stamp that one has done so. The neat twist is that the person cannot report to any police station twice, and thus is forced to go all over town to find a police station to report to that is different from all the previous ones. A "Wolf's Pass" therefore is usually a pass to certain dislocation and often to starvation.

As it was, terrible indeed must have been the time when my mother finally had to stand on the platform waiting for a train out of Kiev, marked as a wife of an enemy of the people and looking at an uncertain future, holding my hand in the bitter cold, while her son, orphaned by the regime, shivered and blue with cold, yet intoned: "I am not c-c-cold, mamma, because I am a hero of Soviet Stalin." Thus a truly totalitarian regime pushes children into partaking of its crimes.

Mother was truly devastated by the loss of her husband and never really got over it. When the mood struck her, she provided a counterpoint to the happy stories about Father and her, saying that in her entire life she experienced only thirteen happy years, the years she spent with Father. When she died at the age of 93 in 1996, I went through her things. Because Alzheimer's disease struck her in her last years, resulting in severe paranoia, she had destroyed most of her photographs, but I found an album and took her favorite picture of my father off the wall of her house. The frame was not in very good shape, and I left the frame, placing the photograph in the album. Only later did I happen to be looking through the album and found faint letters on the back of Father's photo. It was a poem, written by Mother, who was not a bad poet at all. It goes like this:

How can I know you so long after sad separation?
Where's your voice, glance, and face upon which I so strongly depend?

Where's the dear hand that touched me with caring and loving sensation?

Tell me, how can I know you so long after sad separation, after tears without end.

It was so long ago, I don't even remember it clearly,

But the nights without sleep, and the thoughts, and the fears torture me!

How I wish to be joyful! How memories rise up so dearly!

It was so long ago, I don't even remember you clearly,

But you're always with me!

I must be frank with you; I cannot read this poem without tears."

The fate of Sasha's father is similar to millions of other non-offending and innocent people caught in purges that placated a paranoid leader. These lives fed the insatiable appetite for new victims of a state killing machine Stalin created. Now a grandfather, Sasha, can still feel the kiss that his father laid upon his head as he bid farewell and promised to return soon.

The particular purge that killed Sasha's father was the great terror of 1936. Officially, it lasted from 1934 – 1939. Stalin began the terror by giving the order to kill Kirov a rising star in the Soviet leadership. Stalin blamed the assassination on counterrevolutionaries used this as an excuse to begin the purge. Any perceived enemies of Stalin's, old party leaders, influential officers, former landowners, German speakers were targets. A quota existed in each district of how many victims needed to be executed each month, regardless of guilt, and the quota was always filled. Overall, Stalin's great terror of 1936 killed: 2 million civilians, 30,000 officers, the entire politburo, 80% of generals and 90% of colonels.[10]

[10] *Communist Nations Since 1917*. Ch. 3: Russia under Lenin and Stalin, Anna Cienciala, Kansas University, 2010.
http://acienciala.faculty.ku.edu/communistnationssince1917/ch3.html

THE HOLOCAUST (1934 – 1945).

The Charlene Schiff Story.
Individual and Governmental Heroism and Evil.
Pastor Trocme – Simple Resistance.
Un-Police Like Duty.
The Wallenberg-Eichmann Debate.
The 'Europa Plan.'
Bulgaria – Defying Hitler.
Denmark – Widespread Rescue of Jews.
The Wannsee Conference.

"The world is too dangerous a place to live in – not because of the people who do evil, but because of the people who stand by and let them."

Albert Einstein

In the early weeks of the CPG's founding, the Board of Directors invited two speakers who had survived genocide to come speak to us; Charlene Schiff was the first.

The Charlene Schiff Story.

The door to the office opened and a small elderly lady resembling Doctor Ruth Westheimer entered smiling into the board of directors' meeting. I introduced Charlene Schiff to the C.P.G board. We had to place a small platform behind the podium so she could stand and see over it.

59

She thanked us for the invitation to the C.P.G and began to tell her story. She told how her family had lived in Poland and were forced into the Jewish ghetto at the beginning of the war, and how difficult life was in the ghetto. She said it was made bearable because her mother and family were there. One day her mother had found a hole in the wall that led to outside the ghetto. It was just barely large enough for each of them to squeeze through and her mother told her that if trouble began, they would flee through the hole.

Months later when the shots rang out and the screams could be heard, they knew that the ghetto was being liquidated. They ran quickly to the wall in darkness, found the hole and crawled through it. They ran to a wooded area where they hid for the rest of the night. By morning the shots had stopped, and Charlene's mother told her that she would go back quickly to see if any of their family had survived in any of the hiding places. Charlene begged her mother not to go. It was the last time she would see her.

At this point, Charlene stopped speaking to gather herself together. The pain of losing her mother and the thought that she should have begged her to wait longer was always with her. Could she have stopped her from going back? Charlene waited for her mother until late that evening when hunger drove her toward the outskirts of town where she rummaged through trash to find food. For months she lived by scavenging out of garbage and hiding from all human contact. One day she came across a group of twelve other children who were also from the ghetto who had banded together and were surviving much the same way she was. She joined them. She made friends and they bonded together in their common fears and needs. They talked and played and shared the dangers of their existence and the memories of their families. These were the kinds of friends you would keep for life. For twelve of them this was to be true.

One morning as they were gathering food from garbage cans near the outskirts of a town, some town children saw them. There was a moment when neither side moved. Then the town children ran shrieking back to alert the town of the Jewish children's presence. The townspeople roused themselves and headed out to the fields with pitchforks. Charlene and her friends climbed into large rolls of hay. They could just squeeze themselves into the stacks and not be seen from the outside. Yet the villagers found them. They surrounded the big rolls of hay and methodically stabbed the haystack with their pitchforks until the children screamed and their blood flowed. By the end of the morning all twelve of the children were dead, except Charlene.

She dabbed her eyes, and the board room was still. Hers was the story of genocide. Everyone in the room at the Center for the Prevention of Genocide was affected. They now felt genocide.

After she spoke each of the board members approached her and shook her hand and spoke with her for a while. We took a brief break. Then she joined the board at the table.

"Who, after all, speaks today of the annihilation of the Armenians?"[11]

Adolf Hitler

Individual and Governmental Heroism and Evil.

The Holocaust was not a monolithic undertaking by the Third Reich alone. Its success was aided by the collaboration of Nazi allies, the conquered, the disinterested and a lawless international superstructure which was unable or unwilling to block a well-organized genocide. The consequences of the failure to create binding International laws after the Armenian genocide, laws with effective sanctions and mechanisms to prevent genocide, were felt throughout Europe only twenty years later, and throughout the world for the next century.

As incredible as it may seem, some of the Holocaust could have been prevented or curtailed. This goes beyond the scope of theoretical International law, early warning and possible sanctions created at the end of World War One. There existed several means that could have significantly altered the Nazi policy of extermination. For example, there were negotiations to ransom and rescue the Jews across Europe, the 'Europa Plan,' which was tested successfully. There was the military option of bombing the train tracks that led to the Concentration Camps. There was effective action, sabotage and disobedience in governments conquered by and allied with the Third Reich. We will look at some of those governments' responses. In this chapter we will look at three examples of

---

[11] Vahakn Dadrian, *Genocide, A Critical Biographical Review.*
http://cilicia.com/armo10a.html

heroic reactions from individuals to help save lives during the Holocaust. These heroes range from the wealthy diplomat Raoul Wallenberg, who quietly saved tens of thousands of Jews through creative endeavors, paying for it with his freedom. They include a Pastor whose refusal to salute the fascist flag at his school was the first act of defiance that led to a town's almost universal complicity in hiding and saving Jewish children.

These heroes are not, however, the answer for genocide prevention. It is the lesson of this book that the unavoidable answer to genocide is the creation of an early warning system that can trigger a rapid response from the international community including a possible rapid deployment of a standing armed force. A standing UN force should be dedicated to responding to genocide, mass atrocities and the threat of either and be capable of intervening in areas where there is no political interest or will to protect civilians being massacred. A far less effective remedy to genocide is through the action of people who are in a position to help - the ministers and generals, the leaders and administrators who can alter, end or sabotage the process of death. These individuals, in our case, include a diplomat, a pastor and an industrialist.

While not the permanent answer, the following examples provide courageous blueprints for action under the worst duress. Their actions ran counter to the national indifference engulfing their nations. These three examples can give us hope that with clear-headed moral certitude, individuals, even flawed ones, can save thousands of lives. During the Holocaust, many people remained indifferent due to disbelief, callousness, self-preservation, national association and helplessness, among many reasons.

Pastor Trocme – Simple Resistance.

One of the most notable resistances to the policy of deportation and extermination came from a small community named Le Chambon in southeastern France. The people of Le Chambon were a community engaged in the rare fight against persecution in the name of their religious ideals, for the sake of humanity. Some resisted the authorities openly, placing themselves in great personal jeopardy. In an historic account of the actions of Pastor Trocme, his colleagues and the entire town, Philip Hallie's *Lest innocent Blood Be Shed* gives us an account that should be a blueprint for future genocidal resistance by third parties.

Resistance to human rights and genocidal abuse must begin somewhere and can start with simple action. The Vichy government had required that all schools begin their day with a morning salute to the fascist flag. Most members of the faculty went through the daily ritual and thus began their complicity by dull acceptance.

The distinction between the passive collaboration and those who resisted could hinge on a given decision on a given day. But what action or incident can begin to jar the indifferent out of their torpor? At a certain point average men and women who realize the impetus to act, often internalize their commitment to help their fellow man without a word being said. What brings an individual to a point where they must face themselves to assess their morals and the value of their action or inaction? Once a person comes to that turn in the road the road there is no turning back. Even if one were to stop helping, one still knows what should be done. This was the will that flourished in this small town. Throughout Europe, heroism, criminality and indifference occurred often on the same street. In one town, most made the commitment to help.

One morning, at the local school where Pastor Andre Trocme taught, when the fascist Vichy flag was raised, the entire faculty and staff saluted or half saluted it with the notable exception of Pastor Trocme.

> "The government was not aware of what happened (not saluting the flag) at Le Chambon. But the three thousand people of Le Chambon were fully aware. Moreover, they saw that they could resist, that there was a possibility of resisting. For them it was like having a new, beautifully colored bird pointed out, a bird they had never seen before. But now that they saw it…they knew it could come back."[12]

Shortly after Pastor Trocme silently refused to salute the Vichy flag, the trickle of Jewish orphans began to arrive in Le Chambon where they found refuge at the Pastor's home. When the number became unmanageable, he asked parishioners of his church to house some of the orphans; and they agreed. When the number became too great for the congregation, the townspeople were prevailed upon. It was not long before most of Le Chambon was complicit in this openly kept secret mission.

The timing of his simple act of resistance, not saluting the Nazi flag, which led to other activities and inspired his town,

---

[12] Philip Haile, *Lest Innocent Blood Be Shed.*, 91.

could not have been more important. It provides an example of hope that simple resistance can lead to preventing genocide.

When a high-ranked official of the Vichy government visited Le Chambon, the community's resistance was not discussed until a young man approached the minister and delivered the following letter. The unequivocal tenor of the message could have led to the young man's instant death; instead it may have led to the reconsideration of a political crackdown in the area.

"Mr. Minister:

We have learned of the frightening scenes which took place three weeks ago in Paris, where the French police, on orders from the occupying power, arrested in their homes all of the Jewish families in Paris to hold them in the Vel d'Hiv. The fathers were torn from their families and sent to Germany. The children were torn from their mothers, who underwent the same fate as their husbands. Knowing by experience that the decrees of the occupying power are, with brief delay, imposed upon unoccupied France, where they are presented as spontaneous decisions of the head of the French government, we are afraid that the measures of deportation of the Jews will soon be applied to the Southern Zone.

We feel obligated to tell you that there are among us a certain number of Jews. But we make no distinction between Jews and non-Jews. It is contrary to the Gospel teaching.

Of our comrades, whose only fault is to be born of another religion, receive the order to let themselves be deported, or even examined, they would disobey the orders received, and we would try to hide them as best we could."[13]

This firm conviction expressed by the young man and the townspeople surprised the Vichy officials who did not quite know how to react. Later, when the Gestapo freely operated in the South, there would be a telephone call warning of an imminent raid on Chambon warning before one would occur. [14] This implies that this act was one of the Vichy policemen, who had been stationed in Le Chambon. It shows us that courageous defiance can become infectious.

Un-Police-Like Duty.

The people of Le Chambon distinguished themselves in their service to protect Jewish orphans during the Holocaust. But many communities and many average people throughout Europe, would surprisingly participate in the criminal treatment of the Jews. One would expect average fathers and grandfathers to take exception to the policy of extermination and certainly one would not expect them *not* to actively take part in the killing if asked. Christopher Browning's account of average older men doing this unthinkable thing is riveting and a terrible example

---

[13] Ibid., 102-105
[14] Ibid., 114.

of the content of character of some average people when prevailed upon to kill.

Browning's Account of 'Ordinary Men' Committing Genocide

"In the early morning of July 13th, 1942, the men of the Reserve Police Battalion 101 were roused from their bunks. They were middle-aged family men of working and lower middle class background from the City of Hamburg. Considered to be too old to be of use to the German Army, they had been drafted Into the Order Police. Most were raw recruits with no previous experience.. It was still quite dark as the men climbed into the waiting trucks. They were headed toward their first major action, though the men had not yet been told what to expect. (The Convoy arrived in Jozefow and the men climb out of the truck to be addressed by their commander).

Pale and nervous. With choking voice and tears in his eyes, (Papa) Trapp fought to control himself as he spoke. The battalion, he said plaintively, had to perform a frightfully unpleasant task. The assignment was not to his liking, indeed it was highly regrettable, but the orders came from the highest authorities. If it would make their task any easier, the men should remember that in Germany the bombs were falling on women and children.

He then turned to the matter at hand. The Jews had instigated the American boycott that had damaged Germany. There were Jews in Jozefow who were involved with the partisans. The battalion had been ordered to round up these Jews. The male Jews of working age were to be separated and taken to a work camp. The remaining Jews – the women, the children and the elderly – were to be shot on the spot by the battalion. Having explained what awaited the men, Trapp then made an extraordinary offer: if any of the older men among them did not feel up to the task that lay ahead, he should step out.

When Trapp first made his offer early in the morning, the real nature of the action had just been announced and time to think and react had been very short. Only a dozen men instinctively seized the moment to step out, turn in their rifles, and thus excuse themselves from the subsequent killings.

Later during the killing one policeman approached his superior and asked for a different assignment and was given one. Soon another group approached the same Sergeant and asked to be excused from the killing and were given another assignment. Another couple of policemen simply milled around and did not participate to the ire of their colleagues and received no disciplinary action. After the firing squad had finished executing the women and children and during the weeks after the "action" there was not one person in the battalion who did not resent what they had been asked to do....a lieutenant Buchmann, asked to be transferred back to Hamburg. He would not take part in Jewish actions because he was not "suited to certain tasks alien to the police." He was transferred without too much trouble. Only 10-20 percent of the battalion did not take part in the killing, the explanation: wartime brutalization, racism, segmentation and routinization of the task, careerism, obedience to orders, deference to authority, conformity."[15]

Here is the answer to the question, 'what would ordinary, average men do, when confronted with being forced to commit genocide?' Most do. During the four years teaching International Human Rights and Conflict in the Modern World, this quotation caused a great amount of ethical dilemma for my students. What is the correct course of action? A couple brutally honest men disclosed that they hated to think they would do it but didn't see a way out of the situation the above quote described. They wouldn't jeopardize their own family's safety. Most students in my classes indicated they would mill around or un-volunteer like some of the police officers chose to do. The bravest held that they would fiercely argue the 'un-police-like duty' nature of the assignment and verbally resist the order until they held sway over Trapp and his men. One boldly claimed he would turn his attention to Trapp and try to free, or warn, the Jews. As much as we would like to assume we would act heroically, most of us would not. Home, family, safety make cowards of many of us. The impossibility of situations like this makes the creation of early warning and detection more crucial. During and after World War Two a popular refrain was 'we should have stopped Hitler at Munich.' Indeed. We should be stopping all future Hitlers, now.

---

[15] Christopher Browning, "Ordinary Men." In *The Holocaust* (New York: Houghton, Mifflin, Co., 1997), 168-171.

The Wallenberg – Eichmann Debate.

Raoul Wallenburg left the safety of Sweden to save more than 100,000 Jewish lives in Budapest, Hungary.

"(Nazism) It's not really a bona fide ideology. *It's just the political incarnation of a single basic human emotion. Hate.* How can it last?"[16]

> Raoul Wallenberg,
> Heroic Swedish
> Diplomat while arguing
> with Adolf Eichmann.

---

[16] Danny Smith, *Wallenburg.* 1986.

The greatest hero of the Holocaust's name often goes unrecognized by many people today. Raoul Wallenberg is reputed to have saved nearly 100,000 Jewish lives in and around Budapest in the closing months of World War Two. His life and story are astounding and a testimony to the good that can be embodied by the human spirit. As incredible as his life-saving exploits were, the fact that he openly opposed the Holocaust's architect Adolph Eichmann and not only knew him but had dined together and fiercely debated the Nazi doctrine and the Holocaust. This stands as one of the clearest moral debates between good and evil in modern history.

"Budapest, December 1944.

"At the end of private dinner, the small group of men retired to another room for after dinner drinks. The dinner was thrown together quickly by Lars Berg for his colleague, the wealthy Swedish diplomat Raoul Wallenberg. Among the guests was Adolf Eichmann, the Nazi SS officer responsible for the 'final solution' - the murder of all Jews in Third Reich and Axis territory. To this day, Eichmann remains one of the most notorious agents for death and evil in the Twentieth Century. A slight man, Eichmann's mission in Budapest was to finish the deportation of the last 250,000 Hungarian Jews to their death. 400,000 Jews had already been deported under the fascist Hungarian government. Even as the Soviet troops advanced toward Budapest, Eichmann was sent to finish this evil work before Budapest changed hands. By contrast, Raoul Wallenberg's presence in Budapest was as an agent of life, relentlessly pursuing strategies to save as many Jews as possible from the killing machine of the Nazis. He had no delusion about the fate of the Jews being deported, having read the secret reports written by Jews who had escaped Auschwitz. In 1942 after watching a film telling the story of a man saved Jews from German Concentration Camps, He turned to his half-sister Nina and said, 'that's what I want to do.' Two years later he arrived in Budapest as a diplomatic attaché whose mission was to aid endangered Jews."[17]

As soon as Wallenberg arrived to work in the Swedish Legation in Budapest, he used his wealth and untiring energy to create the 'schutzpass' for Jews, a safe-conduct pass for travelers waiting to go to Sweden after the war. This passport was essentially a ruse and had no legal standing except for that which he forced on Hungarian officials. Nonetheless, it provided protection from deportation and death for thousands of Jewish 'schutzpass' holders. Wallenberg paid for a publicity campaign for the official-looking safe-conduct pass with large billboards announcing them throughout Budapest. Before long, Wallenberg was able to obtain large quotas from the fascist government to allow thousands of Jews protection under this passport. He argued, bribed, and threatened a diplomatic incident if the 'schutzpass' was not recognized. When the 'schutzpass' reached its quota limit, he developed another strategy. Leasing entire apartment complexes, Wallenberg claimed them as Swedish diplomatic territory and safely housed hundreds of Jewish families in them. Other neutral countries

---

[17] Ibid.

and humanitarian organizations followed his lead and the number of Jews who were protected in the International ghetto grew. When necessary, Wallenberg would pressure officials with the skill of a lawyer, often forming complex but compelling reasons why the official should give him what he wanted. He even forced a friend to pressure her husband, the Interior Minister of the Arrow Cross fascist government, to reinstate the 'Schutzpass' when it was cancelled. Wallenberg was unstoppable. There are many accounts of Raoul rushing to the river side or to a remote farm where Jews were being lined up to be shot or marched to the death trains. He would go among their number, obtaining names and vital information and issue them protective visas, saving their lives on the spot.

On the last night of the vicious Arrow Cross government, as Budapest was about to fall to the advancing Soviets, the order came to the SS to liquidate the Jewish ghetto of its 60,000 inhabitants. Wallenberg sent a personal note to the SS commander in charge of executing the order. In the note Raoul promised to testify at the officer's trial for crimes against humanity if he gave the order to liquidate the Jewish ghetto. It is likely that Wallenberg's intervention saved those 60,000 lives that night.[18]

> "Eichmann was the guest at Wallenberg's home with excellent food for dinner in Budapest during the last days of the Second World War. After dinner they retired to a room with a view of the Russian artillery shelling in the distance and had after-dinner drinks.

---

[18] Ibid.

The dinner had proved a success and afterwards the group retired to the living room where coffee and brandy were served. On the horizon the Russian guns sounded a distant thunder.

Wallenberg was careful to face Eichmann and Krumey so that they were facing curtains that were covering an east-facing window. Eichmann sat in an overstuffed armchair, brandy snifter in hand. Then Wallenberg told Carlsson to open the curtains. Carlsson did so as Wallenberg turned the lights out. A fierce Soviet barrage lit the horizon to the east with explosives. Gote Carlsson, one of the guests at the dinner party was startled by the effect as the silhouettes in the room were lit up by the crackling gunfire.

"The effect was tremendous" Carlsson recalled. "The horizon was bright red from the fire of thousands of guns as the Russians closed in on Budapest."

Wallenberg stood at the window as Eichmann sat in his armchair, quaffing the brandy. He began to engage Eichmann in a conversation about National Socialism and the likely outcome of the war.

"It's not really a bona fide ideology," said Wallenberg. *It's just the political incarnation of a single basic human emotion, hate.* How can it last?"

Eichmann tried to defend National Socialism spewing poisonous catchphrases about the Jewish-Bolshevik menace and world Jewish conspiracy.'

Fearlessly and brilliantly he (Wallenberg) picked Nazi doctrine apart, piece by piece, and foretold the total defeat of its adherents. Wallenberg's intention was not so much to put his own views forward as to pass on a warning to Eichmann that he would do well to stop the deportation and extermination of Hungarian Jews.

Eichmann could scarcely conceal his amazement that anyone should dare to attack him and criticize the Fuhrer, but he soon seemed to realize that he was getting the worst of the argument. His propaganda phrases sounded hollow compared with Raoul's intelligent reasoning.

"Look how close the Bolsheviks are." Wallenberg told Eichmann. "Your war is almost over. Nazism is doomed, finished and so are those who cling to this hatred until the very last. It's the end of the Nazis and the end of Hitler."

"Finally, Eichmann said: 'I admit that you are right, Herr Wallenberg. I have never believed in Nazism, as such, but it has given me power and wealth. I know that this pleasant life of mine will soon be over. My planes will no longer bring me women and wine from Paris. My horses, my dogs, my luxurious quarters here in Budapest will soon be taken over by the Russians and I myself, as an SS officer, will be shot on the spot.

"For me there's no escape." added Eichmann. "There are, however, some consolations. If I continue to eliminate our enemies until the end, it may delay our defeat – even for just a few days. And then, when I finally do walk the gallows, at least I'll know I've completed my mission. (And) if I obey my orders from

Berlin and exercise my power harshly enough, I may prolong my respite for some time here in Budapest."

"Why don't you call off your people?' asked Wallenberg. "Why not leave now while you still can?"

Eichmann was beginning to lose his temper. "Budapest will be held as though it were Berlin." With that, Eichmann got up to leave. Then turned around to face his host.

"I want to thank you for an exceptionally charming and interesting evening." He said, shaking Wallenberg's hand.

"I warn you, therefore, Herr Legationssekretar, that I will do my best to stop you, and your Swedish diplomatic passport will not help you if I find it necessary to have you removed. Accidents do happen, even to a neutral diplomat."

With these menacing words, Eichmann stood up to leave, but not at all displaying any anger. With the imperturbable politeness of a well-educated German, he bade farewell to Raoul and thanked us for a particularly pleasant evening."[19]

---

[19] *Wallenberg* Danny Smith, 1986. Pp. 107 – 108. *The Envoy: The Epic Rescue of the Last Jews of Europe in the Desperate Closing Months of World War Two* Alex Kershaw, 2011, Pp. 118-119).

At the war's end, Wallenberg was captured and sent to Siberia where he disappeared behind the iron curtain in the Soviet gulags for the rest of his life. I have a hopeful picture in my mind that the memories of the tens of thousands of people he saved helped sustain him in the Siberian cold and isolation.

Joel Brand and Saly Mayer – "The Europa Plan."

"I am prepared to sell you one million Jews. Goods for blood – blood for goods. You can take them from any country you like, Hungary, Poland, the Ostmark, from Theresienstadt, from Auschwitz, wherever you like. I am willing to offer one hundred thousand Jews in advance, and a further ten percent on receipt of the first payment. 1,000 trucks in exchange for every 100,000 Jews. You are getting away cheap."[20]

> Adolf Eichmann, negotiating with Joel Brand to 'sell' 1 million Jews on behalf of Himmler.

It is almost unimaginable to put a price tag on the value of human life. Yet Oscar Schindler, the famed industrialist, found a way to bribe a Nazi official to purchase the safety of his factory workers. This is also the strategy which saved thousands of Jews living in Slovakia and Hungary. It is a policy that might have saved millions more. As far-fetched as it sounds, the practice of ransoming Jews was a very real one among the Gestapo.

There are several examples of both successful negotiating for Jewish Lives and excruciatingly near-successes. Noting a German willingness to negotiate for Jewish lives in

---

[20] Donald Niewyk and Ian Kershaw, ed., *The Holocaust* (New York: Houghton Mifflin Co. 1997).

Slovakia in 1942 and Hungary in 1944, Joel Brand explored possibilities of ransoming Jews. He approached the Gestapo official in charge of exportation with a bribe of $50,000 to stop the deportation of 90,000 Jews. After sending the first half of the payment, the deportations stopped. But the international group of rabbis could not make the second deadline and four transports were sent to Poland. When the other $25,000 was raised the deportations were halted for another two years.[21]

Brand's efforts at first yielded results when Eichmann himself met with him and offered to ransom one million Jews for trucks, coffee and sugar supplies. In a terrible twist of fate, Brand was unable to convince nations, organizations or individuals of the legitimacy of the deal. He was detained and confronted with a bureaucracy and politicians whose priorities were elsewhere during the war and who placed little importance to the offer. This strikes me as criminally negligent indifference, to allow the imminent death of one million souls when a potential solution was at hand. After the invasion at Normandy, communication became difficult and the offer disappeared.

Another successful ransoming intervention example was the effort of Saly Mayer in Hungary.

> "Mayer, a Swiss citizen, was authorized to negotiate for the ransom of the Hungarian Jews in an attempt to gain time but not to offer to make any payments. He actually made a personal goodwill gesture of some Swiss tractors he bought to allow the talks to continue. In return, Himmler stopped the Budapest transports.

---

[21] Donald Niewyk and Ian Kershaw, ed., *The Holocaust* (New York: Houghton Mifflin Co. 1997), 270.

Through undaunted effort, Mayer tempted the Nazis to make some releases of Jews (1,200 from Thersienstadt) by showing he had access to $5 million in a Swiss bank account, controlled by the Americans."[22]

The two examples that follow are frightful. It is difficult to comprehend that a real possibility existed to stop the policy to exterminate the Jews during the height of the killing.

"A letter was sent through Wisliceny (Slovakian Gestapo) to Berlin on behalf of world Jewry the price Nazis had set for stopping all deportations throughout Europe. (Nov. 1942). The Nazis appeared to rise to the bait. After protracted negotiations, Wisleceny offered, in the name of his SS chiefs, to stop deportation from Western Europe and the Balkans for $2 million. Further negotiations on Poland and the actual Reich area might follow."[23]

The world Jewish Congress did not believe the deportations would stop and rejected the plan. They viewed the 'Europa Plan' as a blatant Nazi attempt to extort money. The fact remains that several deportations had been stopped through similar arrangements on the orders of a cash strapped Third Reich. While two million dollars may have aided the Nazi war machine, or more likely gone into the pockets of officials, it was insignificant compared to the lives it may have saved. It would have cost an unfathomable thirty to fifty cents per life saved, if this ransoming effort had been successful.

---

[22] Ibid., 271.
[23] Ibid., 273

Hungary adopted the same strategy to rescue its Jews, while escape routes to Slovakia and Romania were being forged. Toward the end of the war:

> "Eichmann himself ordered Brand to appear before him. He offered to release one million Jews (not only Jews of Hungary) in return for war material and other goods. In subsequent meetings the ransom became more specific: 10,000 trucks and quantities of coffee, tea, sugar and soap. The British, Americans and Russians refused him. It appears that the SS offer was serious. Because the Nazis believed the Jews controlled the West, they could be used as hostages. Their ransom might bring not only valuable war materials to a besieged Germany (this was the story Himmler 'sold' to Hitler) but might well move the Allies toward negotiating with the SS."[24]

The implications are staggering. Could these relatively innocuous deliveries have saved millions of lives? The fact that we can legitimately ask this question within the context of other successful efforts, highlights how many intervention opportunities exist, before and during genocide. These opportunities were present even in what has often been perceived as a monolithic, un-penetrable machine for extermination.

---

[24] Ibid., 274.

Bulgaria – Defying Hitler.

Bulgaria's leader King Boris, who was an ally of Hitler, is an example of how one individual's refusal could stop genocide in its inception and execution. Beyond this, it provides an insight of how a nation that has recently suffered acts of genocide itself (Bulgaria at the hands of Turkey) can have a pronounced and widespread sympathy for others being persecuted and massacred.

Bulgaria government gave some concessions to the Third Reich on Jewish policies, but categorically refused to turn over their Jewish population for deportation. "The plan to persecute the Jews was met with widespread opposition from every corner of the nation. It was strange to point out the dangers of a small number of Jews (50,000) when there were 650,000 Turks (in Bulgaria)."[25]

Bulgaria's refusal to deport their Jews was largely because anti-Semitism was practically non-existent there. Another factor may be that Bulgaria had suffered ethnic massacres at the hands of the Turks in recent years. Is it possible that their more humane policy toward the Jews could be the result of their suffering under similar circumstances? The memory of innocent unarmed Bulgarian villagers being cut down was still fresh in their national psyche. To appease the Reich they passed a few restrictive laws, for example: no Jews could have gentile servants, there were limits on the number of Jews in certain professions, Jews could not send money out of the country, there was a 20% Jewish tax, they were not allowed

---

[25] Marshall Lee Miller, *Bulgaria During the Second World War.* (San Francisco: Stanford University Press, 1975), 96.

to own or possess radios, and Jews were required to wear the Star of David (which few did)."[26] The Minister of the Interior went to the Jews when they protested his decision. He asked them to be patient and explained that the worst was over. Adolph Eichmann, the Nazi officer in charge of the 'final solution' was frustrated by the Bulgarian intransigence He began chipping away by having them allow Bulgarian Jews living abroad or in newly acquired territory to be deported to the camps. Then his representative finally threatened Bulgarian King Boris and he relented and signed the document to allow the Nazis to relocate the entire Bulgarian Jews to the East. Days later, with the pressure off, the King rescinded his decision and the Bulgarian Jews were to be safe until the end of the war.[27]

The newly acquired land of Macedon and Thrace, however, were deemed to be technically out of the national boundaries of the State of Bulgaria, even though they were under Bulgarian administration. Over 11,000 of these Jews were deported directly by the SS and killed. Late in the war, German operatives rounded up the Sophia Jews and sent them to the countryside to await deportation. But through the stalling of the Bulgarian government, this (the deportation) never occurred.[28]

King Boris attempted to get permission to send his Jews to British Palestine. The expense would have been great, due to the German fees to allow this to occur. Ultimately, British

---

[26] Ibid., 96.
[27] Mark Mazower, *Inside Hitler's Greece* (New haven, Yale University Press, 1993) 241.
[28] Ibid., 242.

Foreign Minister Aden blocked the effort.[29] King Boris would oppose Hitler one more time, in a contentious meeting in August of 1943 where Hitler pressured him for troops to oppose the Soviets and to change his Jewish deportation policy. King Boris refused. Two weeks later he was dead shortly after a dinner at the Italian Embassy where, many believed, he was poisoned at the behest of Hitler for opposing his Jewish policy and refusing him troops.

Denmark – Widespread Rescue of Jews.

The Danes had two factors to aid in a credible campaign to oppose to the Third Reich policy of extermination of Jews: strong leadership and favorable geography. In Denmark, King Christian X led the effort to smuggle the Danish Jews to safety and was an important factor in motivating his people. The fall of Denmark to German forces on April 9th, 1940, in six hours, remains one of the quickest military defeats in history. In part, because of this swift and relatively painless fall of Denmark to Germany, the government of Denmark was left largely intact.[30] This was an essential factor of the ability of the society to mobilize the effort to help the Jewish population escape unharmed to Sweden.

The Danish policy on deportation was that the government simply refused to give up their Jewish citizens.

---

[29] *A History of Israel from the Rise of Zionism to Our Time.* Howard M. Sachar, Knopf, New York, 2007

[30] Michael Marrus and Robert O. Paxton, "Western Europeans and the Jews," in *The Holocaust* (New York: Houghton Mifflin Co., 1997), 100.

Denmark was not treated as oppressively and with as much manpower as other Nazi-conquered nations, in part because Danish loyalty to the Third Reich was assumed by the Nazis due to their Germanic/Nordic heritage. This less strict oversight may partially explain the success of their effort to rescue Jews to neutral Sweden. Then during the summer of 1943, in the middle of a turbulent year, the Nazis attempted to forcibly take the Jews for deportation. In a mix of defiance to the Reich authority and humanitarian concern, Danish individuals, the government and neutral third-party agencies such as the Red Cross, all helped to transfer most of the Jewish community to neutral Sweden and safety. It was largely successful, though the Nazis were able to intercept 475 of the 8,000 fleeing Jews.[31] This is one of the most outstanding examples of how unified resistance through strong national and individual leadership can save lives in the most daunting of circumstances. A nation that was conquered in six hours was morally strong enough to save over 94% of their Jews.

The Wannsee Conference.

On January 20th, 1942, fifteen men convened a meeting in a beautiful countryside mansion. The delicious foods and wine were in sharp contrast to the deprivations of the war raging around them. They gathered to enact the 'final solution' of all Jews of Europe and the U.S.S.R. No longer would the Jews emigrate, stay in camped ghettos or be massacred in relatively small numbers by gun or in 'gas vans' that roamed the countryside killing standing Jewish passengers with exhaust

---

[31] Ibid., 104.

fumes. Thirteen of the fifteen present immediately embraced the plan outlined by Reinhart Heydrich and his number two, Adolf Eichmann. All Jews were to be deported to Auschwitz where an industrial production-line of death was being built. There they would go into showers which were actually gas chambers, to be poisoned to death by zyklon B and their bodies burned in industrial crematoriums leaving practically no trace of the person, and the race, that existed before.

Before the end of the meeting, all fifteen agreed on the solution. One transcript of the meeting survived and outlines the gruesome efficiency of these monsters of humanity. Their plan was put into effect almost immediately and the killing machine peaked from 1943-45 decimating more than five million Jews and millions more Slavs, Gypsies, Communists, political prisoners, homosexuals, clergy, captured soldiers and other innocents. The industrial death camp of Auschwitz could murder 2500 per hour, 60,000 per day. Barely an objection arose around the table, with the exception of some political infighting. Alternatives to mass slaughter were briefly discussed including sterilization but none seriously. Dr Wilhelm Stuckart argued against the dismantling of the Nuremburg race Laws that he co-authored but relented. Of the 15 men who attended the Wannsee 'final solution' conference, five survived the war.

Of these five men who survived the war, only Adolf Eichmann was executed for his crimes. The rest lived long, relatively normal lives, some were successful in business and life, and were never punished for the millions of lives they were responsible for murdering. They lived without the stigma or punishment of being the brain trust of one of the worst genocides the world had ever known.

The Cold War Genocides 1965 – 1979.
Indonesia, China, Ibo, Bangladesh and Cambodia.

Indonesia 1965.

> "The fact that a man is a man is more important
> than the fact that he believes what he believes."
> John Hersey.[32]

The vast majority of people killed for ideological reasons in the past one hundred years, perished under communist or fascist regimes. Indonesia, however, offers a good counterexample of a country in which communist party members (P.K.I.) and their families were specifically targeted and massacred.

The Indonesian massacres of communists in 1965-66 killed between 300,000 to 500,000 people according to conservative estimates. These massacres were largely carried out by army units and vigilante militia groups with strong political affiliations. A communist coup attempt in 1965 set off the explosive situation. The reaction to the near coup was a massacre of communist party members and their families ordered by the general who has survived the coup attempt.[33] The reaction of the world was almost non-existent. As word of

---

[32] Irving Louis Horowitz, *Taking Lives: Genocide and State Power*. (New Brunswick: Transaction Publishers, 1997), 69.

[33] Robert Cribb, "The Indonesian Massacres," in *Century of Genocide* (New York: Garland Publishing, 1997), 237.

the ideological genocides of the U.S.S.R had been suppressed, so too had word of the Indonesian massacres disappeared. Few of us in the West have ever heard of the Indonesian or Bangladeshi genocides. This arises from: the inaccessibility of the area, an ideologically charged climate and an emerging dictator who was willing to perpetrate genocide for political advantage, while his allies looked the other way.

China 1966 – 1976.

After a disastrous agrarian reform policy which cost over twenty million lives, China's communist dictator Mao's leadership position was in jeopardy. In the early 1960s he rocketed back to popularity due to his book, 'Mao's Red Book of Quotations.' The zeal with which the youth embraced his concept of perpetual revolution, led the youth to target many of Mao's political enemies and stabilize his place firmly at the head of Chinese leadership again. During this time, millions of Chinese were beaten, tortured, re-socialized, trained to purge themselves of capitalistic thought. Hundreds of thousands died as a result, and palpable fear ran through China during this period of purges. While the Chinese purges were not as brutal or as all-consuming as Stalin's Soviet purges of the 1930s, it devastated millions of lives and families and sapped an ancient civilization of its potential as other world players advanced on the world stage. The 'counter revolutionary' purges ended with Mao's death in 1976 and the eventual rise of Deng, a comparative reformer, in 1978.

The Ibo of Nigeria (Biafra) 1967 - 1970.

In 1967, the Ibo of Nigeria exercised their right to self-determination and declared their independence. The new nation was called Biafra from an ancient name for the area. It separated itself from a Nigeria that was fraught with military dictatorships, political assassinations, and coups. Nigeria has over 350 languages and dialects, three major ethnicities and dozens of minor ethnicities, and two major religions. The war for independence began to go badly for the Ibo when the Nigerian government chose to attack the Ibo food supply and starve the fledgling nation into submission rather than to defeat them militarily. This strategy has been used with the Native American Sioux (1876-7), Ukraine (1932-3), the Nuba of Sudan (2002, 2011), Zimbabwe (2002) and North Korea (2002).

Bangladesh 1971.

One of the least discussed full-scale genocides is the wanton slaughter of Bangladeshis in 1971 by the Pakistani army. It is believed that a staggering 3 million Bangladeshis perished, 10 million were displaced to India, 30 million were internally displaced and 250,000 women were raped in a nine month period of time.[34] The cause of the massacres lay in the Pakistani government's attempt to keep Bangladesh as a part of

---

[34] Rounaq Jahan, "Genocide in Bangladesh," in *Century of Genocide* (New York: Garland Publishing, 1997), 291.

Pakistan. When India gained its independence and broke up, the Muslim Bangladeshis willingly joined in a union with the Pakistanis. It soon became apparent that the union was not to their benefit. Politically and economically the Pakistanis dominated the union without regard for the Bengalis. When the Bengalis began to move for independence in 1971, the Pakistani Yahya regime sent in the army. 'Operation Searchlight' headed by General Khan of Pakistan was responsible for the massive killing and rape that followed, which appalled the international community and galvanized the Bangladeshi Muslims. It took many months before smuggled videos were able to make it to Western media to be broadcast, the first revealing the massacres at Dhaka University. The backdrop to this genocide was, once again, the Cold War. Pakistan was aligned with the U.S while India, and eventually Bangladesh, were Soviet aligned. Did this Cold War alliance play a role in the under reporting of this genocide in the West?

Ultimately the intervention of the Indian army, at the behest of its President Indira Gandhi, combined with Bangladeshi forces defeated the Pakistani forces, stopped the genocide and Bangladesh gained its independence.

Cambodia 1975 - 1979.

> "Saloth Sar would not have killed a chicken."
> A neighbor who knew
> (Pol Pot) as a youth.[35]

After the failure of Mao's Great Leap Forward (1958 – 1961), which cost approximately twenty million lives when people starved due to the collectivization of China's farms, Pol Pot's Khmer Rouge believed that Mao's failure was because he had not gone far enough with his reforms. They believed that the Khmer State (call Kampuchea at the time) should first tear everything down and start at the beginning, at 'year zero.' Toward that end, the Khmer Rouge emptied the cities of people and forced almost the entire Cambodian population into the countryside. The Khmer Rouge taught their captive nation that family ties were counter revolutionary, as was an education and books and they proceeded to kill one out of every three Cambodians in five years. That was 2,400,000 of 7,100,000 people, in an attempt to teach their vision.[36] What was their vision? The creation of a peasant-based agrarian society, one which was anti-intellectual, anti-family and anti-urban. This was a revolution where you could be killed because you wore glasses because it was a sign you were an intellectual.

During the revolution, children who turned on their parents and family were particularly prized and often were elevated in rank at teen and pre-teen years.

---

[35] Ben Kiernan, "The Cambodian Genocide," in *Century of Genocide* (New York: Garland Publishing, 1997), 335.
[36] *Statistics of Democide: Ch 4: Statistics of Cambodian Genocide* Charlottesville, 1997. RJ Rummel.

"In the first few weeks after Cambodia fell to the Khmer Rouge in April 1975, the nation's cities were evacuated, hospitals emptied, schools closed, factories deserted, money and wages abolished...Freedom of press, movement, worship, organization and discussion completely disappeared for nearly four years. So did everyday family life. A whole nation was kidnapped, and then besieged from within. Meals had to be eaten in collective mess halls...it was a prison camp state, and (of the 8 million prisoners)... 1.5 million were worked, starved and beaten to death."[37]

The absolute power with which Pol Pot and his Khmer Rouge ruled Cambodia left the nation utterly silent. No word seeped out of the country. Buddhist monasteries were targeted for annihilation. Two hundred thousand Vietnamese who lived in Cambodia ceased to exist by 1979. Approximately half had fled the country and the rest, almost down to the individual, were murdered. Half the Chinese population (425,000) were annihilated, as well as almost forty percent of the Muslim Cham communities.[38] By targeting specific ethnic groups for extermination the Khmer Rouge fulfilled the technical requirements for the UN Genocide Convention definition of genocide, but ideological or political genocide was their

---

[37] Ibid., 334.
[38] Ibid., 340-341.

clearest intention. The ultimate irony is that it was the Communist government of Vietnam, which was itself guilty of internal purges, and egregious human rights abuse, that finally ended the Cambodian genocide.

The damage of this genocide to Cambodian society is still felt and seen to this day. With the inexplicable death of such a large amount of its population at the hands of some that are still living among them, Cambodia has chosen to try to ignore this horrible chapter in its history, and to bury it, rather than to confront it and heal it. Part of the reason for this was the continued existence of the Khmer Rouge as a military force until recently.

Sierra Leone 1991 – 2002. A Generation Without Limbs.

"The soldiers would come up to you with machetes in their hands and ask you: "Long sleeve, or short sleeve?" If you said short sleeve they would push you down, hold you to a table or tree stump and chop off your arm near the elbow. If you said long sleeve, they would shop your hand off at the wrist."

Eddie Turay, former Presidential candidate in Sierra Leone discussing RUF mutilations.

The Eddie Turay Story – Long Sleeve, Short Sleeve?

When I was attempting to found the Center for the Prevention of Genocide, I had assembled the prospective Board of Directors and invited two speakers who had suffered genocide personally to come speak. Eddie Turay was the second of them.

He lumbered into the board room. He was a large, broad shouldered African man from Sierra Leone who approached the lectern. Eddie Turay had been a presidential candidate for the All African People's Congress Party in Sierra Leone before the war broke out. When the war overran his hometown, he was captured. He told about seeing the hated rebels, the RUF, tossing babies up in the air and catching them with their blades. He told of a popular game that the RUF rebels would play. They would pull a pregnant woman roughly out of line and bet on her.

"25 Leones, it's a boy."

"No man, 50, it's a girl."

"Okay 50."

They would then cut her open and the baby would spill out and one would win the bet and the mother and baby died on the spot. True horror.

Eddie told about how he escaped death through a bizarre mistake of identity. He was rounded up and sent to prison. After a few days they called out the names of approximately fifty known political leaders. These leaders were to step from their cells and marched to the center of the courtyard. Eddie stayed in his cell. He hoped against common sense that they wouldn't notice that he wasn't there. For some inexplicable reason they didn't. Maybe the person who took his place thought that the political leaders were being released so he took Eddie's place. Whatever the reason, the RUF prison guards counted them. The correct number of prisoners was outside. They shot them on the spot. None survived.

He told stories about the procedures the RUF employed to intimidate and take revenge. They were punishing everyone for voting in the recent election which they had boycotted. If you go today to Sierra Leone, you will find tens of thousands of people who are missing hands and arms.

"The soldiers would come up to you with machetes in their hands and ask you. Long sleeve, or short sleeve? An innocent enough sounding question. If you said short sleeve they would push you down, hold you to a table or tree stump and chop off your arm near the elbow. Sometimes they would take both arms. If you said long sleeve, they would shop your hand off at the wrist."

Edward eventually secured his release from prison and made a risky attempt to escape the country. At the border a few days later, a husky, quite manly looking, six foot one, woman, wearing a dress that barely fit her, crossed the border. It was Eddie Turay's first leg of his journey to safety.

The most enduring impression of the war in Sierra Leone is the sight of men, women and children, from the east and west, lining up and to have their limbs cut off. This was as a Revolutionary United Front (RUF) punishment for areas that voted when rebel leader Foday Sankoh had warned the country to boycott the election. This gruesomeness applied to little children as well. There were massacres and other unspeakable acts of barbarity, but the primary characteristic was the disfigurement of a generation.

The highlight of this conflict was the struggle over the lucrative diamond mines in the North. Liberia's President Charles Taylor supported the vicious RUF and benefitted from their control of the mines. Child warriors were used on the RUF side and eventually the government side as well. The British took an interest as the former colony but was confronted with the grim reality that victory involved killing a number of these children warriors in order to disarm the RUF. In this dilemma, the British came up with a unique solution. They hired 'Executive Outcomes' to dislodge the rebel control of the diamond area. While not conclusive, the use of mercenaries did prove effective in this particular conflict. The loss of a large part of their income left the RUF in a more vulnerable position and the British and government forces eventually defeated them. Charles Taylor of Liberia was tried and convicted for war crimes by the I.C.C and RUF leader Foday Sankoh was indicted prior to his death.

There are several salient lessons to be taken away from Sierra Leone's civil war. The first is that there is no end to human depravity. This conflict has child soldiers on both sides, permanent bodily mutilation as a standard form of abuse of bystanders, massacres, and greed. Second, mercenary forces, which are known professional entities beholden to the Geneva and other applicable International Conventions, *may* be a viable option for some of the more complex human rights abuse scenarios which require military intervention. Lastly, in my view, the healing that took place in Sierra Leone and the role of women in that process after the horror was over, was key as well. In Ishmael Beah's book *A Long Way Gone* and in the many interviews subsequent to its release, he credits his recovery from the post-traumatic stress of being a child soldier on his adoptive parents:

> "To get over it, it took the action of selfless people, adults, who were willing to see us as kids and treat us as kids and love us with a depth of compassion that it allowed us to move past what we had seen and done."[39]

We know that mankind is talented at destroying, waging war and committing atrocities. We also know that mankind is learning how to creatively solve those issues and put the pieces together of the lives it effected.

---

[39] Ishmael Beah. *A Long Way Gone.*

Rwanda 1994.

> "People became fools. I don't know why. I kept telling them, 'I don't agree with what you're doing,' just as openly as I'm telling you now. I'm a man who's used to saying no when I have to. That's all I did - what I felt like doing. Because I never agree with killers. I didn't agree with them. I refused, and I told them so."

> Paul Rusesabagina

My interest in nationalism and genocide came from my Armenian heritage. I always wondered how the Armenian genocide could have occurred in full view of the world community without being stopped. Although almost a century ago, it was a defining moment in my family's history. An explanation for this worldwide phenomenon of indifference to genocide occurred to me after the Rwandan genocide took place. In 1994, when the Rwandan genocide occurred, I read U.S newspaper coverage of it hidden beneath the O.J Simpson's trial and thought 'what a shame' and turned to the rest of the newspaper. I had no connection with Rwanda. I wasn't Tutsi, my identities were American, Irish, Italian and Armenian. None of those were being massacred so the impetus for action did not exist in me. It was three years later when I began to research genocide at Georgetown that the subtle danger of nationalism began to occur to me. Because of my lack of connection to those victims of genocide in Rwanda, their humanity was unconsciously and automatically assigned a lesser amount of value to me. Was this not the same phenomenon that occurred to my ancestors as the world failed to respond to their massacre? This is a common and dangerous tendency that still exists today. There are several answers for how to solve this, but it requires action from people like you and me, who are not, and will never be, in jeopardy, to help bring about the solution.

At the end of the Nineteenth Century and the beginning of the Twentieth Century, Armenians were being massacred and the world watched in horror but could do nothing. At the end of the Twentieth Century the world watched Rwanda with disinterest as Tutsis were massacred and chose to do nothing to stop it. Between these two genocides there had been dozens of full-scale, military-sponsored and man-made famine-based genocides. The world was no longer surprised. But the Rwandan genocide is perhaps the most devastating and frustrating because it was so detectable and preventable. Rwanda clearly showed that the world was no closer to preventing genocide than it was one hundred years earlier.

Unsurprisingly, news and other items of interest in the world newspapers eclipsed the genocide in the little known land of Rwanda. In Africa, the headlines focused on the democratization of South Africa and difficulties in Somalia. In Europe, the Bosnian War was raging and the First Chechen War had begun. In the United States, the O.J. Simpson trial reigned supreme and relegated the important issue of the Tutsi genocide to the back pages of most newspapers. Many who were familiar with the situation in Rwanda assumed the disturbance, after the assassination of President Habyarimana, was part of the confusing instability of the region. Few outside Rwanda realized, at the outset, that what was happening was a carefully planned genocide.[40] Few outsiders anticipated that one million people would lose their lives within the next one hundred days. But the few who did know were in strong positions to prevent or mitigate the genocide.

The history of Hutu and Tutsi massacres dates back to colonial times. In the year 1972 alone, over 100,000 Hutus living in Burundi were massacred, in response to a Hutu attempt to seize control of the Burundi government. The Hutu were, indiscriminately, slaughtered regardless of age and sex. In 1988, between 5,000-20,000 Hutus were massacred by the Tutsi-dominated Burundi army. The initial Hutu attempted coup in 1972 had targeted innocent Tutsi men, women and children and the Tutsi response was similarly ugly and wildly disproportionate. These actions were certainly precursors to the full-scale Rwandan genocide of the Tutsis in 1994 at the hands of the Hutus. In fact, some of the perpetrators of the 1994 genocide were survivors of the 1988 massacres.

The Rwandan genocide is distinct from other genocides in that, though initiated by an ethnic political clique trying to remain in power, Rwanda's genocide had the ground swell of popular support from non-targeted citizens. While this was clearly planned from the top, it was carefully orchestrated to encourage average Hutus to help the militia kill the Tutsi. The planners attempted to legitimize the behavior through the idea that "If everybody is implicated, then implication becomes meaningless."[8] After a successful radio campaign vilifying the Tutsi, many average Hutus were swept into the killing frenzy.

---

[40] Fergal Keane, *A Season of Blood: A Rwandan Journey.* (New York: Viking Press, 1995), 7.

After the assassination of President Habyarimana, the sizable Presidential guard and massive Hutu militias, aided by the government executed a long-planned campaign of extermination against the Tutsi minority in Rwanda.

> "Following the militias' example, Hutus' young and old rose to the task. Neighbors hacked neighbors to death in their homes, and colleagues hacked colleagues to death in their workplace. Doctors killed their patients, and schoolteachers killed their pupils."[41]

If a massive number of Hutu were guilty of crimes of genocide, we, the world community, were the neutral third parties who were guilty of passive complicity. A picture comes to mind of German citizens being to look at the concentration camps to force the realization of their passive complicity in the Holocaust. The Rwandan genocide had been predicted and could have been prevented. Just prior to the beginning of the massacres in January, Canadian Brigadier General Dallaire sent a fax to the UN Peacekeeping Headquarters with a very specific warning of the impending genocide. An informant had given Dallaire information about the intentions of the Hutu elite. These intentions included the provocation and massacre of the Belgian UN troops and the registration of all Tutsi for their extermination. The informant noted that the Hutu militia were

---

[41] [8]Philip Gourevitch, *We Wish to Inform You That Tomorrow We Will Be Killed With Our Families*. (New York: Farrar Straus and Giroux, 1998), 115.

trained and capable of killing up to 1,000 Tutsi within twenty minutes. The fax was ignored and General Dallaire was told to hand over his informer to the proper authorities. Everything predicted in that fax transpired exactly as the informer had foretold. The chief of peacekeeping operations was none other than Kofi Annan the future Secretary General of the UN.[42] On April 7th, the day after President Habyarimana's assassination, Belgian UN peacekeepers arrived at the residence of the Rwandan Prime Minister.

> "The Prime Minister fled over her garden wall and was killed nearby. Before the Belgians could leave, a Rwandan officer drove up and ordered them to surrender their arms and come with him. The Belgians, outnumbered, were taken to Camp Kigali where they were held for several hours, then tortured, murdered, and mutilated."[12]

The killing of the Belgian peacekeepers precipitated a large UN withdrawal. But during the first weeks of violence, the UN peacekeeping force of 2,000 soldiers was present in Rwanda. It was soon reduced to less than 200, contrary to General Dallaire's recommendation. This was due to the political concern of those nations who had peacekeepers stationed there. General Dallaire strenuously objected to the withdrawal of troops and petitioned for an increased presence in Rwanda as the killing began to unfold. The General promised that with five thousand UN soldiers he could immediately halt

---

[42] Ibid., 105.

the genocide. The world sat and waited while the UN Security Council debated what to do. What followed was then, and remains now, a dark stain on the reputation of the UN. The UN voted to reduce its forces in Rwanda by 90%. Embassies closed and foreigners were quickly evacuated from the country, leaving the Tutsi remained to face massacre. In the Security Council, the United States had insisted that the events in Rwanda should not be considered a genocide. Politically, there were several missions underway including the costly Bosnian mission and the unpopular Somalian mission. Ultimately, influenced by the US, the Security Council failed to consider Rwanda a genocide and thus UN members were not compelled to act under law. Had they deemed the Rwandan genocide to be what it was, in fact, the Security Council would have been required under international law to respond.

In few instances the killing was temporarily stemmed. In one case the *prefect* was a Tutsi who refused to allow the massacre of his countrymen. He was soon replaced by a Hutu extremist who pursued the task of genocide with vengeful efficiency. The entire structure of Rwandan government, from the national to the local, played active roles in the genocide, with almost no exception. The efficiency of the massacres is a testimony to this horrible fact. When the Tutsis tried to flee, they were immediately executed as they reached the borders. Many local populations, poisoned by the radio broadcasts and fueled by hate and greed, turned on the native Tutsi population with a viciousness which has few parallels in modern history. The number of bodies was so great that garbage trucks were used to clear the towns of bodies.

The international community had not learned from the past, but by knowing the UN did not have the stomach to intervene, the perpetrators showed that they had learned from the history of genocide. In actuality, some of the international community did clamor for an immediate intervention. Czechoslovakia, New Zealand, Spain and several African nations spearheaded a movement to force a humanitarian intervention almost immediately following the UN withdrawal. The eight-member African group which wanted to intervene requested fifty armored personnel carriers to help prevent casualties. The US delayed on this issue, finally agreeing to lend the carriers for a price of 15 million dollars. "Meanwhile the armored personnel carriers sat on a runway in Germany while the UN pleaded for a five million dollar reduction of the rental charge"[43] They remained there until after the killing was over. Ultimately the Rwandan Patriotic Front, a highly disciplined multi-ethnic force, reclaimed most of Rwanda. When the UN finally sanctioned the French-led 'Operation Turquoise,' the killing of the Tutsis continued in those areas that the French had secured! R.P.F advance finally ended the genocide.

There were individuals who simply stood up during the genocide and saved lives without compromising. Paul Rusesebegina, of 'Hotel Rwanda' fame used the valuable commodity of beer to forestall the persecution of his refugee guests. When the situation became grave, he used every political contact, alcohol and money to save the refugees from being evicted from his hotel to their certain death.

It is ironic that the West, which traditionally places a high regard on the sanctity of individual rights, while hundreds of thousands of those individuals were massacred, gave more

---

[43] Ibid.,

media attention to the trial of former U.S. football player O.J Simpson. One American celebrity's trial eclipsed the life and death struggle of almost one million, non-American men, women and children. Are the Tutsi mothers, fathers, sons and daughters less beautiful, less pertinent, less valuable by virtue of their foreign-ness? Was it their foreign-ness that allowed their massacre to become just a footnote in our American daily lives? Our lack of connection to them made us regard them in less than human terms.

We are inoculated to the horrors of genocide, numbed to them because they have become commonplace. Reading accounts such as the following, it is a wonder how we can turn a deaf ear to this horror simply because we have heard it before.

> "As I walk towards the gate, I must make a detour to avoid the bodies of several people. There is a child who has been decapitated and there are three other corpses splayed on the ground. A woman on her side, an expression of surprise on her face, her mouth open and a deep gash in her head. She is wearing a red cardigan and a blue dress."[44]

The Red Cross officially put the death toll in Rwanda at over one million. The UN withdrew its peacekeeping force following the death of ten Belgian peacekeepers.

After the reality of the genocide was revealed, the world reaction, was impressive. The world community

---

[44] [21]Keane Fergal, *A Season of Blood: A Rwandan Journey.* (New York: Viking Press, 1995), 78

launched the largest relief effort by the international humanitarian aid industry of the Twentieth Century, an effort which would have been entirely unnecessary had early warning been heeded with the rapid response to intervene. We are remarkable at sending many firefighters after the house has burned to the ground.

In the immediate aftermath of the Rwandan genocide, Hutu perpetrators fled with the millions of refugees to D R Congo. There they massacred 39,000 Congolese Tutsis called Banyamulenge. Killings occurred in the refugee camps as well.

The very thin silver lining for Rwanda was the 'Gacaca' traveling court that went throughout Rwanda seeking perpetrators to come out publicly and confess and ask for forgiveness of the victims in the community. This courts functioned similar to the 'truth and reconciliation' efforts of South Africa which was occurring around the same time. It promoted healing, and conflict prevention to diffuse the cycle of vengeance likely to occur after trauma where neighbors killed neighbors. While divisions still are present in Rwanda today, the role the 'Gacaca' courts played in helping Rwanda move past the genocide is indisputable.

Bosnia and Kosovo 1994 and 1999.
Ajsha's Story

> Her sister said: "Sister, let's pray sister." 'So we prayed for a miracle.'

> Ajsha Pllana as machine guns were pointed at them as they knelt.

Ajsha's Story.

During one of my last human rights classes at University of South Florida, I was not sure that she would arrive. Fifteen minutes after the beginning of class Ajsha entered quietly, gracefully, sporting a bright bubblegum pink spring dress that was at odds with the discussion about to take place. She turned a little red as she slowly began her story.   Her father had been a Professor at the University for many years and had taught many students, sometimes taking them home to tutor them, free of charge, at his kitchen table, as his wife cooked dinner. It was after the Bosnian War that Yugoslav President Milosevic started a campaign to replace ethnically Albanian teachers and civil servants with Serbs. Her father lost his job at the University.

Ajsha woke up in the middle of the night to screams. Her town was located on a lake surrounded by mountains and sound could echo throughout the lake. She ran to her parents' room and told her mother she heard screams. Her mother assured her it was just some Serbian soldiers who were drinking and their voices had carried.

The next morning the town was evacuated. Serbian

forces watched by NATO observers were ethnically cleansing the village. Ajsha and her family carefully stepped around the bodies of the villagers who were massacred and laid in the streets. Most Kosovars were numb to this scene, but Ajsha remembered how a NATO soldier cried at the sight of the bodies of the late night massacre.

The Pllana family went into hiding with friends at a nearby village. For several months they stayed in a basement, mostly reading, sometimes learning or playing games, rarely ever coming out and then only at night to stretch their legs and breathe in some fresh air. Several months later their friend rushed into the basement and told them 'You have to go, now. They're checking attics and basements and finding people!'

The Professor and Mrs. Pllana had discussed their strategy several times and concluded that trying to leave the country across to Macedonia was too risky. Three young girls and a young attractive mother would be an easy target for the Serbian militias known for rape and they controlled access to the Macedonian border. So they came up with an improbable but potentially good plan. They would go home. They would return to their home in their village which was now abandoned. They had canned food stored and they could stay hidden at home indefinitely until the trouble was over. No one would ever think to look for them in the evacuated town.

They went unseen for the whole trip back and were in their final approach, the last three blocks to their home, hurrying through an open park area, when they saw the car. It was a Yugo. It skittered by them on the nearest street, with its engine making a tinny whirring sound, one block away from the park. It was parallel to them, then past them. Maybe they didn't see them. Then the Yugo slammed on its brakes and backed up.

The Pllanas froze in their tracks in the middle of the green grass. Four men lumbered out of the Yugo carrying machine guns and yelling at them to halt.

The irregular militia men barked an order for papers. They didn't dare show them the real ones or they would be shot on the spot so Professor Pllana started making elaborate searching gestures through his pockets and Mrs. Pllana started to berate him for always forgetting his papers, hoping that the theater they were performing was convincing. Then Ajsha panicked. She knew they were dead. The nine year old blanched and ran blindly. The alarmed men threatened to shoot her if her sister didn't catch her. Her sister ran to her, caught her by the arm and said: 'Sister, let's pray.'

They kneeled and prayed to be delivered from death when the militiaman standing behind the others stepped out and asked: 'Professor Pllana?' They recognized the young man immediately. Professor Pllana had failed him as a student several years before. But then, as was his habit, Professor Pllana took him to his home and tutored him at the kitchen table and he ate dinner with the family, many times, until he passed Professor Pllana's class.

"It's okay, their okay. I'll take care of this." His student said to his unit. Then he took Professor Pllana by the arm and motioned for the rest of the family to follow. 'Where are you going? Do you live close? Show me the house and I'll make sure no one troubles you. But you must never come out."

And so the Pllana family survived. Eventually they were to cross the Macedon border successfully. They stayed in a refugee camp and then immigrated to the United States. Professor Pllana died some years ago. The sisters and mother have gone on to a happy, successful life in the United States.

To me, the author, Ajsha Pllana is the unlikely face of genocide. Young, vibrant and deserving of protection.

The first move toward the disintegration of Yugoslavia during the end of the Cold War, came from Slovenia. With a 97% ethnically Slovene population, the separation from Yugoslavia was relatively quick and painless. When Croatia followed in 1991, the time for peaceful separation was over. Deep scars from the Second World War resurfaced with memories of how the Serb population, previously trapped under fascist Croatian rule in the Krajina, had been persecuted and sent to concentration camps. There were Serbian minorities spread throughout the other Yugoslav Republics and Serbs sought to protect them from the persecution they suffered under Croatian hands during World War Two, and even Muslim hands before then. The Serbians quickly used the Yugoslavian military might to attempt to keep Bosnia and Croatia in the union and protect Serbians in the disputed territories. After arming and securing the Serbian-dominated territory of the Krajina in Croatia, and large portions of Serbian-controlled Bosnian territory, their protective military campaign soon turned into something much worse.

Attempted Interventions and other Possibilities. Allied attempts to mediate and redraw the borders to curtail the ongoing conflict were well-intentioned but fatally half-hearted. Former NATO commander Colin Powell explained logically that no forces should be committed unless victory was possible, sending the unmistakable signal that America's heart was not in the Balkan struggle. Without being able to rely on the force of NATO's major sponsoring member, potential aggressors on all sides of the conflict saw no reason to take the inflexible negotiation terms seriously. "We don't have a dog in that fight," was the way US Secretary of State James A. Baker described American interest in the area. The message was clear. The terms of any agreement would not be backed up by an enforcing power. This fuzzy-minded, vague inaction constitutes fatal and inexcusable indifference. The lessons of disengagement and appeasement prior to World War Two had been long forgotten.

One look at the ethnic map of Yugoslavia puts into perspective the reason why Slovenia would leave peacefully, but Bosnia and Croatia, without negotiations and reformed borders, would leave only through conflict. Bosnia is the very picture of a mixed ethnicity federal nation. Which works well until forces are present which demand its breakup. But if you try to break Bosnia apart, the opposite of indifference needs to occur, great care needs to be applied. One can see form the map the reason Bosnia was the site of most of the Bosnian War.

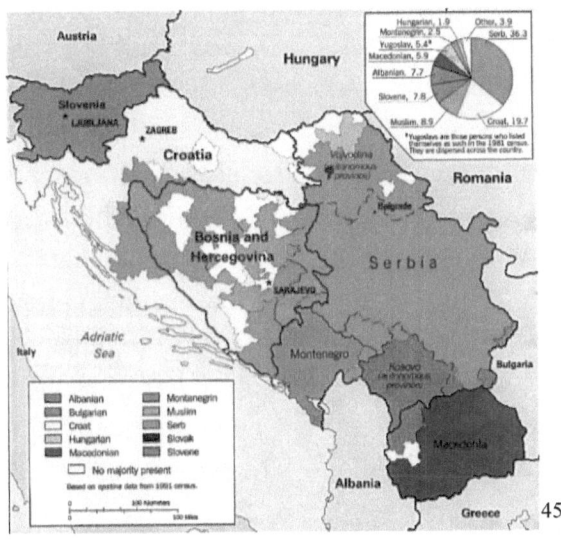

[45] CIA World Factbook 1998, Appendices.

113

Once the mass atrocities of the Yugoslavian soldiers had come to light, including the massacre of over 9,000 Muslim men and boys at Srebrenica, NATO finally woke from its torpor and intervened. A massive bombing campaign ensued which paralyzed practically all Serbian military movement. President Clinton assigned Assistant Secretary of State Richard Holbrooke to lead negotiations in a hard hitting, tough session between Slobodon Milosevic, Franjo Tudman and Alija Izetbegovic on a US military base in Dayton, Ohio. One participant later said they felt like the US would not let them go home unless they came to an agreement to end the war. Agree they did. And the Bosnian War ended with the signing of the Dayton Agreement in December 1995.

In 1999, Ajsha Pllana's family and thousands like them began to flee from the first massacres and Serbian ethnic cleansing of Kosovo. Milosevic had long made the dubious claim that the Serbian minority in Kosovo had been abused by the Muslim, ethnically Albanian, Kosovars. For years Milosevic had forced laws on the small enclave that elevated Serbians and removed Albanians from key positions throughout Kosovo. In several instances, Kosovo Serbians loyal to Milosevic would serve as his proxy throughout what was left of Yugoslavia, storming to any city that Milosevic needed a spontaneous show of strength or support. Under the same pretext of abuse of the Serbian minority, Milosevic invaded Kosovo with regular army and militia to ethnically cleanse the province of Muslims/Albanians. The massacres began almost immediately.

It did not take long this time for the vigilant US Secretary of State Madeleine Albright to utilize satellite imagery of the area to pinpoint mass grave sites. In March 1999,

Finnish forensics specialists confirmed the discovery of the second of two mass graves of civilians butchered in Kosovo. NATO immediately became involved through extensive bombing of Serbian strongholds and transportation hubs and placed NATO boots on the ground to bring this genocide to an end. Kosovo marks one example of excellent response to unfolding genocide. It also marks one of the first major known instances where satellite imaging technology was used successfully for this purpose.

Postscript. I had always known that Ajsha was brilliant. Years after taking my classes and sharing her story, she and her sister graduated Harvard with their master's degrees. Today, they are off making the world a better place.

CHAPTER FOUR: D.R. CONGO (2002-2003): An Emergency Crisis Procedure at the CPG – A Massacre in Bunia.

"We have to control the city with 500 warriors just to observe; we have to be able to fire. We can't remain like that. If we are to settle the situation, the mandate must be changed."

Colonel Daniel Volo
UN Commander, forces in Bunia
prior to mandate change that
allowed force. 2003.[46]

Emergency Crisis Procedure at CPG on D.R. Congo – Bunia Massacre.

It was the end of a productive but uneventful summer at the CPG. We had great office space overlooking the Potomac River, 4,000 square feet of discounted office space as well as an indoor basketball court. We had funding woes, but the professional-looking office space helped us feel more secure. August 9th was the last day all of the interns would be at the

---

[46] http://www.guardian.co.uk/news/guardianfilms YouTube: Bunia Massacre – Democratic Republic of Congo

Center, so we decided we would throw a barbeque. We set up the grill on the penthouse balcony overlooking the river. At the lunch hour the interns handed in their country binders and headed out to the balcony. The stress of the daily work began to melt away. I had prepared thick burgers the night before and they sizzled with the hotdogs on the grill. The smell attracted everyone including the other offices. By 1:00pm the sun arrived, making it one of the most beautiful settings in Washington to say goodbye. Cory and a few others would stay until the end of the summer and of there would be our newly hired skeletal staff but the volunteer human rights monitors were the soul of the operation, and they were leaving. It had the feel of a seasonal hotel closing down for the winter.

I wiped my hands on my apron and added hotdogs to the grill. Cory gestured urgently to me through the window. Yevgeni, who had returned for his second summer, took over at the grill and I went in to see Cory. Her face was serious with worry.

"Rich, it may be nothing, but there's some trouble in Bunia, Congo."

"What's up?"
"Well, C has been emailing me frantically in the past few days and he just sent a note that seems pretty ominous. He's hinting that there may be a massacre occurring right now."

"Lendu on Hema?"

"No Hema on Lendu."

117

I looked at everyone outside relaxing and laughing. My mind went from the tranquil scene outside on the balcony to the flash of machetes and screams of terror in the Ituri Province jungle.

"When will you know?"

"Any minute."

"Okay, tell Roy to grab anyone involved in the emergency crisis procedure for DRC and give them a head's up, and to stop drinking."

She nodded then walked out. How ironic. The season is over. A day later and we would have only limited ability to react, but here it was at the last possible hour. The timing was uncanny. I took up my spatula, flipped a row of burgers and looked at the view of Washington. A helicopter flew low down the Potomac and passed close over the Key Bridge. They were getting closer and closer. One helicopter came so close to our balcony a few days before that it shook the structure and we all thought the tail blades would hit the side of the building. I looked back at the doorway. Cory was already walking back to me reading a printed email as she walked.

"It's happening. It's on. C is confirming a massacre on the ground in Bunia, Hema dialect speaking perpetrators with over a hundred dead and many wounded."

C was one of our best sources on the ground. We had met him when he had visited policy makers in Washington. He was biased, to be sure, but his information was always excellent. The only problem with C's information was that it would need independent confirmation before we could release it.

I looked at Cory:

"Okay, that's it. It's go-time. I want everybody on the emergency crisis team in the boardroom in two minutes. Let's go."

I went outside and handed my apron to Yevgeni. I cleared my throat. I addressed the group on the balcony.

"Well, Cory just received a first-hand ground report of a massacre unfolding in Bunia, Ituri Province, and DR Congo. This is not a drill. I need the five people on the emergency crisis team and everyone on the executive staff and the PR people to head to the boardroom. Now, the rest of you, try to be helpful to the DRC team after the meeting. Otherwise, finish your lunch. Jan take the grill."

The complexity of many ethnic and linguistic areas with a weak central government, a history of genocide and many well-armed militias, made D. R. Congo a constant threat to explode.

At the beginning of the summer, two months earlier, we had tried to get a grasp of the ground situation in DR Congo. It was a mess. We began to meticulously draw a map on our wall-sized blackboard to include each of the several rebel, foreign national armies and D R Congo government controlled areas. We counted at least 18 armed groups, some of whom had shifting loyalties. The list didn't even include the ethnicities like the Hema and the Lendu who were now battling in Ituri Province. Then, we wrote up the names of each of the groups and their alliances, modus operendi and strength. Now came the pivotal question:

"Which of these, are the bad guys?" I had asked.
 Their answer, given in unison without hesitation, was jarring.
"ALL OF THEM."

This would be difficult. We divided the lists into different levels of massive human rights abuse. Those who were directly responsible for massacres were in the worst group. Those that *may* have committed massacres were next. Then we broke the civil war down into its several components. There was the Rwandan government involvement, the Ugandan presence, the RCD Goma proxy war, the Banyamelenge in the area, the Hutu genocidaires leftover from the Rwandan genocide of 1994, the Hema and Lendu militias, the rebel forces in the north, not to mention the several neighboring governments who had sent troops. Nine foreign governments had been heavily involved in the later stages of the DR Congo civil war, and at least fourteen militias were involved in the conflict being called the African World War. Most of these foreign forces had gone home during Joseph Kabila's first term. However, Rwanda and Uganda continued to keep forces there. On the surface, their reasons for being in D.R. Congo were well founded. Rwanda was still seeking the Hutu genocidaires who had fled to the Congo bush after the genocide. The genocidaires from Rwanda killed nearly 40,000 Tutsis living inside the Congo, Banyamelenge and in refugee camps. Uganda was asked to help keep the peace between the warring Hema and Lendu. Neither was exactly as it appeared. Suspiciously, Rwanda and Uganda both had record years of diamond and coltan exports during the time their troops were on the ground in DRC implying a taking of mineral resources that were not theirs. Rwanda also aligned itself with a rebel group called the RCD Goma who were accused of horrendous human rights abuse and employed this group in proxy warfare when it was convenient. Rwanda had agreed to remove troops and had resorted to tricks to keep some of their soldiers in DRC. One example of this was when Rwandan University students were marched from Rwanda to D.R. Congo at night and were marched back across the border to Rwanda in soldier's uniforms, under the eyes of the international observers. This was done briefly to meet the quota of Rwandan troops being withdrawn from D.R. Congo.

In the northeastern province of Ituri the feuding between the Hema and Lendu ethnicities destabilized the area. Uganda, originally asked by the UN to intervene for stability, ended up fueling the Hema and Lendu conflict to unrivalled proportions with the saturation of arms from Uganda. Suspiciously, Uganda's exports of diamonds and coltan also multiplied, raising the likelihood that they, too, were profiting off of the weakened state of the Congolese government. As long as the Hema and Lendu were fighting, Uganda could stay in order to provide stability to the area while benefiting from the Congolese resources. Uganda was asked to step in to keep the peace, twice.

121

The CPG staff looked at motivations, the ground situation, and dangers toward civilian populations until we had a clearer picture. We could not imagine a more complex civil war or human rights picture. Just a quick glance at the main player's acronyms was enough to make your head spin: UPC, RCD-ML, RCD-N, MLC, UPDF, RCD-K-ML, APC, RPF and the MONUC.

In brief, the government controlled the western region near the capital and far from the fighting. It had just made "peace" with one of the war lords in the north, Bemba, and had offered him the VP slot in the government, but unlike Caesar, when it came time to cross his Rubicon, he chose not to return to the capital but remained with his troops in the north – a Vice president on paper only. Years later he would run unsuccessfully for President against Joseph Kabila in a closely watched election. Many of the neighboring governments saw the benefit in supporting Joseph Kabila after the assassination of his father, the former communist guerilla Laurent Kabila. When Joseph Kabila assumed the reins of power, he was committed to a negotiated resolution to the civil war and diplomatically and effectively ushered the 'guest armies' to leave. It was in the East, where there were many armies and militias that the trouble always occurred.

On this day, August 9th, 2002, the day of the barbeque, a band of Hema militia had massacres a Lendu village. It appears that the massacre was a reprisal for an earlier Lendu attack on an unguarded Hema village. Our job was to obtain credible neutral third party confirmation. If we received the confirmation, we would need to get the information to whoever could stop the massacres. We would give the information to the press, but often times that did not have an effect. Even if the press published it, publication alone was not always enough to resolve a major human rights disaster. Our ultimate goal was to resolve the situation.

We closed the Board Room door.

The first step was formulating a strategy and assigning tasks to each person in the room and then agreeing on a second meeting in a short while. We decided to meet in a half an hour. Two people were tasked with drafting the press release. Two people checked the wire services and the regional and international media to see if word of the massacre was out. If the media already had news of the massacre, we could stop trying to get third party confirmation and could concentrate on releasing the information to the right policy makers. The rest of us worked on neutral third party confirmation. Cory and I, who were most familiar with the ground situation, divided the list of field contacts and relief organizations who had people in the area. It was 1:15pm when the meeting adjourned. By 1:45pm Cory and I were still working the phones. We changed the meeting time to 2:00pm.

At 2:00pm we all stepped into the boardroom. No one sat down. The press release first draft was read. It was rough and needed editing. The wire service and media search had produced nothing. It appeared no one was reporting this massacre. Again, we appeared to be among the first in the world outside of D.R. Congo to have the information. But we needed neutral third-party confirmation, and quickly. The UN staff in New York would start to drift toward their weekends in about two hours. It was crucial to get the information to the UNHCHR (now OHCHR) in New York because they were helping to draft the language for the new UN-flagged, French troops soon to be deployed to the area. I put John on the draft and everybody else starting hitting the phones with instructions if they got ahold of someone who could confirm the massacre, to get Cory and me immediately.

Around 2:30 Cory came into my office.

"Richard, call this number and ask for Jacques."

"Who is he?" I asked as I dialed the very long number.

"He is with the UNHCHR in Kinshasa."

I stopped. Good thinking. Smart. Who would know better than the UN High Commissioner for Human Rights Office in Kinshasa? Well, actually the UN presence in Bukavu would know better because they were within 300 miles of the massacre. But we couldn't get them on the phone because it was the middle of the night and the middle of a massacre. Even if we could get them on the phone, they would be very busy securing staff, protecting people, receiving and writing reports to send back to the UN. But the local office would certainly have called Kinshasa with the information so they could begin to file their report and request help as needed. But it was very possible that neither office had thought to call the UN offices in New York because they were swamped. That was where we could help.

"Ah qui?" Jacques hurriedly answered the phone.

"Bonjour, est-ce que Jacques?"

I introduced myself in my high school French. After one sentence of my French he broke into fluent English. I asked about the Bunia massacre.

"Yes, we heard about the massacre," he confirmed:

"Yes, at least 100 dead by the count right now."

"Jacques, we have information that the perpetrators were speaking a Hema dialect. Do you have that?"

"Yes, we also have other credible information that the perpetrators were Hema."

Now for the crucial question.

"Did you," I asked
"Pass the information on to UNHCHR in New York?"

"Mais non! Do you know how late it is here? There is too much to do. I have to go home and get some sleep to be any use tomorrow. I am going home." He sounded exhausted and said goodnight.

That was the confirmation we needed. We called another board room meeting. This was a strategy session to determine which agency was best suited to respond to the massacre.

Most of the four years at the Center were filled with research, editing, interviewing, developing contacts, phoning, emailing, writing, fundraising, and selling donated computers. Reacting to unfolding emergencies like the one in this story was rare. This was the time when all the preparation paid off with information that could save lives. For every one report the center published that had a tangible effect there were a half a dozen that achieved little except increasing awareness. But when our action did have an effect, I was always surprised at the timing of how close we would come to failing. Examples of this were; the phone cards running out just moments after we obtained the critical confirmation of the Sulawesi massacre; our asking the right bush pilots for information on Nuba just before USAID made some significant decisions regarding deliveries to the starving Nuba. A third coincidence was our fortunate timing as we called the UN offices in New York with the fresh confirmation from C and their *own Office* in Kinshasa.

After the phone call with the UNHCHR Kinshasa office we convened another brief meeting. We agreed that the UNHCHR was best positioned to help in light of the imminent troop deployment to the area. We called a UNHCHR contact in New York. After a series of transfers, I was required to have the same conversation with three highly placed officers inside the UN who were working on DR Congo.

"Hello Pierre, my name is Richard O'Brien. I am from the Center for the Prevention of Genocide. We are a nonpolitical, non-religious, nonprofit organization that serves as an early warning system for massacres worldwide. Our purpose is to bring breaking news of massacres to agencies and policy makers such as yourself. Pierre, the reason I am calling you today, as you may be aware by now, is that there has been a

126

massacre in Bunia just a couple of hours ago. Approximately 100 unarmed Lendu, mostly women and children, were massacred by a Hema militia. It is likely a reprisal attack for the recent Lendu on Hema massacre."

"Are you certain of your information, I mean, who are your sources?"

"Well I cannot reveal our primary source to you for reasons you can understand. However, our confirmation source is the UNHCHR Office in Kinshasa."

There was a pause at the other end of the line.

"Now why in the world would you have that information and we wouldn't?"

"Well, Pierre, they are writing up the report as the information is coming in. It is also in the middle of the night there so many of them have gone home. You know they probably have a few ground concerns as well."

"Who did you speak to in Kinshasa?"

"Jacques."

"How long ago?"

"Just a few minutes."

"You know the timing on this is extraordinary. Did you know that we are set to have an interdepartmental meeting about the level of the UN peacekeeping deployment and mandate recommendations for Ituri Province on Monday?"

"One of your colleagues had just mentioned it to me."

"That's quite extraordinary information, because, you know with an immediate threat that gives new importance to the numbers of peacekeepers and the strength of the mandate, their response ability."

"We thought the information could be used by your office." I offered.

"Can you send us the information you have?"

He gave me his fax and email and we sent the information off.

It really was amazing timing. If we had not taken the initiative, it is likely the exhausted Kinshasa UN office would not have had the time to submit the report to the New York UN office before the Monday meeting to determine the mandate language. When Pierre left the phone, they held a quick meeting at the UN regarding the breaking news in order to incorporate the information into the Monday meeting agenda.

In Monday meeting in New York, the UN raised their levels of peacekeepers in the area and included 'use of force' in the mandate language to protect innocent lives on the ground. This was language the UN peacekeeping force commander had

128

requested for months. By having an early warning system in place, we helped make sure that the information, in a world where there is an overabundance of information, did not get lost in the noise or bureaucracy.

When trouble occurred in Ituri Province between the Hema and the Lendu and the Ugandans were in the process of pulling out due to international pressure, something unexpected happened on the UN Security Council. One of the Security Council members stepped up and took responsibility to stop the massacres. In Sierra Leone several years earlier, it had been the British, aided by some unusually effective mercenaries that had ended the massacres. But this time, unexpectedly, it was the French. Within one month of becoming fed up with international indifference to massacres in DR Congo, the French forces, under EU and UN auspices, arrived and halted the massacres in the Ituri and South Kivu Provinces.

While DR Congo has some of the most valuable resources of any nation in the world, today it remains fragmented and stymied by warfare and disease. The French force that went in, however briefly, showed again, that genocide can be combated by vigilance and action.

The stars sparkled under a clear Washington summer sky. The heat of the day had evaporated and a nice warm breeze passed over the penthouse balcony. Cory, Madoko. John, Yevgeni, Roy, Jan and I lounged on the outdoor chairs and took in the majesty of the view. Everyone was subdued. The significance of the events of the day was on everyone's minds. We fired up the grill and broke out the beer and at the end of the evening began to say our goodbyes.

CHAPTER FIVE: GUJARAT, INDIA (2002): INTERVENTION AND CONFESSIONS.
Confessions Caught on Tape. Bloodbath Averted by Sikh Police.

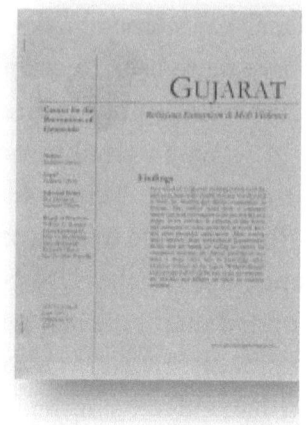

"We showed them what's what."

Babu Bajrangi, massacre participant bragging, Gujarat, India.[47]

On February 27th, 2002, a trainload of Hindu pilgrims, returning from a pilgrimage to sacred Ayodha, caught fire in the Godhra station and fifty-eight people perished in the blaze. The gruesome sight of the sheets covering the bodies, contorted in the shapes of the victims last desperate moments, enflamed the outrage of the majority Hindu population. A story immediately circulated about Muslims fire-bombing the train as revenge for an ongoing dispute between Muslim vendors who sold refreshments through the train windows and the Hindu pilgrimage passengers. Weeks later, the Indian government created a commission to investigate the fire. It found no credible evidence for this claim of Muslim responsibility. It defied logic that any person could climb into the cars, spread an incendiary,

---

[47] YouTube: Gujarat Massacre of Muslims Undercover Footage 1 of 3.

start the fire and escape unharmed and unnoticed. Nonetheless, radical Hindu nationalists produced lists of names and addresses of Muslims throughout Gujarat, distributed them to radical members and initiated large-scale killing. When it ended a few days later, more than 2,000 innocent Muslims had been murdered, including former Member of Parliament Ehsan Jafri. Parliamentarian Jafri had tried to intervene to stop the rape and killing of Muslim women and children in his apartment building. When he slipped money out of his narrowly opened door to the perpetrators, in an attempt to pay them to leave the innocents alone, the radical Hindu men pulled him outside and, in full view of his family watching from the balcony, hacked him to pieces.[48]

The tensions between the Hindu majority and Muslim minority dates back, in the modern age, to the separation of the newly independent Indian state into Muslim-majority Pakistan and Bangladesh (originally East Pakistan) and Hindu-majority India. The minorities of Hindus and Muslims remaining in these nations experienced the brunt of antagonism between these countries during times of tension.

Following the train fire at Godhra station, radical Hindus scoured communities looking for Muslims, some carrying lists of Muslims to target. The police stood aside as children, women and men were hacked to death and set on fire. Groups of radicals had their eyes on the Muslim minority, waiting for such an excuse to attack.

A few aspects to note on the Gujarat massacre and the government reaction make it unique. Not only was the violence unleashed not justified, but it was based completely on a

---

[48] Ibid., Video 1.

misinformation – an assumption that the train caught fire because of a Muslim bomb. This first disaster compounded into one of geometrically larger proportions. The government reaction to prevent further massacres was praiseworthy and effective. It is also unique because several perpetrators were caught on film bragging about their exploits in murder.

Confessions Caught on Tape.

An industrious journalist went undercover to infiltrate the Hindu national groups that perpetrated the massacres. Once he was accepted as part of their group, he inquired about their roles in the Gujarat Muslim massacre. Surprisingly, several of the leaders and perpetrators proudly told him of their roles in the killing spree. Their new recruit carried a very small video camera which recorded through a buttonhole in his shirt or a tiny hole in a book he held. Caught on camera were 'confessions' of these average men who took extraordinary measures to kill innocent Muslims. One radical Hindu killer described the plan: "What happened was, the people we've had in our sight for the past twenty, twenty-five years, we selectively killed those people." Another describes their plan to kill the Muslims as a 'Hindu Jihad.'[49]

Babu Bajrangi appeared to be the most talkative of the perpetrators as he gleefully described the horror he perpetrated, as if it were a sports game. "There was this pregnant woman, I slit her open. We showed them what's what."[50]

---

[49] Ibid., video 1.
[50] Ibid., video 2.

Most police stood aside as the killing occurred. One victim, Fatima, described the police response when she asked for help for her family. "They said (the police) 'we have not been ordered to spare your lives. Our orders are to kill you'"[51] Almost all of Fatima's family died.

This type of journalism, facilitated by the improvements in technology, helps make the world a more transparent place. The prosecution of these men was slow, yet after years of delay, this stark video evidence was used to prosecute a portion of these perpetrators. The unfiltered view into the minds of perpetrators is eye-opening. Evil is present in the human heart everywhere, in every continent and in every nation.

Bloodbath Averted by Sikh Police.

While heroism is always praiseworthy in these circumstances, the most effective way to combat the next instance of genocide or mass atrocities is prevention. Early warning and education are cornerstones of that prevention. It is interesting to note the different reactions between authoritarian governments, which usually do not act to prevent these types of abuse, with the responses of democracies, when confronted with internal massacres or genocide. India, the world's most populous democracy, attempted to grapple for a solution to help prevent future reoccurrences of violence in Gujarat. While the two activities they undertook did not receive much press attention – they were, nonetheless, very effective in preventing continued massacres of the Muslim minority. First, they

---

[51] Ibid., video 1.

published a report which concluded that Muslim vendors were *not* responsible for the fire. This helped reduce tension. The danger remained, however, that in large public celebrations, especially religious celebrations, misunderstandings and tempers could flare, or lists could be maliciously distributed again and massacres reignited. The government of India chose to be proactive. They hired several hundred Sikh police officers, as Sikh's were neutral in this conflict, to show a strong presence at all public events and celebrations. Those Sikh officers acted as a buffer between these groups, helping to prevent tensions from flaring into violence. They succeeded, as the police presence diffused the situation. This is a classic conflict-prevention strategy. It was not front page news but it is likely that it saved lives and allowed a nation to move forward.

CHAPTER SIX: UGANDA
L.R.A CHILD-MILITIA
MASSACRE ACHOLI.
A Ugandan Boy.
Alice and the Spirit of an Italian
Soldier. Testifying Against the LRA

"They looked for students who wore
our shirts and killed them. They
reversed years of work in hours.
They're gone."

> Aid worker in Northern Uganda
> after massacre of their students
> by the LRA.

A Ugandan Boy.

The LRA militia, mostly teenagers, came into town on
horseback, in vehicles and by foot. Many of the boy's family
fled and were cut down in their tracks. Others tried to hide and
were discovered. Many were raped before they were butchered.
The dead bodies were stripped of valuables. He hid, then fled
to another burned out hut and then to some bushes. The militia
caught him near the edge of the village, beat him with rifle butts
and left him for dead. He woke in pain when they were gone.
His eye was swollen shut. He began wandering for days. His
feet, face and arms swelled with infection and disease. He
survived on plants and collapsed on the roadside miles outside

135

of a protected camp where he was discovered near death. After a while he could stand and talk a little. He was six years old. To me, his swollen face is the face of genocide.

The photo of the little boy who was almost beaten to death was the most poignant thing I had ever seen. It came to us from a Christian aid group in the area that helped build and supply schools for the Acholi. Three British nationals from the relief group that had provided the photo, met us to discuss the region. They were charming people who were serious about their work. They told us how despite their hard work to provide Acholi children a safe haven, the LRA had swept into one of their camps, seeking any of the children wearing the camp tee shirts and killing many of them. It had disheartened even the most diehard relief workers from their organization.

Alice and the Spirit of an Italian Soldier.

The LRA is the militia the Lord's Resistance Army, a cult militia that used children to fight while they operated in northern Uganda. The movement started in 1985 when Alice Lakwena (Auma), was struck by an illness and emerged claiming she had been taken over by a spirit of a dead World War One Italian Captain who was infused with Christ's spirit reborn. Many other spirits shared her body and she convened meetings with these spirits in the wilderness.[52] She developed a following among some of supporters of deposed President Okello and declared war on the government. Her group armed itself with hymns, Shea-nut oil and strode into battle against

---

[52] *The Economist*, Obituary 1/25/2007

Ugandan government troops in 1986-7. The frightened government soldiers fled the battlefield from this hymn singing display. Ultimately, a government artillery barrage in the summer of 1987 showed the thinness of Alice's spiritual

CPG Publication.

protection as the Holy Spiritual Movement warriors were killed and dispersed on the battlefield. Alice fled by bicycle and said the spirits had left her. She spent most of the rest of her fifty years in the Dadaab refugee camp. But a fragment of her militia continued under the leadership of Joseph Kony, who claimed to be her cousin. Kony declared himself to be filled with the same

Holy Spirit as Alice.[53] The newly named LRA (Lord's Resistance Army) claimed to be fighting to install a government ruled by the Ten Commandments. Kony and the LRA proceeded to break almost all of them, especially 'thou shalt not kill.' From a seemingly non-violent cult movement under Lakwena (Auma), the LRA transformed into one of the most viciously cruel child militias on the continent.

In 1987, Joseph Kony began a guerilla warfare campaign against the government using child soldiers to attack local Acholi villagers in northern Uganda. The campaign targeted local Acholi villages, travelers, clergy, schools and anyone that had food or money. They raped, abducted children and killed many villagers. Their primary goals were their own survival and to instill terror and their chosen method was to live off of the belongings of the villages they massacred. The children they abducted were forced to kill other children to prove their loyalty to the LRA. A boy, asked who in the crowd was his friend, would hesitatingly point to a friend. A pistol with a single bullet would be placed in the young boy's hand, 'kill your friend,' he would be told. When he hesitated, the militia would threaten, 'kill your friend or we will kill you.' Either the boy would comply and be bonded to the other LRA boys in a bond of shame and murder, or he would be killed and the LRA would continue the gruesome initiation with another young boy.

At the height and through the end of the LRA presence in northern Uganda, thousands, then tens of thousands of women and children walked dozens of miles every night to the relative safety of the government-protected camps. They were

---

[53] Ibid.

fleeing the LRA violence that often came at night. They would walk back to their unprotected villages in the early morning hours. This was a man-made migration to preserve life. It is almost as strange an activity as the child cult-militia it was fleeing from.

Testifying Against the LRA.

The longstanding President of Uganda, Yoweri Museveni, attempted to disarm and defeat the LRA several times, the most notable effort being 'Operation Iron Fist.' The porous Sudanese border, however, and a complicit al Bashir Sudanese government gave the LRA a safe haven. Eventually, Sudan closed its borders to Kony's militia and the Ugandan government was faced with the unpleasant challenge to disarm or kill abducted child soldiers, in order to protect the innocent. To get out of this Catch 22 situation, Museveni chose a controversial course of action; he let them leave Uganda. He offered Kony safe passage to D.R. Congo with the promise he and his militia would be unharmed as long as Kony pledged to never return to Uganda. When Kony and the remnants of the LRA fled to eastern D.R. Congo, they brought their madness with them and have been directly responsible for several large-scale massacres in D.R Congo since their arrival. Recently the LRA has also been active in the Central African Republic as that nation plunges into civil war, mass atrocities and chaos, largely unrelated to the LRA presence. While there now exists a large reward for the capture of Kony, and the U.S has forces tracking him, one cannot help but wonder whether the best opportunity to capture him was when Museveni willingly let Kony slip through his hands years earlier.

The Center for the Prevention of Genocide (CPG) published four full reports on the LRA massacres in the area. Our first report came out in 2001, and then one in each of the following years. Because places existed where people were dying in greater number, Uganda was always overshadowed. In the other countries tens of thousands were dying or were in danger: Nuba, Sudan, Sulawesi, Indonesia, Ituri Province, D.R. Congo, Darfur, Sudan In Uganda, the LRA massacres would stop for months at a time, the LRA would disappear, then begin again when they reappeared. Unlike other places that had garnered international front page attention, the numbers of victims in Uganda were in the dozens, not the hundreds or thousands. It was more difficult to get anyone to notice an area with no strategic importance, no lobby power, a low grade war and a low grade genocide. However for the Acholi people living there, it was pure hell.

Early in 2004, we lobbied Congress and the Africa Sub-Committee to take more action regarding the LRA. We found that most of the offices clearly needed a tutorial. Uganda's LRA was a group with which most lawmakers and staffs were unfamiliar. The CPG worked with the Africa Sub-Committee to appear with Acholi local leaders, flown in by Human Rights Watch, to inform the Congressional Africa Sub-Committee of the LRA terror. We provided detailed testimony in Congressional staff briefings. But it was not enough. Over a decade later, the LRA continues to function in the bush of central Africa today.

The author testifying in U.S. Congressional Sub-Committee hearing on the
massacre of Acholi by LRA in Uganda, March, 2004.

Letter of firsthand atrocities committed by the LRA – referred to as rebels.

CHAPTER SEVEN: NUBA, SUDAN: INTERNS EXPOSE MAN_MADE FAMINE.

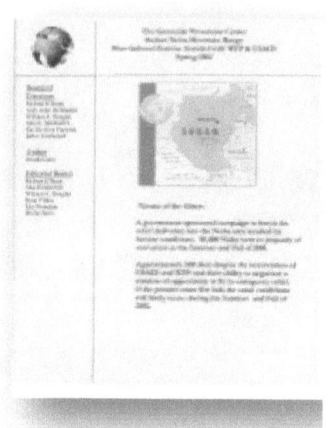

"Where the hell did you people come from? We can't get any information out of Nuba."

Roger Winters, US AID

Interns Help Prevent a Man-Made Famine Against Nuba.

Joanna and Yevgeni, two new interns, were assigned to research and make contacts in the South of Sudan and to follow up on reports of massacres, human rights violation, ethnic cleansing and slavery. Many human rights organizations had been monitoring South Sudan for years. Militias hired by the Sudanese government had ethnically cleansed, massacred, starved, raped and enslaved the Nuer and the Dinka among other ethnicities of the South. The abuse was a continuation of the jihad which had led to the civil war and an effort to depopulate the oil concession areas that the government had sold to foreign corporations. Until the Comprehensive Peace Accord of 2005 was signed, slavery was actively practiced and entire regions had been depopulated by Baggara militias hired by the government. It was perhaps the most likely place where

142

we might find genocide occurring. Our pair of interns emailed, phoned and laid out maps to track activities in the region. They approached human rights NGOs, aid groups and UN agencies to get a better understanding of the ground situation. After a week of research they approached me with an unusual revelation.

"Rich, we want to ask if we can change the scope of the area we are working on?"

Yevgeni started. Joanna continued. "We think that there are a lot of human rights organizations concentrating on the South of Sudan and the information is pretty much getting out to the press and policy makers. But we wanted to take a closer look at an area in the Central part of Sudan, the Nuba Mountain range."

"Why, what's going on there?"

"Well, we're not sure yet. But there is a government ban on travel there so there are very few relief organizations except for small ones that don't worry about the danger to themselves and are mostly Christian based. But the thing is, it seems that the government is bombing the relief as it comes in, so that the Nuba will starve and have to leave."

"Bombing them, really? Are there oil field in the area like in the South?"

"No, that's the strange part. This area seems not to be so strategically important. But we'd like to ask your permission to change our focus, contact people there, the relief organizations, and the bush pilots, to get a better picture of what's happening there."

"Okay but know your stuff before you hit the phones. Know your towns and questions. You can try the Colonel next door, he may know some pilots in the area."

"Thanks Rich."

They left my office with beaming smiles. That was to change two days later.

Joanna and Yevgeni came back to see me, two days later in the afternoon. They looked miserable. They had contacted a number of the relief organizations on the ground to no avail: wrong numbers, disconnected lines, no answer and messages left unreturned, but then they turned their attention to the bush pilots. Their first call was a disaster. On the same floor as the CPG in the white building on the corner of King Street and Payne Street in Old Town Alexandria, there was a Colonel who flew aid missions to Central America. We believed our gruff neighbor was a CIA operative. Yevgeni and Joanna wondered if he knew any bush pilots currently flying into Sudan. He did. The Colonel met with them late the previous day and gave them contact numbers of a friend of his who flew relief flights in and out of the Central areas of Sudan. In their excitement to contact the pilot, they mismanaged the call. Having woken up very early that morning to take account of the time difference, they made the call with a phone card for Africa. They successfully got through to the pilot but, in the course of the conversation with the tough, no-nonsense military vet, they forgot to lay out a map out and got some names of towns confused, and instead asked about massacres and relief work that was occurring several hundred miles away. Their inexperience and lack of preparation was apparent. He told them off and hung up. Not quite the reaction they expected from a pilot doing what they considered to be noble work.

"You don't even know where El Obeid is? What the hell are you doing wasting my time? What organization is this? Make sure you don't call me again."

The pilot's criticism was tough. They felt sufficiently bad that I tried to encourage them.

"Okay, good. What did you learn?" I asked.

"Not to get on the phone until we're really prepared."

"Right, well that's fair enough. You two are off the phones until you are tested to make sure you're ready. This is a good lesson. It's the real world. Brush yourselves off, go get a bite and then do your research. Learn what you need to know to speak authoritatively on the area, read the UN reports, look on the internet, find out what the ex-pat Nuba community is saying then come back to me."
"Okay."

They looked devastated. I continued.

"Look, we're flying blind here. We're all trying to do something that we've never done before and maybe no one has. We're going to make mistakes. But the only way you're going to make a difference and help these people is if you suck it up, work harder and learn from your mistakes. Don't take it so hard but also don't put yourself and the Center in that position again."

They smiled at the prospect of actually getting out of the Center for lunch as well as the chance to redeem themselves. And so it became policy, that before reaching out to contacts, every human rights violation monitors who worked in our office had to take a quiz and do a presentation to an executive staff member before contacting sources or policymakers by phone, email or in person.

A few days later, Joanna and Yevgeni presented marvelously, were quizzed flawlessly and were back on the phones calling everyone and anyone on the ground they could contact. They developed a good lead with some of the bush pilots. These pilots were those who would fly the aid into the Nuba Mountain area in spite of the government ban on travel. However, these pilots had never heard of us and they were wary that the Sudanese government was setting them up. Joanna and Yevgeni felt that some confidence-building measures were in order. They asked if we could help the pilots in some way in order to earn their trust. They felt the pilots could become an invaluable source of information. Time would prove Yevgeni and Joanna right.

They asked the pilots what we could give them that would help them in their job of delivering aid to the Nuba. The answer was startlingly clear: they wanted Cold War-era maps of the area. During the cold war both the US and the Soviet Union produced maps of the area that still remain the best and most accurate since the end of the Cold War. Recently, cheaper and less accurate maps had proliferated the market. The good maps were no longer easily found, increasing the danger for the pilots. The government did not hesitate to target these planes that brought the aid, because they were in violation of the no-travel ban. Often the maps would be inaccurate by several miles and would lead to needless flying or force additional approaches to the landing strip, all of which subjected the pilots to extended time as targets for the artillery.

Joanna and Yevgeni, along with four other volunteers went to the US Archives and the Library of Congress, to find the maps. We purchased hundreds of dollars' worth of maps. They were huge: two of them covered an entire wall in the boardroom. We sent these to Nairobi where most of the pilots originated. Within days the pilots received the high quality maps, and we began receiving some of the best information anyone could get out of the area.

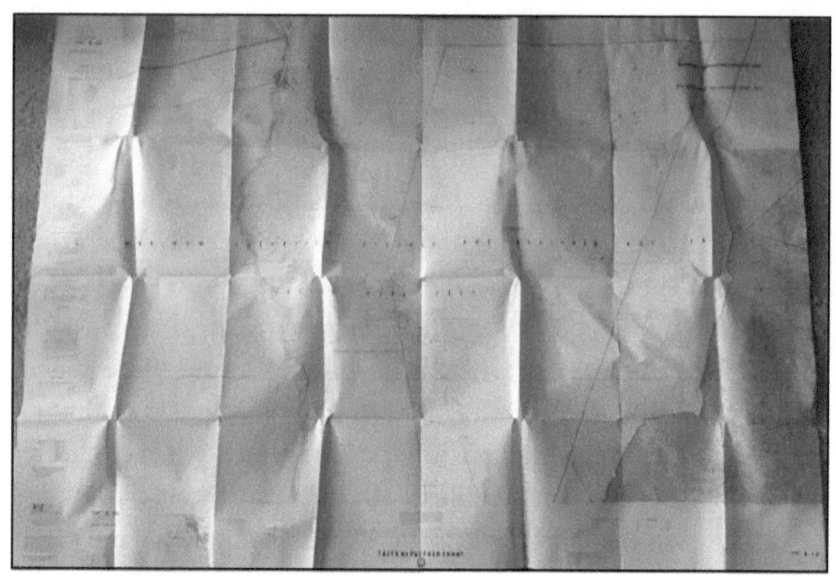
Photos of wall-sized map sent to Nuba relief pilots.

The first piece of information we needed was 'why.'
The narrative we told to policymakers must be accurate,
compelling and make sense. The question of, 'why would the
government care enough to bomb the Nuba?' was one we would
have to answer. The pilots felt that there were two reasons; first,
that the oil pipelines passed through the area and, second,
because the Nuba Mountains was a place where moderate
Muslims lived peaceably with the Christians and animists. The
radical regime in Khartoum wanted to rid Sudan of its
Christians and depopulate the oil regions to give them easy
access to the concessions they were selling to foreign
companies. As a peaceful region of moderation, the government
saw the Nuba area as a threat to their radical religious agenda.
In order to depopulate the area, the government began sending
planes into Nuba to bomb the fields during planting season and
attack the farmers with machine gun fire. An area that had been

self-sufficient for most of its recorded history was now without crops and the relief couldn't get through because of the travel ban. So the diehard smaller Christian charities like Samaritan's Purse, Christian Solidarity Worldwide (and International) and others would fly illegally into the area, land and unload quickly and get out. In any case the government would target any planes before, after or as they unloaded.

The information began to come to us daily. When the pilots returned to Nairobi at night, they would send us an email outlining how many people had been killed in the most recent bombings. They even included how many cows and chickens were killed and wounded. One report read:

"No fatalities but four cows dead, three injured, fourteen chickens dead, and eight injured."

We thought reporting on the number of chickens injured or killed was strange. Later it became apparent that these figures were important because it strengthened the case for man-induced famine that we were to make at USAID.

Within weeks we had enough thorough evidence of a man-induced famine that was sponsored by the government of Sudan. We began the process of writing the report. While the government was not massacring the Nuba, nor sending them to gas chambers, the willful blockading and purposeful bombing of the civilian food supply fit clearly under the Genocide Convention. Article 2, Section C "bringing about conditions in order to destroy a race, religious, ethnic or national group." It would be a while before the full report would be written, edited, re-written and printed, so I asked Yevgeni, Joanna and others to compile an advanced report for presentation at USAID.

A nutritional analysis based on ground information had predicted that 30,000 Nuba would perish within months, even

149

weeks, if 2400 to 3000 metric tons of aid didn't reach the Nuba. The rainy season was approaching and if the aid wasn't delivered before then many would perish. Urgency was crucial.

As the staff worked on the advanced report, the US was taking an increased interest in Sudan, thanks to the efforts of many human rights and relief organizations, as well as indigenous groups. One such person was Jemera Rone of Human Rights Watch who had consistently gathered and released massive amounts of information each day from the region. She monitored all goings on in Sudan like a watchful, concerned and protective mother. She worked hard and ceaselessly as one personally charged with the protection of the victims of Sudan. Eventually her information, combined with the work of scores of organizations, had brought the plight of the Southern Sudanese to attention of the US policy makers. The result: former Senator Danforth, accompanied by USAID Director Natsios, went to Sudan on a widely reported fact-finding mission. The government of Sudan, however, denied them access to the Nuba Mountain area, under the guise of protecting them from the dangers in the area. One of the parties was able to make a brief landing at one of the stable government-approved sites where there was no violence. By the time the US delegation left, USAID and the State Department were very concerned about conditions in Nuba.

The Center made the appointment with USAID at this critical moment when they sought legitimate information on Nuba. Roger Winters, one the most influential Africa specialists at USAID, sat across the table from me and as I ended my presentation said:

"Where the hell did you guys come from?" Before continuing.

"We can't get a thing out of Nuba and you've got the bombings down to the cows and chickens!"

We explained we had canvassed the small religious based relief organizations in the field as well as the bush pilots who flew in their aid and he was satisfied.

Our meeting was in a basement USAID office without frills. It was Winters and one aid. Our papers that outlined the first-hand accounts of the abuse were spread across the table. The premise of the meeting was that the Center for the Prevention of Genocide was about to make its first determination of genocidal conduct. It would be in the Nuba Mountain Range of Sudan and it would be a man-induced famine. The findings, I added, would also highlight the likelihood that USAID was one of only a few organization that could pull off the rescue in time. We covered the information one more time and went through the integrity of the informational sources without compromising their identities. We ended with a specific request for USAID to undertake strategies to deliver the 3,000 metric tons of sorghum to the area. When we finished, he looked like a man on a mission.

One week later USAID officially requested the Sudanese government lift the travel ban to the Nuba Mountain range for the expressed purpose of avoiding the man-induced famine. One week later, with permission in hand, under Natsios's supervision, USAID began delivering the 3,000 metric tons of Sorghum to the Nuba and staved off starvation for 84,500.

* * *

Over the next several months we were to meet with and become familiar with many of the Nuba leadership in exile in the US. They helped provide pinpoints for massive human rights violations in the area. While we couldn't use their information without independent neutral confirmation, they proved to be invaluable in knowing where to look. Some of the Nuba wives would bring in a tomato and peanut-paste eggplant dish that I still remember fondly.

Akila was the tallest Nuba with a charming smile and a gentle way. He was 6'7' and had to duck when he entered and exited doorways. He had briefly played at the top level in college basketball until injuries sidelined him. One evening he stopped by my office to say hello. As he sat his unfolding legs took up most of the free space in my office. We talked about our families. He was regretful that he could not go home and help his grandfather before he died. For Akila, it was impossible to get there. As a known Nuba leader, the danger of returning to the Mountains was severe at the time. I asked what his grandfather died of. His grandfather, he told me, had died of starvation. I was shocked. There was no one left of the family in the village. No one to take care of him. They found him dead and alone in his dwelling. He had been too weak to go to town during the government man-induced famine. There had been nothing Akila could do about it a half a world away.

The USAID had saved 85,000 Nuba. Approximately 500 Nuba starved. That number did not seem high until Akila said his grandfather was among them.

CHAPTER EIGHT: DARFUR, SUDAN (2003–2004)
Lists of the Dead.
The Credible I.C.C Threat and Sudan's Hitler.

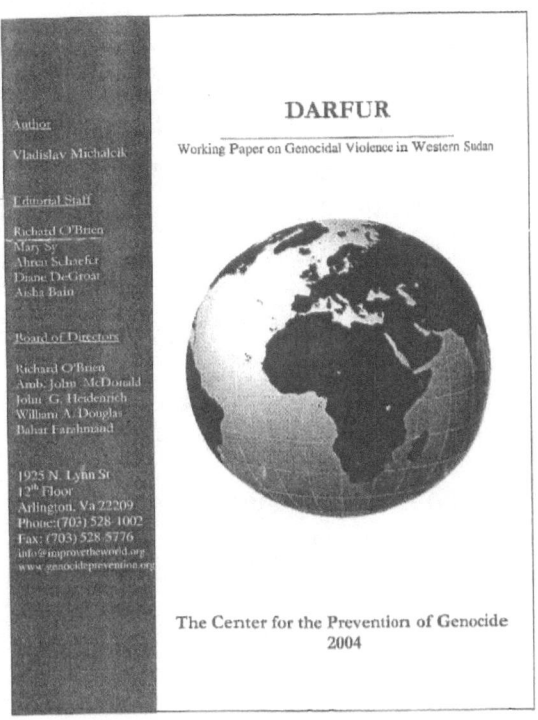

"In the time we have been here today, more women and children will die violently in the Darfur region than in Iraq, Afghanistan, Palestine, Israel or Lebanon. So, you won't need the UN – you will simply need men with shovels and bleached white linen and headstones."

George Clooney, American Actor, Activist

Lists of the Dead.

The lists came to us late in 2003. They were handwritten names of boys and men who were all dead. We were asked by the Nuba leadership to meet with a group of Darfurians who wanted to share urgent information about government abuse in Darfur. We met with them in the board room of the CPG and they unfolded the lists of the dead in front of us. We spread them out and studied them. After a few minutes I asked the delegation if we could be excused for a few minutes. My executive staff and I went to my office.

"What strikes you about these lists? What do you notice?" I asked.

"They're all Muslim names" one responded,

"They're all men." another added.

"That's it. What else? Look carefully."

They looked for a few seconds until someone pointed out the ages.

"That's right. These are all men and boys between 16 – 62 years of age. These could be considered fighting-age males. There are no female names among several pages of the dead. So, what happened? That's what we need to know. What's the context, the story here? Were the men and women separated and only the men executed? Was this a pitched battle and these are the names of the dead? Are there any neutral third parties in the area that can

154

confirm the context of these deaths? These are questions we need to ask."

We returned to the meeting room and explained our dilemma. We needed context and neutral third-party confirmation before we could publish. The list could be the dead from a civil war or rebel clash. The man who provided the list explained that he had simply received the list from his cousin who had said these were the names of the dead in the village they were from, and that the government had killed

them. This explanation brought up another issue. He was the second or third hand source. We would be the third or fourth hand source, without confirmation or context. I knew immediately we could not publish the list. While we resisted red tape preventing us from doing our jobs effectively, there still needed to be certain ground rules for confirmation of the information. Otherwise, it was likely that we would report incorrect information and hurt our credibility. Credibility was crucial with policymakers.

> "Can you go back to your cousin and get the context of what is happening. What was the story? How did these people die? Also, are there any aid groups, humanitarian, human rights or any other neutral groups that may be in the area that we can reach to confirm this information?"

CPG Compilation of Confirmed Massacres in Darfur, Sudan

The Center for the Prevention of Genocide has monitored conditions in Darfur since the summer of 2003. On January 20, 2004, eleven elderly people perished in a massacre, which occurred in villages north and south of Kuttum. In addition to the massacres, numerous incidents of looting, rape, torture, and abduction have been reported. Unfortunately, the travel ban on the region has made neutral third party confirmation extraordinarily difficult to obtain.

Date: February 10, 2004
Location: Shatatya
Victims: 81 civilians killed during an attack on Shatatya and surrounding villages

Date: January 20, 2004
Location: Various villages to the north and south of Kuttum
Victims: 11 elderly civilians killed and 24 villages destroyed in *Janjaweed* raids

Civilians Killed:
1. Mohammed Adam Kahleel
2. Issa Abakar Khaleel
3. Abdulaziz Mohammed Noor
4. Yousid Mohammed Jummah
5. Tiganie Ahmed Yagoub
6. Mohammed Abdulmajeed
7. Ismael Yahya
8. Yousif Abdullah
9. Maryam Ishag
10. Khadeeja Yagoub Mohammed
11. Khadeeja Ahmed

Villages Destroyed:
1. Jakhana
2. Tarainga
3. Loobous
4. Naro
5. Boori
6. Taraigna
7. Amoo
8. Bargna

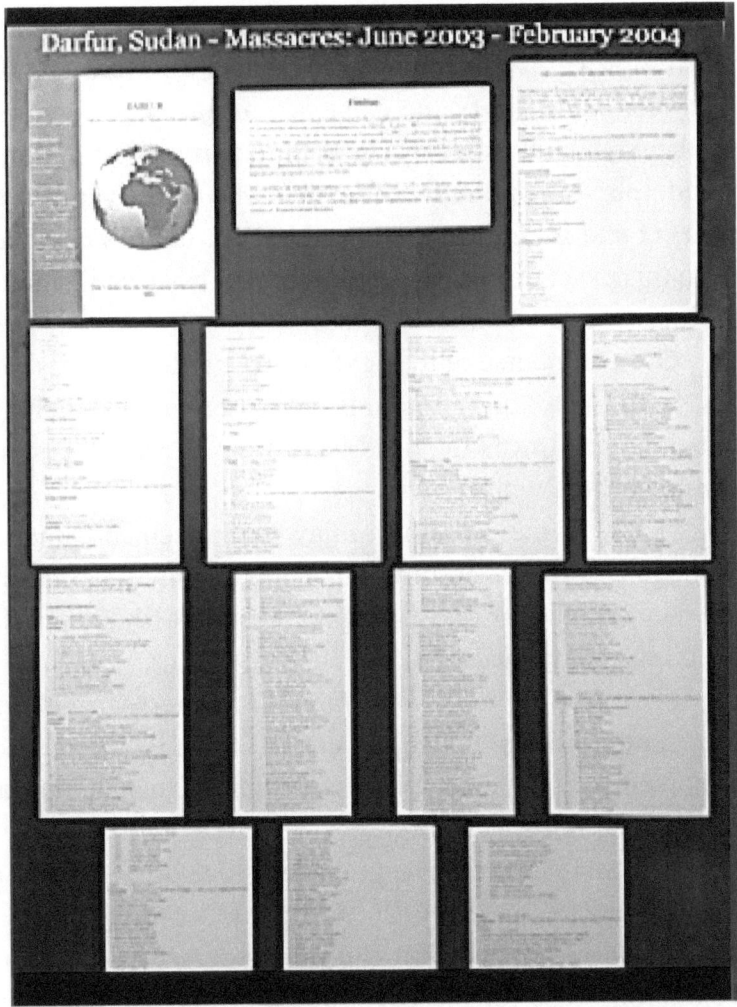

Lists given to CPG of the dead by genocide in Darfur, Sudan.

He was pretty sure there was nothing but Darfurians there, but he would ask. We explained why we couldn't move forward with the report until we could get confirmation. There was a possibility that we could move forward if we had significant detail of the context, and so declare it an unconfirmed report. After all, if Jewish escapees from the concentration camps during World War Two were the only people who could verify the existence of gas chambers at the time, one would not expect Nazi, or third party confirmation. In fact Rudolph Vrba and Alfred Wetzler, who actually did escape Auschwitz and tried to tell the world about the gas chambers, ran into this exact difficulty – without third-party confirmation, their story was questioned.

Over the course of the next two months, more lists came to us with increasing amounts of information, including occupations and towns the dead were from. Eventually stories and context came with the lists.

"Early in the morning Janjaweed horsemen came into our village and began burning our grain supplies, killing men where they found them and raping the women who had not fled. The men were unarmed…"

The stories took on familiar patterns, with the government providing helicopter cover fire while these deadly Arab horsemen conducted policies of ethnic cleansing, rape and what appeared to be, genocide.

A combination of events made us decide to declare the situation genocide in early 2004. In our working paper on genocide, we concluded that the preponderance of evidence made a strong case for the government of Sudan's complicity in genocide in Darfur. The Board of Directors knew that the CPG would probably close its doors when we lost our leased/donated space at the end of April. We were in debt, had no working capital, and the prospect of losing our space meant we could no longer fulfill our mission. With this knowledge, we made the decision that it was better to call Darfur what all evidence indicated it was: genocide, rather than waiting with the information for independent confirmation while innocent people continued to die. The massacres and ethnic cleansing in Darfur needed to be published and word of the genocide needed to be put into the mainstream media. While I spoke out on national public radio about Darfur during those weeks, more needed to happen.

***

During the last board meeting there was a lot to cover over and the mood was very somber. The only bright news was that I was finally able to push four names through for the CPG Humanitarian Awards. With no resistance, it passed. We would give out our human rights award. There were several individuals who had sacrificed much and had accomplished an incredible amount of life saving, genocide preventing work. For years I had wanted to acknowledge them. Now we had a chance to do that, and to help Darfur's cause and to do one last thing. It was the ten year anniversary of the genocide in Rwanda: it was time to remember their loss as well.

The four individuals were quite unique and spanned the political spectrum but were similar in one very important way. Each had moved mountains to save lives that, had it not been for their effort, would have been lost. The Reverend Steven Snyder was one of the individuals who directed the 'help us were being massacred' email to us, regarding the slaughter in Sulawesi. (See Introduction chapter) We had approached him when we were compiling our Moluccas Report and he shared information freely. He had provided photographs to be used in a national PBS special on genocide (Genocide Factor) for the section on Indonesia. His mission was both religious and humanitarian, and he was passionate about both. The reverend selflessly ministered to Indonesians in danger, provided aid as well as human rights reports that had proven instrumental in stopping massacres in Sulawesi and elsewhere. His altruism had cost him his life. He had died of kidney failure after becoming ill while in Indonesia.

Andrew Natsios, our second choice, had to cancel the receipt of his award as he flew across the globe to respond to an emergency. Natsios, as the head of USAID, had on several occasions lead the charge or even put himself in physical or professional peril to fulfill USAID's mission. He authorized the aid for the starving Nuba in Sudan during the man-induced famine in 2001. He personally had nudged both the US and the Sudanese government to make this happen. When North Korea teetered on the brink of another man-induced famine, he worked to make ensure there was no repeat famine and wrote an authoritative book on the subject. There are a host of countries and ethnicities that owe a debt of thanks to Natsios's efforts though he is rarely mentioned in the press. He helped bring attention to the plight of the Darfurians in western Sudan, even placing himself in danger when a riot broke out at one of the refugee camps. He placed himself in the way of an angry mob that wanted to kill a government spokesman. While he probably understood the crowd's anger toward the official who had threatened the already displaced crowd, his appreciation for life made him naturally step into the breach to stop the killing. When others might have been reluctant to overburden the work, he pushed forward to assure massive aid reached those in need. He represents what is best about US foreign policy.

The last two awarded are human rights icons. The calm and laid back John Prendergast had worked in the Clinton administration before establishing himself in the ICG concentrating his efforts on D.R. Congo and Sudan as well as the Great Lakes region. Unpretentious, straightforward, with long hair and a sometimes shaved face, John could break down a question or explain a complicated situation in the simplest and easiest of terms. Sometimes he would just shrug and say something casual like 'you got me on that one, I'm not sure, maybe one of the other panelists would like to tackle that one. His business was human rights and his casual appearance belied his seriousness of purpose. He deserved to be acknowledged not for his cool demeanor but for his timely information and fact finding throughout the region. He lived and slept in these conflicts, knew most of the nuances and was, in my estimation, the second most influential NGO person in the United States regarding the eastern region of Africa, where so much of our work was concentrated.

Finally, Jemera Rone. I knew her name long before I met her. Day in and day out we would receive reports about the most detailed human rights abuse in the South of Sudan. It was easy to receive 4-10 emails a day from her listserv. Her information was excellent, her sources outstanding, and her timing, impeccable. I sincerely believe that had she not been born, the 17 year civil war in Sudan, with its slavery, massacres, ethnic cleansing, rape, torture and man-induced famine, would still be going on today. Many of us wouldn't have known where to look for information. When Jemera smelled smoke, you could be sure there was a human rights fire going on in Sudan. We wanted to acknowledge the work of Prendergast and Rone in human rights, but we also had a hidden agenda. We wanted the Darfurian community to link up with these two human rights specialists on Sudan. When I presented her the CPG Humanitarian Award I said:

> "Like a Chinese water torture, drip by drip, she constantly reminded the international community and policy makers about the horrors in Sudan until they broke down and paid attention to it."

Her tenacity saves lives. Though she hated it, she should be applauded and upheld to the next generation as a model, a challenge to the saying 'you cannot possibly make a difference.' In places as hopeless as Sudan, remember Jemera Rone.

We decided to hold one final big event that would encompass several ideas. It was the ten year remembrance of the Rwandan genocide: we would walk with a candlelight procession from the American University to the Rwandan Embassy, where the Rwandan Ambassador would greet us and give a speech. Before the walk, at American University, we would have an awards ceremony for the four award recipients. This event would be a rare opportunity to help the struggling Darfurian community, who needed word of the genocide they faced to reach the right hands. It was a success on each of these levels. After securing the march route permit from the American University to the Rwandan Embassy, we confirmed the Rwandan Ambassador as a speaker. We created the award plaques and invited many communities. But we especially targeted the Darfurian community in exile.

The award ceremony was flawless. The speeches were touching. The Reverend's widow steeped her statement with Christian references. Jemera and John spoke well and were honored. As the ceremony broke and we began to form up for the candlelight walk, three and a half miles to the Rwandan Embassy, the Darfurian leadership crowded around the podium.

They had come from Arkansas, California, Canada, Florida and elsewhere across the US with the sole purpose of bringing attention to the plight of their people. They had driven, taken buses and flown to get here. They crowded in to thank me for the invitation and the work we had done, but this was not the time for it.

"Guys, listen. This is a big opportunity for you. There are two of the biggest forces in the US for human rights, specifically regarding Sudan. They are standing there holding plaques that tell the world that they are the best at this. This is the time to meet them, make appointments, tell them the stories of your family members being killed and figure out how you can coordinate your activities with them."

"Jemera!" I called out. She came over as did John Prendergast, and introductions were made all around and the buzz began.

"The next time you folks are coming to town we should definitely put some time together to meet and coordinate events." The words just came naturally out of her mouth.

"That's part of the problem Jemera, they are scattered and it's difficult for them to organize as spread out as they are. But, as you can see, they are willing to get their

163

message out policy makers on the hill and elsewhere, they'll show up in full force."

The Darfurians and Jemera and John did the rest of the talking. Numbers were exchanged, appointments were made and over the next months as I moved to Florida, I read report after report that stemmed from the American Darfurian community, through Jemera and John. Within three months Congress used the term genocide to describe the situation in Darfur as well as the US Secretary of State.

I felt that Darfur was finally getting the attention it deserved when during the presidential debate both George W. Bush and John Kerry called the situation in Darfur by its proper name – genocide. I let out a battle cry whoop during the debate when I heard it. John, Skee and several others who had worked at the Center, separated by thousands of miles from each other, let out similar battle cries of satisfaction, long after the Center had closed its doors.

The Credible I.C.C Threat and Sudan's Hitler.

Postscript on Darfur. In the nine years since I wrote the first part of this chapter, Darfur worsened with three million of its people internally displaced within Sudan and externally in neighboring Chad. Hundreds of thousands remain displaced today. The massacres, burning of villages and ethnic cleansing slowed down in 2009 but the fallout was enormous. Sudan remains devastated through displacement and hardship and the perpetual fear of further government repression. Significantly, it was not the dozen of human rights organizations, nor was it the policy makers, politicians or even the 9,000 person African Union force, that ended the genocide in Darfur. It was the I.C.C When the International Criminal Court handed down its indictment of Omar al-Bashir for crimes against humanity and then genocide, it was impactful. Even though Bashir said he would kick out the aid organizations, as punishment for the ICC indictment, he relented. Omar al Bashir did what was unthinkable only a few years before: he allowed the southern part of Sudan to have its referendum on independence. When South Sudan voted overwhelmingly for independent, al Bashir, unbelievably, let it go. The split happened and South Sudan became independent. A reason why this was relatively easy for al Bashir was that much of the oil concessions had already been sold to foreign companies and the treaty did not challenge that ownership. Finally, al Bashir scaled down and eventually stopped the scorched earth policy for Darfur.

When I think of Omar al-Bashir, I think of Hitler. This man is evil. But even evil men try to protect their own skin. I firmly believe that the I.C.C indictment and the resulting travel restrictions that accompany it were instrumental in ending the genocide in Sudan. It irks me that he is still in power there. But the lesson here is that a single piece of paper, backed up with the force of international law and potential consequences can prove to be a very powerful tool against even the most evil of powerful men.

The crowd of 400 begin to gather at American University for the C.P.G Awards Ceremony and Darfur/Rwanda March. Next Page: The author, Jemera Rone, Widow Snyder and John Prendergast of ICG, and below, Jemera speaking with the Darfurian leadership. At least 100 Darfurian leaders and their families were present from across North America.

Jemera Rone meets the Darfurian leadership during the rally.

The author encouraging the Darfurian leadership to advocate to Jemera and John during the march.

Hundreds marched from American University in DC to
the Rwandan Embassy to commemorate the anniversary of
the Rwandan genocide and draw attention to Darfur, Sudan.

CHAPTER NINE: THE CENTER FOR THE PREVENTION OF GENOCIDE: STORIES OF A STUDENT-LED EARLY WARNING SYSTEM.

Sergio Vieira De Mello Lay Dying.

"Help Me, Help You."

India-Pakistan Nuclear Non-Proliferation Report

Chechen Refugee Camps

CPG staff in October of 2001. Next page, CPG staffs and interns, 2002 – 2004.

Sergio Vieira de Mello Lay Dying.

Laying underneath tons of rubble, whispering his last words to his wife 'I love you, hurry back' was the end of the life of Sergio Veira de Mello.

His wife frantically ran from soldiers to administrators trying to get their attention to focus on digging Sergio out from under the ruble. You can see her doing this on the films of the aftermath of the bombing. His death is symbolic of the failure of the UN and the world community to properly gauge the needs when responding to world dangers, whether genocide, warfare, terrorism or even natural disasters. Sergio's death was due to an al Qaida bomb, but it was also due to the ineptitude of the rescue mission. When they finally lifted the body of the dead hero out of the rubble, unbelievably the two UN flags that adorned his office were draped underneath him.[54] He died on a bed of UN flags.

A few hours before he had felt a sense of relief to pack his belongings and prepare to return to his position as High Commissioner for Human Rights at the United Nations in Geneva and then back to his native Brazil for a brief visit with his family.

De Mello had been hand-picked to help oversee the writing of the new Iraqi government's Constitution. The position would, on the surface, be a step backward or, at best, laterally, for his career, but de Mello did not hesitate to go where he could do the most good. There were already rumors that he was an emerging favorite pick for the UN Secretary

---

[54] *Sergio*: One *Man's Fight to Save the World*. Introduction. Samantha Power, Penguin Books, 2008.

General position. The Constitutional Assembly was difficult to manage and the tempers ran very hot on several issues. But in the end, they finally drafted a document that enshrined individual rights, the rule of law and protection of minorities – and put that power in the hands of a people who had never known this right or power.

The al Qaida-built bomb destroyed part of the compound and took the man's life but did not undo the work of a lifetime. De Mello died, but the Iraqi Constitution lived.

Eight months before this, I met Human Rights High Commissioner de Mello for only a few minutes on his first day on the job. That chance meeting lead to our little-known CPG reports being read and considered at the highest levels of the United Nation. He was a class act in his bearing and his life's missions had an effect on millions. His name should be remembered and life's mission should be continued.

"Help me, Help You."

I arrived at the UNHCHR headquarters, showed my ID at the security booth and waited inside. As I was escorted upstairs, I noticed the hushed tones and politeness. It struck me as a very civil place, not overly stuffy, but a building maintained with class. Everyone's behavior was impeccable but personable. Allison LesBlanc met me at the office door.

"Mr. O'Brien, so good of you to come."

We sat across her desk in her small office and I thought,

'This is the desk where the problems that plague the humanity of Sudan come.'

It wasn't quite as simple as that, but she certainly was one of the people you would want to reach if your Sudanese cousin was in danger.

I asked if she would mind if I presented for ten minutes about the Center's work, the reason why I was in Geneva, and what I would like from her. She agreed. I began by telling her about the Center's purpose, that it was created to anticipate massacres and was often among the first organizations in the world to obtain information of impending or unfolding massacres. I told her about our rigorous standards, how we confirmed with neutral third party sources, reached out before the trouble began so we would have a working relationship with people on the ground. I told her of the inroads we had made with policymakers in order for them to take us seriously. It was important for her to note that we were not religiously or politically aligned, and that we responded with urgency to all major human rights violations that had an aspect of genocide to it.

I explained that before the beginning of each new college semester season we go through an extensive hiring phase where we review the resumes and interview the top candidates who apply to serve as Human Rights Violation Monitors. We identify the areas where genocidal conduct is most likely to occur, looking primarily at factors that include recent history, predisposition to massacres and the presence of any trigger mechanisms. Trigger mechanisms can be any one of a number of actions: ranging from an assassination of a crucial leader, an election, a food shortage, or the forecast of reprisal massacres. Then, we assign one, two or three volunteers to each 'hot spot.' They learn the history, the key players and the indicators of likely trouble that may occur. They reach out to established contacts on the ground to introduce themselves, and they create links with new contacts to get better real-time information out of the country. They monitor their area and watch for danger signs. If nothing happens, good, they can work or their secondary country or aid with the editing of a report. But if something does occur - a trigger to a massacre, a militia surrounding an unarmed town, relief deliveries being restricted so that man-induced starvation ensues - if anything like that occurs, the volunteer has to be ready to work with the executive staff in the emergency crisis procedure. That procedure includes confirming the incident with a known neutral third party, or finding an independent, credible and neutral source to confirm it. The next challenge is getting the information into the hands of those who are in a position to stop the massacres. We had developed extensive contact lists of people in-the-field for each country we monitored, as well as comprehensive lists, phone numbers, faxes and email for every policy maker in each agency, government or national body that could possibly affect a positive outcome for the area. We also kept extensive local, regional, national and international press lists and cultivated relationships with journalists in the areas we were looking both as sources for us and to enlist to publish our breaking news. (See the Appendices for examples) The key to our success, as a small operation, was planning ahead of the emergency crisis to build relationships with people who could help resolve the situation.

Some of the contacts would come from unusual and unexpected sources. We found one in a bar in Nairobi. We were given the number of a reporter from an internationally respected

174

media outlet, with a satellite phone. This particular reporter had not been getting published as much as he thought he would like and felt neglected. He had excellent, thorough information, and he had risked his life to gain it, yet it was hardly being published. We could understand his predicament; he was sitting on a treasure trove of information but was unable to convince the editors back home of the pertinence to the home readership of a D.R. Congolese guerilla war. We found him, over the phone, as he sat in a bar in Nairobi. He was willing to talk and had excellent information on the ground situation. His help pointed us in the right direction of Bukavu just before it exploded.

The second part of my presentation to Allison LesBlanc was to recount our actions in the Nuba Mountain range, our work getting the information to USAID and their subsequent reaction. This was her area of expertise. I concluded with a summary of the hotspots we were presently working on and the likely aspects of genocide in those conflicts. She looked impressed. We discussed Sudan for a few minutes and ways we could collaborate in the future on mutually confirming human rights violation information. Then she looked at me askance,

"Who else do you have appointments to see?"

"No one."

"No one? Why not? You really should see John at D.R. Congo, Allyssa at Uganda, Boris at Chechnya, Claude at Burundi."

"Yes, I know. The trip was very last minute and Geneva wasn't even on the agenda until I had your appointment. I think it would be a great idea to get together with each of them to see how we could collaborate. But that depends on one thing."

"What is that?" she asked,

"You." She looked at me for a few moments, and I continued,

"If you can commit some time, let's say fifteen minutes on the phone, sometime today, to just pick up the phone and call ten of your colleagues for a minute each. Be my scheduler for fifteen minutes. I'm at your disposal, as many meetings as you can schedule, whenever, late this afternoon and tomorrow. It would be an indispensable service and I honestly believe it is true to say, no one else can do it for me but you."

I paused, let her think, then I asked:

"Can you help set that up?"

She looked again at me and smiled.

"You picked a great time for it. I have a meeting literally in a couple of minutes. But, hmmm."

She seemed to be going over her tight schedule in her mind.

"Okay, right after that meeting I will get on the phone and see if I can set something up for today and certainly a few meetings for tomorrow. But give me a little time."

It was 3:30 when she called back.

"Okay Richard, if you are still available, I have set you up for four brief appointments today and two tomorrow. The appointments today are at 4:00, 4:15, 4:30 and 4:45 at the following desks, Uganda, Chechnya, D.R. Congo and Burundi."

She gave me the names and advised me to get to the security booth soon so I could make all the meetings and then instructed me to come by her office at 5:00pm for details of the next day's meetings. I hung up impressed. Whoever thought that the UN was just an ineffective bureaucracy should have experienced her efficiency.

The first meeting was with the stern faced Allyssa regarding Uganda. She actually produced our Uganda report out of her top desk drawer, and said it was the most thorough report of massacres in Uganda she had seen to date. We discussed channels of information and, as we spoke, I noted the universal sadness in her tone and expression. I realized her sense of despair was well grounded not only because of the massacres in Northern Uganda, but also because she was responsible for five other countries in the area – an unfathomable amount of human rights violations for one individual to police effectively. I understood why her eyes were so heavy.

The next meeting was conducted entirely in French with the desk officer for DR Congo. Surprised at myself for agreeing to conduct the meeting in French, I squeezed my brain hard for the right words or close approximations and turns of phrases to express my points and the purpose of the visit. When I couldn't remember the words, I would rattle off a sentence in English and Jean was comfortable with that. He had a warm personality and detailed knowledge of the complexities of the ground situation in DR Congo. It was fortunate that my needs were simple to communicate. I needed two things. First, contacts at UN agencies on the ground in DR Congo and, second, his assurance that if we passed him breaking news, he would pass it up the chain of command at the UN. He instantly agreed to both and began jotting down the number of a contact who was on the ground near the massacres in the lawless eastern regions of DR Congo. (See Chapter Ten – D.R. Congo – Bunia Massacre). We parted with a genuine amiable grasp of each other's forearms and a half embrace.

The last scheduled meeting that afternoon was with Boris, a Bulgarian responsible for monitoring the Caucuses. He was amiable and collaborative. We agreed that the most pressing danger to unarmed civilians in Chechnya was the impending liquidation of the Chechen refugee camps in Ingushetia. At the end of our meeting he asked me if I would be attending the reception that evening for Sergio Vieira de Mello. I couldn't believe my luck. De Mello was recently appointed to direct the UNHCHR (OHCHR today) and could probably be counted among the top three people at the time to influence human rights endeavor in the world. I naturally agreed to attend the reception.

After the last meeting I returned to Allison's office.

"So, you wrangled an invitation to tonight's event, did you?"

"Actually, Boris was kind enough to invite me."

"Well that was another thing I was going to talk to you about."

Boris arrived at the door and we made our way to the reception downstairs.

Sergio Vieira de Mello was arriving today and the reception was his introduction to his Geneva UNHCHR staff. De Mello was a well-liked and well-travelled Brazilian diplomat. He was tall, distinguished and youthful looking. He had impressed U.S. President G.W Bush despite political differences. His reputation as a fearless trouble shooter helped place him as High Commissioner for Human Rights at the UN. Less than a year later, in a magnanimous act of courage, de Mello temporarily stepped down as High Commissioner for Human Rights, a safe and influential job in Geneva, and assumed another UN mission in Iraq. He was placed at the head of the UN's effort to oversee the creation of a legitimate Iraqi interim government and constitution. De Mello went to Baghdad, oversaw the creation of a respectable interim government and a well drafted constitution. Before he packed his bags to return to his High Commissioner position in Geneva, a van loaded with a massive bomb detonated right beneath his window at the Canal Hotel. The bomb ripped through his building and trapped him under tons of concrete. He lived for few hours as he lay pinned by the enormous immovable weight. There the refined gentleman died alone, after bidding his wife return with help. The soldiers at the scene could not or would not listen to De Mello's wife's pleas to help him. She and his surviving staff tried digging him out of the rubble with their hands with no success.

I walked into the open area, crowded with about 75 UNHCHR staff. Eight months before the bombing, he was alive and well and surrounded by well-wishers who vied for his attention and favor. I turned my attention to the buffet of food that was spread out along three tables, and the good wine that flowed easily. I made a point of limiting my wine intake to a glass and a half. It would be good to be a little relaxed. As I looked around the room and was introduced, I found that I was the only non-UN person present. At one point I saw Bernard from Burundi light up as he saw an old friend and fellow Burundian from across the room. As they approached each other slowly and smiling, the two old men neither shook hands nor embraced, nor did they kiss cheeks. They smiled and then slowly and affectionately lowered their heads and touched foreheads in one of the simplest, most graceful greetings I've ever seen. They smiled and laughed as old friends.

I watched de Mello and was surprised by two things; first, he had a polished, rich cadence in his voice. He exuded wealth and elegance. He held his mouth down around the corners and spoke with what appeared to me to be an aristocratic clipped tone. The second surprise was that he seemed supremely bored or perhaps just tired. He appeared to give the person introducing themselves about ten to fifteen seconds to engage him before his eyes would glaze over and he would occupy himself looking elsewhere in the room, occasionally saying, "Oh, yes, yes, yes, yes," "I see, quite interesting, yes-yes." It seemed like he wished to will himself out of the situation.

I needed a good hook to catch and keep his attention. Years of teaching high school and the book *How to get your Point Across in 30 seconds or Less* by Milo Frank had taught me the value of getting your subject's attention right from the start. I thought for a while then decided on the memorable lines from the movie *Jerry McGuire*. In the movie, the main character is a sports agent whose career has taken a bad turn and his only client is a surly, but talented, football receiver whose attitude is preventing both of them from making the big pay day. The film is known for many famous lines including *'show me the money,' 'You had me at hello'* and *'Help me, help you.'* I knew which one was perfect for this occasion. I waited a long time until there was a lull in the conversation. De Mello had just informed the crowd that his door was always open and that any new, fresh ideas about how the UNHCHR could work better he would be interested to hear them. Despite giving a meaningful pause, it seemed that everyone there was intimidated to make a suggestion of any kind and to risk their relative anonymity and security. Perhaps they just didn't want to show off. But I took the cue and said:

"Early warning systems are a great way to save thousands of lives and millions of dollars and almost no one uses them."

I stuck my hand into his and introduced myself to him. By the time I said my name and the name of the CPG, his eyes were already moving on. They had glazed over and he was already gazing off into the distance. So, in a familiar way, I put my other hand around his elbow; he wasn't going anywhere. I asked;

"Do you remember the movie, *Jerry McGuire*?"

He stopped the progress of his eyes away from me and came back to regard me.

"Yes. I remember the movie."

"What was the famous quote from that movie? There were many of them, you remember? One was 'you had me at hello,' but the most famous one. Do you remember it?" I asked him.

"Ah, yes, yes, oh what was it." The schoolboy, brightest kid in the class machinery was spinning, working trying to retrieve the long ago stored information. I offered a hint:
"Show, me…the?

"Ah, yes-yes, I know this, yes SHOW ME THE *MONEY!*" He said loudly, like the character in the movie.
"That's right! Good job!" He looked pleased.

"Now, Commissioner, there were many good quotes in that movie. Do you remember when Tom Cruise's character, the sport's agent, was talking to his hardheaded football player in the locker room? He finally gets frustrated and what does he say to the football player. De Mello looked puzzled, so I gave him another hint:

'Help, me…help…"

De Mello's face was searching his memory, he knew it.

"Oh, yes-yes, HELP ME, HELP *YOU*!"

"You've got it!" I encouraged. I paused and waited for his attention.

"Well, that's why I'm here."

I said and stopped short. He looked at me mystified.

"I am sure I don't know what you mean, but I am interested."

He seemed genuinely puzzled and intrigued and smiled.

"High Commissioner, I run an early warning system that watches for genocide and massacres. Often times we know of massacres well before the rest of the world. What a monumental shame it would be if we had information that your staff was in danger, or their charges were in danger, and we couldn't navigate your chain of command quickly enough to get the warning into the right hands. So, 'help me, help you.'"

"Oh." He paused and thought this over for a moment.

"Hmmm, 'help me, help you'. Ah, that's terrific. I quite see it now. Brilliant."

He smiled at the simplicity of it, then said the magic words:

"Have you met Bertie Ramcharam, yet?"

I hadn't and I had been hoping to. Ramcharam was number two under De Mello and was the glue which was pivotal to the smooth operation of the UNHCHR. Knowing him meant potential access to the top UN Human Rights agency. De Mello led me by my elbow to his office manager, who arranged the appointment with Bertie Ramcharam for the next morning.

Milo O. Frank's *How to Get Your Point Across in 30 Seconds or Less* had shown me how to strike effectively in business, politics, human rights, job interviews and personally, when time was limited. But it was Mark McCormack's *What They Don't Teach You in Harvard Business School* that taught me when to say 'no' in business, how to observe and listen 'aggressively' and when to leave after you have achieved your goal. Satisfied, I smiled, finished my drink and returned to the hotel.

As I waited in Bertie Ramcharam's office I surveyed Lake Geneva from his office. The CPG had a great view of the Potomac River, but somehow his view seemed more majestic, more significant, more fitting for an influential UN office. Ramcharam was professional and vastly intelligent. He made the persuasive case that while the Geneva contacts would be no doubt good for collaboration; the best contacts for effective

184

results for the CPG were the UNHCHR (now OHCHR) at the UN in New York. By virtue of their proximity to the most powerful people in the General Assembly and staff, the UNHCHR in New York had more influence and the ability to get things done. He provided me with a list of names of desk officers and regional supervisors to meet with when I returned to the States. I could use his name to open doors.

On the way back to the States, I stopped in Reykjavik, Iceland. Despite missing the auroras borealis and their famous puffins, I could not stop smiling. I was amazed and kept thinking: 'the UN will work with us!'

CPG staff/interns at Mishas Café, King and Payne Sts, Alexandria, VA.

India-Pakistan Nuclear Non-Proliferation Report.

The C.P.G India-Pakistan Nuclear Threat Report and the original C.P.G HQ on the corner of King St and Payne St in Olde Towne, Alexandria, VA 2000 – 2002.

I remember Chris Forster's first day at the CPG, clearly, because it started out embarrassingly for me. I was alone in my corner office with no one due for an hour. I was alternately checking my email, reading my paper and spinning in my chair over to the other desk to check wire reports and press. My desktop had the radio on with Madonna's 'Celebrate' playing. The music had just brought me to my feet when the celebration was interrupted by a voice and a cough.

"Ah-hem." In a British tone.

"Ah, Rich"

It was Skee and behind him was a distinguished looking gentleman. The Brit behind him, Chris, coughed and looked away uneasy.

"Yes?"

I tried to sound in charge as Madonna blared in the background.

"I'd like to introduce Chris Forster. Chris, Richard, Richard, Chris."

"Oh, yes, Cambridge, right?"

"No, Oxford, actually." He looked blandly at me.
"Great, well Chris, you are a little earlier than we expected so why don't you have a cup of coffee, look at the paper and I'll sit down with you in a bit?"

"Ah, right."

"Skee, would you show Chris to the coffee, the newspapers and the board room."

"Sure Rich."

I gestured for Skee to come back afterward. When he returned, I pulled him in close.

"Skee, do you know why we come back and tell a person that they have a visitor first before bringing them back?"

"I think I now know why."

"Because they could be dancing, badly, to Madonna and fall immeasurably in the eyes of a future employee."

"Not to mention mine." He smiled.

I finished reviewing a report, put on a professional demeanor and went to the board room. Orientation with Chris took 45 minutes before we headed back to my office to discuss his schedule.

During the whole meeting Chris was very rigid, almost unfriendly. He answered questions stiffly with a minimum of syllables and I foresaw difficult times ahead if this was his manner of communication. Previous experience told me to discuss the communication differences right away.

"You know Chris, it's good that you approach the work seriously, it is serious work. However, the work is so serious that we try to lighten things up around here when we're not in a crisis. The workplace culture here is much more laid back than I imagine you are used to in London. I want you to feel free to be yourself, let your personality come through while being respectful of others."

He looked somewhat confused for a second.

"I see." He said.

"Your serious demeanor is right and correct for the work, but just be yourself with the staff. They're a good bunch, easy to get along with."

"Mr. O'Brien, back at Oxford," he deadpanned,

"I was the life of the party,"

His face looked straight ahead and then a slight smile crept across his face.

I laughed. You could immediately tell that he had a good sense of humor and would fit in. And he did. By the end of the summer he had helped produce one high quality report and laid the groundwork for the India and Pakistan report, one of our best reports ever. He also pitched in and helped move hundreds of computers the CPG sold to stay open, played some basketball and made some good friends.

It was at the time Chris was compiling sources for our India and Pakistan Nuclear report that our website was hacked. We did not even realize that a hacker had intruded. Apparently, some hackers like to crack the site and just look around. According to our technologically skilled neighbors, this particular hacker was about fourteen years old and lived in London. One of their technology company employees was Mo. Chris had asked Mo to take a look at some technical problems and server issues we were having and, as a good neighbor, he did so without charging. A little later on in the day Mo came back laughing to us.

"Well I fixed your server, you had a routing problem where signals were bouncing back and forth because of your wiring and hubs."

"In English?" Chris asked.

"I fixed your server problem?"

"Ah, right, good man." A relaxed Chris smiled.

"But there was another issue that took a little more effort and finesse."

After he told Chris the story, Chris brought Mo back to my office and he told the executive staff.

"Well, you had a hacker. Nothing serious just someone looking around, a kid actually, fourteen years old."

"Fourteen!"

"Yeah, well, it's pretty easy stuff. So I researched him and got his address and emailed him that I was the authorities and that if he didn't cease and desist this type of activity, we would send a squad car over to him from Scotland Yard."

"That's priceless, how did you get his address?"

"Trade secret. Anyway, he tells me he doesn't believe me. So I asked him if he had a fax machine and he says yes and gives me the fax number. When I send him this fax he gets back online and he's crying, begging me not to tell his parents, promising he'll never do it again."

"What was in the fax?" Someone asked.

"Do I want to know" I added.

He flipped a piece of paper he was holding over to show a detailed satellite image map with a large Ferris wheel in it. The kid's house was circled. When the kid saw the satellite image of his house, he immediately thought that Mo was the authorities and shut his intrusion down immediately.

Chris Forster was the lead on our India-Pakistan Report. Unlike the Gujarat Report that concentrated on massacres of Muslims by Hindus in India, this report stepped outside of the CPG traditional reporting areas. During our research into the near war between India and Pakistan in 2002, a report quoting Pakistani dictator Musharraf leapt off the page. He indicated that when the Indians had amassed their troops on the Pakistani border in response to the bombing of the Indian Parliament (by terrorists who had links to the Pakistani government), that Musharraf had decided if India were to invade to use 'non-conventional' weapons. Pakistan is not known to have ever possessed chemical weapons and so the assumption is he was speaking about his willingness to use the dozen or so nuclear warheads Pakistan possessed against India.

While this was not genocide in the strictest sense, we found it difficult to justify away the potential threat to hundreds of thousands and potentially millions of unarmed civilians on both sides of the border. The more we looked into it, the more disturbing the reports were. India and Pakistan have no 'hotline' for communications like the US and the USSR had during much of the Cold War. They shared no military protocol for escalation and de-escalation like the US and the USSR, so when the passions are running high, there is a realistic possibility of unbridled escalation without proper protocols to slow and check the military atavism. Lastly, there were no confidence-building measures in place which could undermine the distrust between the two nations. Essentially each nation had first strike capability, with massive destructive results for each country. But with less than three minutes response time between launch and arrival of missiles, in some cases, narrowed the capability for containment or the ability to pull back on a false alarm. A nuclear confrontation could happen, quite easily, by accident. And there would be no time, no mechanism and no trust in the information to put the genie back in the bottle.

We realized that we were not qualified to write the report because we had no nuclear non-proliferation, analysis or safety experts on staff. We looked for an expert who could write the report and attract top experts in the field to do the same for the price of lunch. We found him. Congressman Kopetski was a forty-something, youthful, recently retired member of the US House who had led the recent effort to ratify the START II Treaty. Because his retirement was not voluntary (he lost his re-election) he had time on his hands and agreed to meet us for lunch. After two hours of interns and staff entreating him to come on board and help write and attract specialists, he relented. The sushi lunch was his only compensation with the notable exception being the success of the report he and Chris Forster helped create.

Chris facilitated Kopetski's outreach to nuclear non-proliferation experts. Within three months the report was finished and available for placement at the first India-Pakistan governmental meeting since the near war of 2002. We managed for the report and a letter paper clipped onto it to be in front of every participant at the conference. The general in charge of the conference allowed it. The report showed the projected number of Indians and Pakistanis who would die in the short and long term during several accidental and intentional nuclear warhead detonations. It spelled out clearly in the report and the letter the heightened risk present without military protocol, 'hotline' communications and confidence-building measures.

When the participants left, newspapers reported that they agreed on nothing, nothing except that the next meeting should include on the agenda – military protocol, a communications 'hotline' and confidence-building measures regarding nuclear protocols. These were covered in the June 2004 conference between India and Pakistan. The Institute for Defense Studies and Analysis recognized in the pictured report that the areas our report emphasized were discussed and worked on between the two nations, perhaps because of our nudging.

Center for the Prevention of Genocide
an affiliate of Improve the World International
1925 N Lynn St., 12th Floor • Arlington, VA 22209
Phone: (703) 528-1002 • Fax: (703) 528-5776
E-mail: info@improvetheworld.org • http://www.genocideprevention.org

February 12, 2004

Peace Conference Attendees,

The Center for the Prevention of Genocide is presenting the attached Nuclear Threat Report authored by leading non-proliferation experts in the hope to elevate efforts to address the issue of nuclear tensions between India and Pakistan.

The Center encourages participants to consider several important issues highlighted in the report. These concerns include the significant risk of nuclear conflict between India and Pakistan, given the lack of established nuclear protocol. The report further demonstrates the catastrophic implications for the populations of both countries if nuclear weapons are employed.

Finally, in the interest of preserving future peace, the Center calls on the representatives of both India and Pakistan to place a high priority on continued communication to establish a future agenda that includes risk reduction, the development of nuclear protocol, and confidence building measures. Such measures are imperative in promoting a stable and peaceful future.

Regards,

Ahren Schaefer
Fellow

The India-Pakistan cover letter attached to the report was featured on the negotiations table for each participant.

194

From the Institute for Defense Studies and Analysis

Nuclear Confidence Building Measures (June 19- 20, 2004)

The June talks on nuclear confidence building measures (CBMs) dealt with measures to 'reduce risks relevant to nuclear issues'.

Hotlines

Some old CBMs were given a facelift and some new ones agreed upon. For instance, the two sides agreed to 'upgrade', the 'dedicated' and 'secure' hotline between the Director Generals of Military Operations (DGMOs). It was also agreed that one more line between the Foreign Secretaries should be established. Thus, there would be three hotlines, 'upgraded', 'dedicated', and 'secure' for handling crises. If the two sides are still not able to establish a connection, the fault may not lie in the cables but in other exchanges in New Delhi and Islamabad.

1999 Lahore Agreement Re-Invigorated

The Lahore Declaration was followed by a Memorandum of Understanding (MoU) signed by the two Foreign Secretaries (K. Raghunath and Shamshad Ahmed). It reiterates the determination of both the countries in implementing the Simla Agreement in letter and spirit. It encompasses the gamut of issues which are now being pursued and calls upon the two sides to undertake "bilateral consultations on security concepts and nuclear doctrines, with a view to developing measures for confidence building in the nuclear and conventional fields, aimed at avoidance of conflict". It also calls for the two sides to "provide each other with advance notification in respect of ballistic missile flight tests"; "undertake national measures to reduce the risks of accidental or unauthorized use of nuclear weapons"; "abide by the respective unilateral moratorium on further nuclear tests"; and "periodically review the implementation of existing CBMs", including links between the respective Director Generals, Military Operations.

Nuclear CBMs

On the nuclear issue, the two sides have reaffirmed their 'unilateral moratorium' on conducting further nuclear tests until 'extraordinary events jeopardize their supreme interests'. Further, both have called for "regular working level meetings to be held among all the nuclear powers to discuss issues of common concern". It suggests a welcome understanding between India and Pakistan to take the nuclear debate from the regional to the global level.

A report highlighting the immediate focus after the Conference on Confidence Building Measures (CBMs) and other specific recommendations of the CPG India-Pakistan Nuclear Danger Taskforce.

Chechen Refugee Camps.

Approaching winter of 2003 reports began to filter out from Helsinki Watch and other sources close to Chechnya, that Russian leader Putin planned to dismantle the Chechen refugee camps that winter and send them home to Chechnya. The obvious intentional cruelty of this potential action cannot be overstated. The Caucus winters

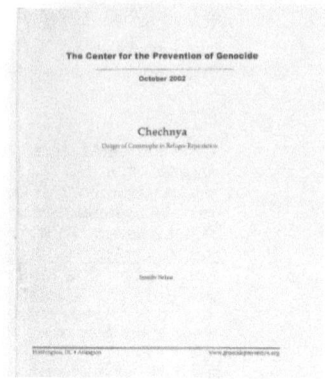

can be as brutal as any on the Siberian steppes. Most of the Chechen homes in Grozny had been levelled and livestock were gone. To return civilians, children and elderly, with the clothes on their backs, through the winter elements to homes that didn't exist felt like Putin seeking vengeance on the stubborn Chechen independence movement.

We joined voices with several human rights organizations to protest and push to rescind the decision Putin was moving toward. Rather than target the UN, or US policymakers, we targeted other aid groups to join in a chorus decrying the proposed action. Most importantly, we reached out to the Russian government, to its foreign ministry and interior ministry to inform it that we were aware of its intentions and would decry it and publish it until international outcry stopped it. We pointed out the flagrant cruelty. We were pleasantly surprised when the order was cancelled. Russia indicated that they would break the camps down in the spring. The delay saved the elderly and infant exposure to deadly winter elements.

CHAPTER TEN: IT CONTINUES TODAY: D.R. CONGO, CENTRAL AFRICAN REPUBLIC, NIGERIA AND SYRIA.
D.R. Congo: Rape Capital of the World.
Central African Republic (CAR): Christian and Muslim Massacres.
Syria: Unlimited Cruelty and Genocide.

This book is about solutions for genocide and several examples are discussed but it is also important to mention what this book does not cover. It does not cover the South American massacres and genocide that occurred in Guatemala during the 1980s under the dictator Montt, and the massacres in Colombia at the hands of the FARC, ELN and AUC. The narco-terrorism and kidnapping that were the primary characteristics of the Colombian human rights abuse paled when compared to the civilian massacres from 2000 – 2004. In

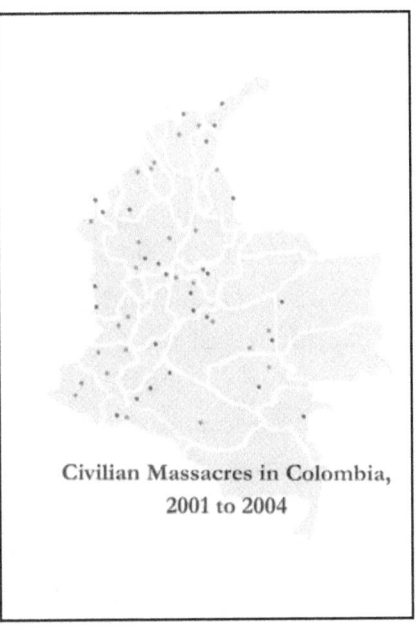

Civilian Massacres in Colombia, 2001 to 2004

addition, Chile and Argentina witnessed some of the worst South American dictatorships that 'disappeared' members of the opposition and other civilians. These also are not included here. The lives lost are no less precious.

In Africa, the terrible dictatorship of Nguema in

Equatorial Guinea that more than 50,000 dead in a nation of only 500,000 is an area of research that deserves more attention and study. The Tutsi massacres of Hutu in Burundi in 1972 and 1988 are historically overlooked and are crucial to understanding the cycles of violence between these two ethnicities. Without taking these into account, true healing cannot happen between the two. Mugabe's man-exacerbated famine of 2002 in Zimbabwe targeted political adversaries through starvation, plundered the resources of a nation and deprived whole generations of their potential.

In Asia, the horror of North Korea and the ideological genocide that has used torture and starvation as a tool against its own people is an ever present danger. The case for man-exacerbated famine as genocide was particularly strong in 1994 and 2002 as a series of classifications of its citizens according to perceived loyalty, allowed Kim Jong Il to callously claim that North Korea could lose 2/3rds of its population and be stronger for it. It remains one of the worst human rights offenders in the world. All of the CPG reports on these areas are included on this book's website. Burma (Myanmar) has ethnically cleansed and marginalized its Karen, Shen, Mon and Rohingya minorities. Millions are displaced in a society where the military junta represses almost all freedom. In Indonesia, several areas experienced massacres: the Maduras in Borneo at the hands of the Dayaks, in East Timor during the movement for independence, of course, the Moluccas Muslims killed by Christians which prompted the Muslim Jihad against the Christians in Sulawesi discussed in the introduction. The two largest repressive regimes in Asia remain Russia and China. The repression of Soviet times, with its deadly purges of millions and political gulags, is over. But Russian President

Putin's use of intimidation and jail to quell political adversaries and critics represents a lighter version of repression that exists today. Critics of the regime have been assassinated and Russia continues to bully its neighbors Georgia and Ukraine by invading democratic Georgia and annexing parts of Ukraine and shutting off their gas in their harsh winter. Early in Putin's first term, he ordered the obliteration of Grozny during the war with Chechnya. While Putin's behavior is authoritarian and not genocide, it warrants attention. Today's bullies are tomorrow's genocidaires. China, while not as repressive as under Mao, or even Deng, continues to repress independence movements. Internet service in the Western Xinjiang province has been blacked out to restrict information about the restive Muslim province. Tibet has seen the 'sinoization' of its nation both through the mass immigration of ethnic Chinese to dilute the Tibetan population, and through the official restriction of Tibetan culture and language. This is a subtle form of genocide when a nation or ethnicity is slowly extinguished.

In summary of what this book is *not* about, there are few places in the world which have not seen massive human rights abuse, massacres or genocide in the past 100 years. I have covered the most impactful ones or the ones I had significant background information on. Many of these areas were reported on by the CPG and those reports are available on this book's website for you.

Lastly, this book does not cover femicide, an emerging concept in genocide prevention. In many places around the world, policies exist that encourage the abandoning of female children. These deadly and restrictive policies qualify women and girls as targets for genocide if they constituted a group in the genocide convention.

***

I have been writing some part of this book, on and off, since 1997, when I began writing my master's thesis at Georgetown University on indifference to genocide. My last rewrite occurred in 2014 and took almost a year as a Visiting Scholar at George mason University's S-CAR – now Carter School. Since I began writing the book, there is good news and bad news. The good news is that successful prevention strategies are beginning to be used more often. The Mass Atrocities Prevention Board, the Right to Protect Working Group, CSO and other Departments at US State and USAID, the UNOSAGP and the Great Lakes Conference on Genocide Prevention, as well as several schools and nonprofit organizations, are all undertaking steps toward early warning and prevention.

The bad news, though, is that throughout the twenty years from 2004 – 2024, since the CPG closed, genocide and massive human rights violations have not abated. Subsequently genocide has occurring in Nigeria, Syria, Central African Republic, Myanmar, and possibly in Nuba, and Darfur, Sudan. I no longer have a staff watching every hotspot in the world, but there are easily more than a dozen places that warrant close watching beyond those mentioned earlier: Syria, Iraq, Pakistan, Guinea, Niger, Yemen, Ukraine, Ethiopia Afghanistan, DR Congo, Turkey, Azerbaijan, Lebanon and Haiti.

D.R. Congo: Rape Capital of the World.

There has been some progress in eastern D.R. Congo in recent years. UN ground troop campaigns in eastern Congo in 2003 and 2007 have proved successful defeating and disarming rebel militias and keeping the peace during the past ten years. The disputing Hema and the Lendu have ceased hostilities, which were usually characterized by massacres. In late 2013, the vicious militia M23, considered a Rwandan proxy militia, was abandoned by Rwanda and the UN chased the vestiges of it from its last strong holds. Unfortunately D R Congo remains one of the most dangerous places in the world, especially for women. It is the 'rape capital of the world' with one woman being raped nearly every minute.[55] The perpetrators of rape were initially members of the assorted militias who were unchecked in their attacks on women.

Today, some of the perpetrators are members of the Congolese government army, whose ranks have been swelled by militias joining without the proper training in human rights and a code of conduct. The following are excerpt of interviews of some of these soldiers and details their justification for rape. Former Mai-Mai militia who were absorbed into the DRC army were interviewed about their practice of raping women. Each of the several men interviewed admitted to raping between two to twenty women.

Soldier One: "We know that it is not a good thing but what do you expect? We spend a long time in the bush

---

[55] www.stoprapeinconflict.org/dr_congo

and when we meet a woman and she will not accept us then we must take her by force."

Soldier Two: "It's all about control. Before raping them, I made sure that the women were in good health. Just by looking at her, I could tell if she was sick or not."

Soldier Three: "…Well, we were just abiding by the conditions of our magic potion. We had to rape women in order to make it work and beat the enemy."

Soldier Four: "For myself, I'm doing just like everybody else."

Soldier Number Two: "We raped as we advanced from village to village."

All except one soldier interviewed had a double standard, when asked if it would be okay if their sister or mother were to be raped by soldiers.[56]

Parts of eastern D.R. Congo are stable due to successful UN military peacekeeping missions. The most recent of these successes was the military defeat of the vicious rebel group the M23. However, women and children remain in constant jeopardy of being violated, often with irreparable injury, rendering the victim's incapable of reproduction and shunned by their family. Some die from the attacks.

---

[56] https://www.youtube.com/watch?v=ZbZIK9Ce0yM

Central African Republic (C.A.R): Christian and Muslim Massacres and a *Late* Response.

"Central African Republic is the worst crisis people have *never* heard of. "[57]

Samantha Power, US UN Ambassador

Central African Republic is the site of the world's latest genocide. After the overthrow of the unpopular despot Bouazizi, Seleka, the largely Muslim coalition of rebels that replaced him, could not be controlled by the coup leader Michel Djotodia. Looting and pillaging led to brutality and then wanton massacres of unarmed Christian civilians by the Seleka rebels. In November 2013, the ground situation had already led to thousands dead and tens of thousands fleeing. The tide of Muslim on Christian massacres began to turn with the advent of the 'Anti-Balaka' (anti-machete) Christian vigilante/rebel groups that began to massacre unarmed Muslims. By January 2014, Djotodia bowed to regional pressure and went into exile. The Muslim Seleka rebels began to fall apart and were unable to protect Muslim communities. As a result, there have been massacres against Muslims throughout the North, brutality is common and more than 8,000 Muslims remain trapped in Bozoum. 60,000 fled in two months, further destabilizing an

---

[57] http://www.theguardian.com/world/2013/nov/22/central-african-republic-verge-of-genocide

already very unstable region.[58] The 8,000 trapped Muslims are in clear danger. Both the Muslim massacre of Christians and the Christian massacre of Muslims are genocide. They each were intentional, habitual and clearly one of the primary characteristics of the ongoing abuse. 6,500 U.N and A.U peacekeepers currently deployed in C.A.R have been unable to curtail the violence or control the situation.[59] The remoteness of C.A.R, lack of early warning and lack of a standing rapid deploy force cost the few pivotal months that may have allowed for this force to have been effective. It does not matter how many firefighters one sends when the house is already burned down. The problems of mankind do not disappear as time passes, but they continue like time, seasons and everything else. Proactive work and resources need to be invested now to prevent the next generation of problems approaching down the road. We must be ready. These problems are coming, guaranteed.

---

[58] http://www.washingtonpost.com/world/africa/tens-of-thousands-of-muslims-flee-christian-militias-in-central-african-republic/2014/02/07/5a1adbb2-9032-11e3-84e1-27626c5ef5fb_story.html
[59] http://www.washingtonpost.com/world/africa/tens-of-thousands-of-muslims-flee-christian-militias-in-central-african-republic/2014/02/07/5a1adbb2-9032-11e3-84e1-27626c5ef5fb_story.html

Syria: Unlimited Cruelty and Genocide.

> "How can you sit there and eat your dinner and
> go about your lives when they are killing us?"

> Syrian Mourner on blog site

Consider Syria: over 130,000 souls have been lost to warfare and genocide over two years, with fitful international efforts to end the conflict. None of the major players, Russia, China, Iran, U.S., Saudi Arabia or the UN, seem to be acting with the necessary sense of urgency that these lives deserve. The failure to work effectively in late 2011 or early 2012 to prevent the Syria catastrophe means that over 7 million people are now affected, and an already volatile region is enflamed. After drawing a firm line, President Obama's tepid response to the massacres in Syria and the use of chemical weapons, has done little or nothing to end a horrible ground situation. Here are seven million more lessons that early warning and prevention would have been the best course of action.

Some genocide's have relatively straight forward fixes that can save lives. Whether we, as the international community, do anything about it is another story. Rwanda was relatively straight forward. Rewrite the UN mandate for its 2,000 troops already on the ground to include permission to use force to protect civilians, increase a stabilizing presence with thousands of additional UN or African Union troops, with armored personnel carriers, immediately and, of course, *call* it genocide. Bosnia and Kosovo, too, were relatively straight forward. As massacres and genocide were detected, NATO bombing commenced until peace was agreed upon. Even the complexities of the Holocaust had some clear-cut lessons: bomb the train tracks to Auschwitz and the gas chambers and facilitate the *Europa Plan* and heroes like Wallenberg with the means to save as many Jews as possible. Of course, recognizing Hitler's hate speech as dangerous and responding *before* there was a war, would have been the best response. There are, however, complex genocide's which do not offer an easy fix – Armenia was in a remote location and the genocide occurred during a world war without real warning. Ukraine's Stalin-induced famine also similarly occurred in a remote location, and in an area where there was no free press. Cambodia's genocide, also in a remote area, was an area with a recently reduced strategic interest. Most of these countries have little strategic interest to major economic players of the world, otherwise the urgency would be self-evident. Whenever governments, armed *with unlimited cruelty*, decide to victimize their own people, they can. The complexity, difficulty and international indifference conspire to assign a deadly fate. Consider the case of 130,000 unsuspecting Syrians.

Definitively, genocide has occurred in Syria. The U.N. Genocide Convention defines genocide as 'any of the following acts committed with the intent to destroy, in part or whole, a national, ethnical, racial or religious group (by) (a) killing members of the group." Syrian nationals have been targeted because they live in rebel stronghold areas. Massacres at the government's hands have occurred in Syria. The three standards held by the Center for the Prevention of Genocide when it was open have been met here:

206

1. *Is it intentional?* Clearly, these villagers were not caught in crossfire or accidentally gassed, so this is an easy yes.
2. *Is it habitual?* As the list of massacres indicates, yes, there are now dozens of examples of massacres at the government's hands including four UN-documented cases of the government of Syria using gas against its own people.
3. *Are massacres a primary characteristic of the abuse?* While there is torture and other mass atrocities present, the primary characteristics of the abuse are massacre, genocide and the internal and external displacement of people. This, too, is a simple yes. The UN Genocide Convention plus these three CPG standards makes this an iron clad yes. President Bashir al Assad is a genocidaire. Period.

The Syrian crisis began as part of the Arab Spring movement of 2011 to remove the autocratic Assad regime. When protesters and activists were killed and tortured, the movement grew into armed rebel action. A full blown civil war, massacres and genocide followed. The solution became geometrically more difficult and complex as the situation was allowed to run its course. The simplest and easiest time to intervene to prevent genocide was early during the Arab Spring. Pressure to transition the Bashir al Assad regime into exile or engage in the first steps of the process of democratization to a post-authoritarian government, should have been strenuously applied. As each month passed and the damage became permanent, different players from across the region entered the picture making a clear solution far more complex.

Today there is a slow-motion war in Syria which started as a popular uprising to unseat an unpopular despot. It has devolved into a regional conflagration that is slowly drawing in all of its neighbors. The quickest resolution to the Syrian catastrophe is that Bashir al Assad has to go, and quickly. Russia's Putin and perhaps Iran are in the strongest positions to exert influence on Assad's decision to step aside for the good of his nation. A national reconciliation government needs to begin the healing process and everyone else needs to go home.

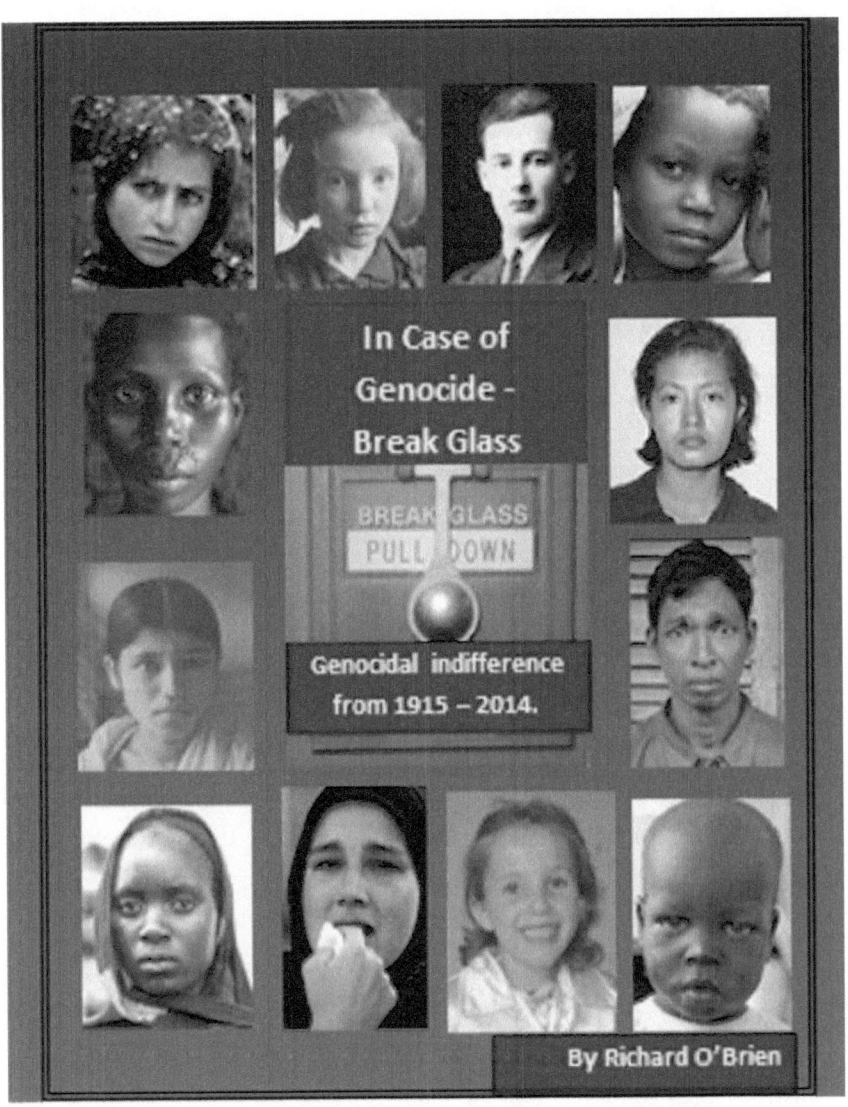

The original mock-up cover for the 2014 version of this book, reviewed and presented but never released. These are a handful of the beautiful faces who were victims of genocide and one hero. As a visiting Scholar at the Carter School (S-CAR), George Mason University, I spent most of 2014 compiling materials for this book.

CHAPTER ELEVEN: ENDING GENOCIDE PERMANENTLY.

Successful Interventions.
The Multi-Track Diplomacy Practice.
U.S Holocaust Museum Recommendations.
U.N. Early Warning and Rapid Response.
R2P. Aggressively Seeking Peace.
Amending the Genocide Convention.

"It always seems impossible until it's done."

Nelson Mandela

Successful Interventions.

There are several points during genocide when lives can be saved. The best known of these is heroism, which usually occurs *after* the danger has begun to unfold. It is, however, the least effective and most harrowing of preventative actions. Raoul Wallenberg, Andre Trocme, Oskar Schindler and Paul Rusesebegina, as well as other heroes of the world, are needed when the international community fails to prevent these man-made disasters from occurring. This reactionary, inconsistent effort will be the standard operating procedure of the world until we improve the other preventative types of action.

A second point at which lives can be saved is *as the danger begins*. When a life-threatening situation is starting to unfold, preventative action is absolutely vital. Many cases demonstrate this throughout the past one-hundred years: the

Armenians arming themselves at Musa Dagh and surviving, the Indian government sending Sikh police officers to serve as a buffer between the Hindus and Muslims and stopped the killing in Gujarat in 2003, and the UN-flagged French and Pakistani army missions to Eastern D.R. Congo which stopped massacres and defeated dangerous rebel groups in 2003 and 2007. These preventative missions, at the time when the situation is unfolding, are crucial until we develop better early warning and response systems. The impact of these missions cannot be underestimated. The lives saved are incalculable. Intervention is the second most effective approach. The world has begun to embrace this strategy more in recent years.

The third and the most effective way to combat massive human rights abuse is to anticipate and eclipses it *before* it begins. These life-saving actions almost never receive front page coverage. Rarely does a reporter file stories about a massacre that was prevented. But massacres and bloodshed which occur are considered newsworthy. It is human nature to take an interest in the sensational and not the mundane. Today, governments, non-government organizations and individuals, without fanfare or recognition, work on successful conflict preventative projects around the world. These programs receive a small fraction of the funding they need. Regardless, their cost is miniscule compared to the amount it costs to repair these human rights and humanitarian catastrophes after they unravel. The amount of money saved by early preventative action does not even begin to take into account the irreplaceable loss of life and human potential which is lost. In 2003, the Burundi election brought to the surface ethnic and rebel tensions similar to Rwanda in 1994. The danger of an imminent explosion in 2003 was obvious to most observers. NGOs and governments worked extensively to successfully defuse Burundi. Few outside of Burundi noticed. But this type of effort works. The US State Department prevention team worked on diffusing the 2014 Kenyan election results. The State Department's CSO Bureau is working to reduce the homicide rate in Honduras, to reduce tensions in Central African Republic and to attempt peaceful engagement in Syria. The countries of Norway and Denmark have human rights and humanitarian missions around the world, as does the E.U. Early intervention can diffuse volatile events and tensions and prevent the potential loss of life and mass atrocities. These strategies are being developed at foreign ministries, nonprofit organizations, Universities, and religious organizations around the world.

One of my favorite examples of a successful conflict prevention organization is the institution in which I wrote part of this book – George Mason University's Carter School for Peace and Conflict Resolution (formerly S-CAR). The Carter School has over a dozen missions around the world. It works in citizen diplomacy in the Caucuses, the Middle East, Asia, Africa, South America and locally. Students and graduates of this school are spread across the globe engaged in conflict resolution efforts. One is working in Burma to develop a Buddhist-based approach to conflict prevention among the groups. Others are engaged in track two diplomacy (citizen-diplomacy) and track one (government-diplomacy) between China and Japan regarding the disputed Senkaku/Diaoyu Islands. Their mission here is not to solve the conflict but to more clearly envision it and to clarify the differences. If the conflict is to be mediated or adjudicated by an international court, the research of Carter School will be a good starting point to clearly understand what the conflict is about. Another S-CAR project works to facilitate Syrian groups to meet together and attempt to envision a post-civil war Syria rebuilding process. Though the Carter School is one of the very earliest of such schools, several Universities now have schools and programs for peace and conflict resolution around the world. The Munk School of the University of Toronto, in Canada, is reputed to have a large monetary endowment – something that was unheard of twenty years ago. These programs yield tangible and intangible results, often beginning dialogues, methods and relationships that are pivotal to future successful peace efforts. But funding of conflict prevention, intervention and resolution work has lagged behind the field's rate of success and should be a priority if we are to move beyond the ever-repeating cycles of human violence.

Multi-Track Diplomacy – IMTD.

Ambassador John McDonald, Multi-Track Diplomacy Pioneer.

The Institute for Multi-Track Diplomacy (IMTD) has been led by Ambassador McDonald for more than twenty years. It has worked on well over fifty projects worldwide. The approach is guided by innovation in the field of diplomacy:

'multi-track' diplomacy. The I.M.T.D expanded the diplomatic paradigm from only two tracks (government and citizen) to include seven more tracks. The additional tracks are

---

60 Wikimedia Commons.

professional conflict resolution practice, business, religion, education research and training, peace activism, funding, and media and public opinion. These have the potential to revolutionize diplomacy and conflict prevention and resolution throughout the world. Multi-track diplomacy acknowledges a larger, more complex picture of human interaction. It assumes that when countries, groups and entities have more connections with each other and understand each other better, they will be far less likely to engage in bloody conflict. Jean Monnet used the 'business track' concept when he helped form the ECSC in 1951, which reduced tensions between Germany, France, Italy and the Benelux nations over the coal and iron ore resources in the ground. The reduction and disappearance of tariffs between these nations, and the joint ownership of resources fostered an era of economic cooperation which became the groundwork for the European Union. Today, the 27 nations of the EU are linked closely in a unique type of political and economic super-federation. These relationships were created on the bedrock of business and economic cooperation. This is a good example of the power of business diplomacy. There is another advantage of business-to-business track diplomacy. Nations and peoples who do business together often develop links with the local communities in which they conduct their business. In times of track-one (government) diplomatic stagnation, there are countless businesspeople whose self-interest makes them ideal for initiating other types of diplomatic ventures and outreach based on business relationships.

The 'religious track' has been a long standing vehicle for peace activism and dissent. Religious diplomatic activities can inform citizens and policymakers and curtail misinformation about perceived enemies with different religions. Religious organizations have a long history of peace-related activities during times of war and peace. This track acknowledges, as a fact, a track that has long been useful in both challenging preconceived notions and helping those victimized through man-made disasters.

The 'education, research and training track' is a quite large and innovative track of diplomacy. Educational student exchanges, classes, seminars, educational projects, and lecture series are some examples of educational-track diplomacy. Projects like those described at S-CAR, which are taking place around the world represent effective educational track diplomacy. Take the recent agreement between Israel and Palestine on shared water usage, a combination of citizen diplomacy and research diplomacy. IMTD was asked to mediate between technical experts on water, brought in from both the Palestinian and Israeli sides. After confidence building measures, each group wrote solutions where the two sides could collaborate. The similarities between the two proposals were the starting point of a relatively straight-forward agreement that is in effect today. Having the technical experts take the lead and design a mutually beneficial agreement based on research and science was something that politicians would not have been able to craft. The training aspect of this track is also fascinating. Just as the US Pentagon trains military commanders from around the world, IMTD and other organizations trains generals, politicians, business and other leaders drawn across civil society in the practice of conflict prevention, resolution and intervention strategies. After one class, the Colonel heading the Marines stationed in Iraq said to Ambassador McDonald: "We should have taken that class *before* we were deployed to Iraq. Do you know how many lives that could save?" While training leaders and citizens around the world in these practices is invaluable, it is rarely done due to the limited financial resources of these small NGOs. Another example of this is *peer mediation*. Consider the debate about gun control in the US. On one side people are very concerned about gun violence and death, especially among children victims at recent school shootings. On the other side, second amendment advocates believe that it is their inalienable right to protect themselves and to hunt. Both sides agreed at a recent debate in Washington, DC, however, that *peer mediation* is one of the best options to reduce gun violence in schools. IMTD, in conjunction with districts in the Maryland school system and in several other school districts around the US, trained entire schools in 'peer mediation and conflict prevention and resolution.' Rather than a small number of teachers, administrators and counselors trained, these schools now have hundreds of trained people, including all the students. The amount of conflict decreased in these schools dramatically because hundreds of trained eyes were better than a few.

'Peace activism' is another track of diplomacy, including protests and awareness-raising that are a staple of many democracies around the world. This type of activity has a long record of effectiveness. Peace activism has used art or even sports as an effective dialogue-initiating medium. In 2005, IMTD sponsored a sports tour of Indian and Pakistani soccer teams, trained in conflict prevention, to take a bus throughout the disputed region of Kashmir and play exhibition games with each other. This is just another strand in the web of peacebuilding that, together with other strands, can lead to substantive change. The 'funding track' of diplomacy includes 'carrot and stick' diplomacy. This involves nonprofits,

217

private donors, international institutions, banks and governmental resources. It was used in Burundi in 2003. The promise of funding for various projects to various sectors helped keep the country stable after the results of the election were in.

Diplomacy through media and public opinion are fairly self-explanatory. As the media focuses more attention, and public opinion is informed on choices for peace over conflict and war, the public capital to will its politicians and leaders into making life-saving choices can be created.

Multiple approaches to diplomacy are essential in an ever-changing and complex world. Strengthening the strands of those in potential conflict serves to counterbalance the impetus to make war or break the peace. If Track One, government to government diplomacy struggles, there exist other options in the diplomatic tool bag which we must use.

In 1978 US President Jimmy Carter achieved a diplomatic success when he convened the Camp David Accords between Israel and Egypt. Before the meeting, the prospects for reconciliation after the recent war were poor. But in a salute to traditional diplomacy, Prime Minister Begin and President Sadat defied the odds and signed the Camp David Accords which remains in effect today. While a huge success, the result set an unrealistically high bar of expectation for future presidents and negotiators. These diplomatic sessions involve two political leaders who represent opposing viewpoints, who are pressured by their constituents to relinquish nothing and to gain everything that their side wants. They arrive at a highly charged environment in which failure is the default. But, in order to conduct a lasting treaty, compromise is required. Each side must give up something they cherish and face criticism and danger for the end result of peace. In Sadat's case, he was assassinated because of his compromise with the Israelis. Similarly, Israeli Prime Minister Rabin, who signed the Oslo Accord with Yasser Arafat of the PLO was assassinated for his role in the peace process. It is a wonder that any of these sessions work. But occasionally they do. The Camp David Accords of 1978, the Oslo Accords of 1992, the Dayton Accords (Bosnian War) of 1995 are prime examples of this kind of success. The Comprehensive Treaty of Sudan of 2005 was distinct in that both governmental and non-profit organizations played major roles to end the conflict and encourage both sides to negotiate. But Track One Diplomacy is often a long shot. Hoping that the personal touch of an experienced hand can affect a successful resolution against the most daunting of odds, should not be the 101 plan of successful diplomacy. A better game plan and stronger long-term strategy relies less on personality and chance and more on having many strands of diplomacy working toward the same end goals at the same time. Thus multi-track diplomacy.

The better plan is to build the web of diplomacy through business, education, religious, training, research, peace activism, professional mediators, citizen diplomacy as well as track one – governmental diplomacy. This web of diplomacy geometrically increases the likelihood that a political climate at home will welcome the politicians negotiating and signing the final treaties.

I also have wondered if there are other undiscovered tracks of diplomacy. Are sports and recreation a form of diplomacy? Are women and women's groups another? Are

219

non-profits and NGOs, such as IMTD different from track two? Do these links, currently labeled as citizen's diplomacy or educational diplomacy deserve study as possible new tracks? At an Ashoka-sponsored women's peace conference in 2001, there was a session moderated by an Israeli woman and a Palestinian woman. Each one had suffered personal loss due to the conflict between the two peoples. At the end of a 90 minute very tense session, which included audience participation, the two women did something I was surprised to see. They looked at each other, paused and embraced and kissed with tears flowing. I could not imagine this happening at any other conference. This represents another potential track of diplomacy: gender diplomacy.

Building multiple strands of diplomatic bonds between peoples in potential conflict is the brilliance of multi-track diplomacy. The liaisons created bring a dynamic aspect to the very old field of diplomacy that is groundbreaking. The concept builds the process of diplomacy by strengthening the web existence of positive, productive, conflict preventing networks to serve as a bridge between conflicting nations and parties. Peace is more obtainable when these networks are built and embedded in daily life.

The crucial short term methods to end genocide are early warning and forecasting, political will and rapid response. The long term solutions include multi-track diplomacy, education, spreading democracy through civic building, and building a permanent national and international political constituency to help pressure policymakers. These practices will help end genocide and create foreign policies that reflect the values and morals of the individuals that comprise great nations.

U.S. Holocaust's Museum's Committee on Conscience's Blueprint for Genocide Prevention.

In 2008 the US Holocaust Museum came out with its *Blueprint for Genocide Prevention*. The committee was chaired by former US Secretary of State Madeleine Albright and US Defense Secretary William Cohen. It is brilliant. It provides a clear cut path to genocide prevention if policy makers and citizens are willing to walk it. If you don't have time to read the 100 page publication, read the four pages of recommendations. They advise everyone, from the US President to American citizens of their role and responsibilities in the solution. Core to their recommendations is treating genocide and genocide prevention with the importance and urgency it deserves.

The President is asked to raise the issue of genocide prevention to an NSC and comprehensive US policy level, spanning the methodologies of many US government agencies. President Obama fulfilled part of this recommendation by creating the Atrocities Prevention Board at the NSC which Samantha Power headed. The inter-department *Atrocities Prevention Board* spans the State Department, USAID, the Defense Department, other US agencies and several key NGOs. The two biggest drawbacks of this effort so far are its ineffectiveness and lack of transparency. Nonetheless, the APB exists and that is an important *start*. The blueprint also recommended that: the U.S Congress fund a Genocide Prevention Office, U.S foreign policy institutions to use preventative diplomacy, early warning, and carrot and stick diplomacy, de-escalation measures, and use military measures when the situation requires it. Lastly to build the international institutions and norms to respond to these threats.

The most urgent of all the recommendations is to create a Genocide Prevention Office. This is timely and crucial. The report estimated the cost would be $250 million per year to administer it. This is a very high estimate of costs. During our four years, the CPG never had a budget of more than $250,000 with a full time staff of six. We utilized fellowships, interns and volunteers. The CPG example is not a stable or permanent model because we were too underfunded and ultimately went out of business for lack of money and donations. Both models represent extremes of resources – the CPG had an extreme lack of them and the USHM has called for an extreme over-abundance of funding. Somewhere in between is a reasonable figure that could assure that these man-made disasters would be a rare occurrence and eventually disappear from human conduct.   A permanent, nonpolitically affiliated, non-religiously affiliated genocide prevention center is long overdue and is in the world's interest to fund completely, immediately.

U.N. Early Warning and Rapid Response.

Aggressively Seeking Peace.

The United Nations, by its charter, is a passive organization. It was not envisioned to be aggressive or to sanction military involvement of its troops, except in a reactive, peace-monitoring role. There is much frustration that the UN can only provide reactive help with refugees or wounded. But as any nation or organization built on democratic principles and 'living documents' the purpose and vision of the United Nations has evolved as the need to protect vulnerable people has changed. Practical measures had to be taken to be more forceful and proactive. The ad hoc nature of each mission is part of the founding principles of the UN to protect against UN abuse. This inherently inhibits a quick response time for proactive intervention to prevent useless loss of human life. There are two specific steps that can be taken to address this. A well-trained, multi-national standing army should be maintained for surgical as well as full-scale involvement for the specific purpose of preventing genocidal or large-scale abuses of humanity. Both Boutros Ghali and Kofi Annan, former Secretary Generals of the UN, called for such a standing rapid deployment force for the UN, in order to better respond to emergencies as they escalate toward genocide. It is no longer sufficient to state that the will or political capital for an intervention does not exist, a mechanism must be created to insure that in the future, resources to save lives will be there regardless of the political climate strategic importance e of the victims or geopolitical relations between powerful nations.

223

In recent years, we have seen a transformation of the mandate language which defines UN peacekeeping missions to include language more conducive for military operations, with specific language allowing the "use of force" to protect civilian life. D.R Congo has benefitted greatly from this with successes in the field in 2003, 2007 and 2012 against militias that perpetrated mass atrocities. But the issue remains, that if there are Security Council members that oppose intervention for political reasons, how do nations seeking to help alter the ground situation to protect civilians?

The Responsibility to Protect.

In October 2005, the United Nations passed a resolution on the 'responsibility to protect civilians from war crimes, genocide, ethnic cleansing and crimes against humanity. It marked the first step the international community has taken to make the concept of early warning and rapid response a functioning reality. Together with the UN Secretary General's report on the Responsibility to Protect (R2P) in 2009, these are good pronouncements and declarations of intentions and ideals. Like the Genocide Convention of 1948, its impact is a question mark. On one hand, the UN is a living body reflecting the will and complexity of the peoples of our world, so this may very well be a first step in the institutionalization of that commitment to protect over time. It does begin to provide an international legal framework for UN General Assembly member nation action. On the other hand, without significant commitment to early warning and rapid response institutions, non-political trigger mechanisms and an ever-building consensus of political will to support these reforms, R2P will remain only a resolution, a declaration of principle. It also requires UN Security Council action, which is heart of the problem of failure to act.

U.N Early Warning Office: Three is not Enough.

I visited the United Nation's Special Advisor Dieng's Office for Genocide Prevention in 2014 . His staff of ten is assigned between himself and the 'Right to Protect' Special Advisor. I met with his office manager, a competent genocide scholar who had significant field experience. By the end of the meeting I understood that there was an early warning system at that office for genocide prevention and for a moment my heart sang. The office manager informed me that it had three people and my heart sank. The world is too big, there are too many massive human rights violations for three people to handle.

The early warning system that the US Holocaust Museum's (USHM) 'blueprint' envisioned does not exists anywhere yet. Though there are several noble efforts. For example the USHM's 'genocide prevention center' is an attempt to create a forecasting mechanism to predict the likelihood of genocide in various areas once enough data is collected. The effort employs part-time staff who work from home and seem to be brilliant at what they do. But this is not the early warning system the US Holocaust Museum envisioned in its blueprint.

Genocide Watch is a longstanding organization founded and run by Dr. Gregory Stanton, usually with one to two interns, which does significant work with its limited resources. Aside from generating accurate and timely warnings, Stanton was a prime moving force behind the creation of an alliance which pushed the USHM's blueprint with policymakers to help create the Atrocities Prevention Board. He never ceases in his work.

There are several other notable and respectable human rights organizations: Human Rights Watch, International Crisis Group and Amnesty International are among the better known and active ones. Their missions are not specifically attuned to genocidal activities, but to human rights and mass atrocities in general, though these areas overlap. The point here is that despite the specific need for one or several major organizations dedicated specifically to genocide prevention – there are practically none.

Rapid Response.

An essential part of ending genocide is having a rapid response team poised to intervene when the situation warrants. In the near future, the United Nations should create a standing armed force for humanitarian and human rights intervention. Other regional authorities can institutionalize their local cooperation to create a worldwide network for genocide prevention and mass atrocities rapid response. Organizations such as the African Union, North Atlantic Treaty Organization, the European Union, the Organization for American States and Economic Community of West African States, not to mention other regional authorities and alliances, a framework can be created for rapid response to genocides, mass atrocities and other significant man-made and natural disasters. While ultimate options for intervention currently rests with the Security Council, as with any democratic institutions, checks and balances must exist to allow for alternate action in case the Security Council fails to act. The implicit charge of the genocide convention is that failure to act during times of genocide leaves the UNSC culpable. Essentially, if one nation leader with a Security Council veto chooses moral indifference to genocide, the principles of 'right to protect', democracy, and our moral convictions are substantial enough to outweigh the UNSC protocol. The current R2P (Responsibility to Protect) discussion focuses on whether R2P redefines sovereignty in such a way that empowers other UN nations to intervene to preserve life.

When the UN Early Warning Office predicts genocide and unfolding actions and confirms unfolding dangers – it must inform a mechanism in the UN that triggers the UNSC or the General Assembly to action for the deployment of the pre-existing standing army with life-protecting "use of force" mandate language. Once the precedent and effectiveness become standard and routine, a large portion of human rights violations will decrease. It is the same simple concept of having an effective police unit poised and ready to respond to crime. Some of that crime will not occur when the consequences are known and immediate. While this does not solve the underlying roots of these conflicts, it certainly aids in reducing the human rights and humanitarian tragedies related to these man-made problems and crimes.

The standing force should be comprised of UN troops uniquely committed to the principles for which the UN stands and the applicable conventions. The mandate would be to secure the safety of those endangered by the genocidal activity, using any means within the scope of the international laws of war. This well-prepared force would prevent the need for international politicians to convince an involvement-wary audience at home, because no domestic soldiers would officially be put in danger. The UN soldiers would have a dual status, as citizens of their home nation and as soldiers of the UN.

Amending the Genocide Convention.

Another potential strategy to enable timely intervention when the UN Security Council is bogged down is to amend the Genocide Convention. When I returned to Washington, DC following a ten year absence, my old mentor and colleague Ambassador McDonald handed me a piece of paper and asked me: 'What do you think of this?' It read:

"State Parties to the Present Protocol

Considering that in order to further the purpose of the Genocide Convention and its provisions, it would be appropriate to make an exception to the principle of national sovereignty, as described by International Law and the United Nations Charter in particular; and allow the international community to intervene with military force in the territory of the state that fails to protect its own nationals who are targets of genocidal acts described by Article 3 of the Genocide Convention, entered into force January 12, 1951.

Article 1

A State party to the Genocide Convention that becomes a Party to this Protocol, recognizes the authority of the General

Assembly and the Security Council, to declare a situation occurring on the soil of any UN member state against its own nationals as, 'Genocide' according to the Genocide Convention, in particular Article 3, and the jurisprudence of international tribunals applying the Genocide Convention.

Article 2

In the absence of action by the General Assembly and Security Council, to an act of Genocide, a State Party to the Genocide Convention that becomes a Party to this Protocol acknowledges the right of the international community to intervene with military force to protect the nationals of a State in a case described in Article 2. Such actions shall not be considered a breach of the Principle of National Sovereignty as described in the United Nations Charter, and relevant norms if International Law, and shall respect the remaining relevant norms and principles of International and Humanitarian Law in particular.

Article 3

This protocol shall come into force when fifteen members of the UN general Assembly ratify it.

Proposed by John W. McDonald, U.S. Ambassador, (Ret.). Chairman and CEO Institute of Multi-Track Diplomacy"

This may well be another good concept for an end run around the UN Security Council when it is caught in paralysis and the people who are dying need swift response. A low threshold for coming into force (15 members) has precedent with the establishment of the International Criminal Court and would apply only to those countries that ratify it. Democracies are based on principles of checks and balances. As the world's largest democratic organization, the United Nations' executive leadership, the Security Council, should have balances built in that weigh world opinion, world morality, the emerging Responsibility to Protect and the spirit of the Genocide Convention against a flawed Security Council mechanism that allows one nation to veto and stop life-saving activities. This is one such tool to rectify this genocide-enabling oversight.

CHAPTER TWELVE: ENDING THE PHILOSOPHY OF INDIFFERENCE.

The Timothy Principle and the Total War Concept.
Creating Permanent Institutional and Political Will.
Internalize World Citizenship – Jean Monnet's Lessons.
Ending War through Democracy-Building.
Our Best Practices.
The Philosophy of Not Helping.
The Unfinished Recipe. The Missing Ingredient is You.

The TIMOTHY Principle and the Total War Concept.

"It wasn't necessary to use that awful thing."[61]

> General Dwight D. Eisenhower on using the nuclear bomb during World War Two.

To be effective in the prevention of genocide and crimes against humanity, international treaties must be binding and enforceable. They must have teeth. As the Armenians, Jews, Poles, Gypsies, Serbs, Bengalis, Tutsis and others were to find out, sympathy, and even the will to act, are often not enough. Aside from effective early warning, there need to be treaties, arrest warrants and mechanisms which can legitimately empower proactive human rights and humanitarian solutions.

---

[61] Peter Calvocoressi, *Total War*, P.83.

We have seen clear evidence of the power of the ICC's indictment with Sudan's al Bashir's curtailing of abuse in Darfur and allowing the South to break away. Without treaties and mechanisms with 'teeth,' perpetrators are unlikely to yield and are less likely to be defeated or stopped. *Treaties which are International Must Often Have Teeth to Yield results* – or, *TIMOTHY,* the Timothy Principle. The missions of the UN are done on an *ad hoc* basis. When an emergency arises there are two time-consuming stumbling blocks: the political will of the UN Security Council must be garnered, and then the actual physical resources must be made available. Transports may arrive from one nation, air coverage from NATO, and troops from several nearby states. Logistically, it is very difficult to coordinate these activities, not to mention deciding who is to pay the bill. This inefficient approach has caused immobility in several situations, unconscionable delays that indirectly lead to the death of thousands. This approach is further hampered by the indifference or intransigence of key players. However, when treaties, conventions and other mechanisms which empower enforcement have clear paths and consequences, the results improve when the 'teeth' in these mechanisms are explicit. Rwanda was a particularly good example of this inefficiency at the United Nations. Armored personnel carriers waited at a US base in Germany for deployment which was held up over a budget debate as an average of nearly 10,000 Tutsis perished each day. Treaties which are International must spell out consequences for both the perpetrators and the Security Council members who obfuscate in the face of deadly results. These members must be held accountable and, in a strict sense, legally liable for a failure to intervene in the most egregious types of human rights abuses. In determining this, a greater emphasis must be placed on the recognition of unfolding genocide through clear verifiable standards.

At the Center for the Prevention of Genocide, we used the UN Genocide Convention definition, but recognized ideological groups as potential victims as well. We emphasized three standards to answer the question of 'what is the magic number for genocide to have occurred?' Currently the number of 5,000 is loosely discussed as a potential standard for genocide in the mass atrocities prevention community. This arbitrary figure denies context and the preciousness of individual life. The CPG instead emphasized whether the massacre of unarmed civilians was *habitual*, *intentional*, and among the *primary* conditions of abuse. If these factors were all met, we declared that genocide was taking place and required an immediate, vigorous response. Whether standards follow these conditions or any one of a number of potential conditions, it must be clearly defined and, when reached, trigger an automatic legally sanctioned response.

Punitive measures under modern international law are taking shape with the reparation rulings of several European nations on behalf of the persecuted Jews of the Second World War. Restitution of personal property, cultural property and territory has expanded to include the return of civilians to their hometowns in Bosnia and Rwanda. These are precisely the kind of teeth that international law must have in order to be effective.

In order to apply the *Timothy Principle* effectively and give teeth to international prevention, intervention and sanctions, it is essential that the UN trigger mechanism for issues of genocide is de-politicized. The UN Security Council naturally brings into its meetings the domestic and international policies of its member nations. But the political climate at home, during a given election year, should have no bearing on the Security Council's decisions to intervene in acts of genocide. It is no longer acceptable that one nation's domestic political climate can determine whether genocidal activities are acknowledged and halted.

The UN would not function properly without a Security Council. The veto of each of its member nations is an important 'check' against any nation dominating the Council. Conversely, if there is a standing UN force ready for humanitarian intervention, political vetoes of an action will decrease. This would be the 'de-politicization' of the UN Security Council's decision-making process regarding issues of dire humanitarian concern. If the main impetus for domestic politics to conflict with the Security Council is removed, then the danger it has posed in vital humanitarian interventions will lessen. Through the professionalization of the UN armed forces, Security Council members will have less face to lose if a peacekeeping or humanitarian mission goes wrong. The troops involved will be acting as citizens of the UN in humanitarian or peacekeeping instances alone. If the lens of nationalism is removed regarding these brave blue helmets, perhaps the significance of their UN mission will take priority over the significance of their home nation. If the resources are there, perhaps the proactive blue helmet humanitarian missions will find broader UN Security Council support.

***

The 'total war' concept should also be considered in as a component of genocidal activity. Few genocides have occurred without being accompanied by war that often masks the severity of the civilian targeting. Since World War Two, there has been a growing historical trend toward the 'total war' theory's inclusion of civilian targeting. Not only is this a monumental step backward for humanity but it has also led to the political justification of genocidal conduct.

There are aspects of the 'total war' concept which warrant an expansion of the definition of genocide to include some conduct during wartime activity. Most wartime civilian dead and wounded are primarily considered under rulings concerning mass-atrocities or crimes against humanity, or a byproduct of the dangers of the war. But there is an aspect of genocidal conduct if the perpetrator is indiscriminately killing civilians without specific military objectives. Examples of this include the firebombing of civilian population centers during World War Two to the Syrian government 'barrel bombing' neighborhoods and entire cities in rebel controlled areas indiscriminately. The burden should be on the aggressor to justify the overwhelming targeting of civilians for a military goal.

The blurring of the line of military action specifically targeting civilians can be traced back to the Nazi blunder of the bombing of Rotterdam, Netherlands after it had just surrendered. Until May of 1940, both sides had followed relative international standards of warfare regarding the targeting of civilians in the theater of war. Civilians were not usually specifically targeted during military operations with the exception of two circumstances: the city where they lived housed a legitimate enemy unit or target or if the entire region had surrendered but this particular city was had not. When the Nazi's bombed Rotterdam, in what was a clear blunder, the

British responded with a blanket bombing of German cities. One wonders whether the gloves coming off at this particular juncture in the war making civilians 'fair game,' set the precedent for the horrible criminal activity of the Nazi regime crimes of the Holocaust.

Creating Permanent Institutional and Political Will.

There is no point to sending firefighters when the house has already burned down.

If a Congressman or woman were to assume a leadership role on the U.S House Appropriations Committee, they could help ensure a serious Congressional funding commitment to genocide prevention. Until that person arrives, or in case they never do, we as unelected citizens, will have to make the difference. We can help create a national and international constituency who believe in this issue and expect our policy makers and elected officials to work to fund these preventative strategies. Demanding 'best-practice' solutions of your government is not just an ideal, it is a right that you have and a responsibility you share if you agree with the premise of this book. Genocide and many of the other ills of humankind are preventable, but an investment in that process needs to be tangible and permanent.

The founding fathers of the United States created a Republic based on sharing power because we are all flawed and the risk for abuse is great. The US Constitution created a successful democracy, in part, because of the wisdom that assumes human nature includes bad behavior. The absolute corruption that goes with absolute power is an absolute part of human nature. This was recognized in the innate skepticism of man's unchecked behavior by many of the Eighteenth Century political writers. It was based on the tyrannical behavior of King George III toward the American colonies. Many of the pilgrims and settlers of the colonies left the countries of their origins because of the oppressive role religion played in their home governments, rendering them outcasts. To break away from those oppressive conditions elsewhere, the American founding fathers sought a 'balance of power' between the Executive and Legislative branches of government with the Judicial Branch aiding with additional oversight and powers. Religion and state were separated lest the abuse of religious minorities occur in the new American nation. The First Amendment in the Bill of Rights allows the individual to defend himself from the corruption and cruelty of individuals and governments through the balancing powers of freedom of speech, assembly and press. If great democracies are built with these protections in mind *against* the worst characteristics in man, should we not make the same assumption in the democratic community of nations? Should we not protect ourselves *against* the worst characteristics in man, on the world stage?

The knowledge that mankind can be evil helps democracies to protect themselves with checks and balances. We need to assume, similarly about leaders and characteristics of leaders throughout the world, so that when the next Adolf Hitler, Joseph Stalin, Pol Pot, or Omar al Bashir appears, there are measures to keep them in check. On the international level that means early warning to predict and detect when that inevitable part of human nature rears its ugly head. It also means having a rapid deploy force at the ready to intervene when evil thought becomes evil deed. Becoming a person who believes in this and will stand for these protections at the international level is the beginning of a constituency of one.

***

Some children have imaginary friends. When I was a boy, I had an imaginary planet - called Jenoco. I wrote the history and treaties, drew maps for years of my childhood. When entered boarding school, it was time to end Jenoco and put childish things aside. I wanted to conclude Jenoco in a way that the imaginary planet would live in peace. It ended when a federation was created that allowed any nation to join if they were committed to three things: democracy, nuclear non-proliferation, safe and clean environmental practices. This Federation, 'the Green States,' grew until more than 70% of Jenoco was part of it and this heralded in a period of long uninterrupted peace. As childish as 'Jenoco' may have been, there were some assumptions which I took for granted for peace. Democracies do not fight democracies is one such assumption which is true.(see the statistician RJ Rummel's work). The European Union today has the 'feel' of how I envisioned 'Jenoco.' Democracies functioned in a way that their people could go about their lives trying to enjoy their friends and family and make a living. Ending genocide, famine, preventable disease and conflict is not as daunting a task as we may think. As with most things, the most difficult part, really, is getting started. In centuries and millennium from now, will

238

we still be struggling with the same problems that plague us now? Will the history of humanity be long periods of struggle, briefly illuminated with periods of democracy and peace, only to fall back into periods of darkness? Or will we learn from our mistakes and finally push away from our long periods of warfare and genocide by developing perpetual democracy and perpetual human rights protection?

***

When a teacher imparts the lessons of conflict and genocide prevention to a class of eager minds, or when an author finishes a book on genocide prevention, these are acts which attempts to build a national and international constituency for this type of belief and work. There is today no real genocide-prevention lobby. Sometimes outraged relatives or human rights activists may lobby congress with varying degrees of success to change other nation's policies of repression and killing. What real power does the Nuba lobby have, or the Northern Nigerian lobby? What power do the Syrian victims' lobby wield in the hall of Congress? About as much as the Tutsi, Acholi, Hema and Lendu lobbied did before them during their massacre – practically none. In recent years, we have seen the rise in popularity of *Save Darfur* and other similar national nonprofit organizations that raise the awareness of millions of people on an issue of suffering which they were previously unaware. In an age of crowdsourcing, crowd funding, Twitter, Facebook and YouTube, the possibility of building a collective consciousness of a people on an issue is as great as ever. To help people realize and internalize their refusal to accept massive human rights violations as business as usual is possible today more than ever.

Take Norway for example. This nation of five million does more to combat human rights violations around the world, per capita, than any other nation. Denmark and Sweden are close behind. These nations have internalized their commitments at an individual level and a national political level in support of human rights and it is a very cornerstone of their foreign policy. The US briefly considered human rights as a cornerstone of its foreign policy under the Carter Administration. When this awareness permeates the national consciousness again and an urgency is built to permanently change our foreign policy – the global impact will be significant.

Ending War Through Democracy-Building.

Since the 1920s, the United States and American organizations have been sending civic-building associations to South America, to aid in building the backbone of democracies. The U.S has, to be sure, also been responsible for its share of coup d'états, supported dictators and pillaged natural resources in South America and elsewhere. But American-sponsored civic building associations and those organic to South America have, however, borne fruit in the past twenty years. Today, almost all of the governments in South America are functioning democracies with democratically elected governments, successful opposition transition in the position of President, freedom of speech, assembly and press with functioning checks and balances form other branches, Venezuela notwithstanding. There was hardly a time in the past Century when there were more than two or three functioning democracies in South America at one time. Civic building associations and democracy movements work – they just take time and several attempts.

The rise of democracies in Africa and Asia is a long and bumpy road. The glorious flash of the 'Arab Spring' of 2011 – 2012, shows that the will for freedom is universal and stirring underneath even the strongest authoritarian governments. The fact that the wave of revolution failed to immediately create democratic governments is not surprising. The military in Egypt, for example, rightly deduced that the civic building associations were helping cause the undercurrent of democratic movement. They closed them all and jailed their leaders. These authoritarian regimes had been strictly curtailing the development of civic-building associations. Over time, as political parties are legalized, and unions and business organizations develop the backbone of civil society, reforms will take place which will give democracy a better chance of survival.

Inherent to well-functioning and mature democracies is the protection of minorities through the court system and the authority and power of the government. When the world is filled with functioning, stable democracies, the vehicles will exist to mitigate conflicts and strife's that have typically led to genocide and mass atrocities. When added to those stable governments are international early warning and rapid response systems for when an occasional situation gets beyond a government's control, then the world will be well on its way to ending genocide in human conduct. As democracies do not fight democracies, nor do they commit genocide.

Internalize World Citizenship: E.U Founding Father Jean Monnet's Lessons.

The European Union was the brainchild of Jean Monnet. He served as the Deputy Secretary General of the League of Nations when he was thirty-one years old. During World War Two he helped coordinate logistics for the transport of war materials from the US to Europe. He was also involved in the Marshall Plan in Europe after the war. After spending much of his life dedicated to assisting Europe after the two world wars, Monnet established some ideas about how to stop the countries on the continent from fighting each other again. One of the underlying keys to Jean Monnet's success in Europe becoming the EU was his assumption that nations that did business together, and had to share resources, would not fight wars with each other. The ECSC founded in 1951 put traditional enemies Germany and France (with Italy and the Benelux nations) together on the same economic path by internationalizing the steel and coal in the ground in those nations requiring joint management of it. Eventually this led to the dissolving of tariffs and taxes, and essentially the creation of an economic free enterprise zone. If you lived in any of the member nations, you could own property or businesses in any of the other member nations without punitive tax consequences. This union gradually expanded to include other members and to become one political union. In 1993, the Maastricht Treaty laid out the structure of a European Super-State, a pseudo-federation with a unique executive and legislative structure, based on cooperation rather than competition. With the Euro and coordinated banking, trade, labor and commerce policies, a true super structure became to evolve where none had existed before. This was the framework for the European Union. Today it is both an economic and political union with 28 members, and has transformed the way a continent approaches business, quality of life and efficiency. None of these nations have fought in any kind of war or conflict against each other, while a member, during the EU's existence. They share a currency, economic and political cooperation, a no-visa border and a vision for the future of which few countries can boast. Monnet knew that this type of transformation of Europe would have to be gradual, so gradual it would hardly be noticeable at first. Over time, even the most fiercely proud nationalists came to associate themselves with their home nation and the greater EU. They have *internalized* their EU citizenship.

People unconsciously internalize many concepts. We are socialized to behave in certain ways, and we internalize those behaviors as part of the package of our identity. For example, four hundred years ago, if we asked a person 'what are you?' Their answer would likely be 'I'm an Alsatian, I'm Christian. I'm a villager. A farmer. A father, A daughter' Today we have expanded these categories to include the larger idea of our nationalism. Even during the fragmentation of Yugoslavia, when the combatants had been separated and plebiscites taken, 15-25% of the population polled considered themselves to be Yugoslavian. They had internalized this Pan-Slavic idea and remained committed to it. When people immigrate to a country, after a number of years, they sometimes begin to feel like members of the new nation in which they live. Sometimes it takes a generation or two before the child internalizes the new identity of the adopted homeland. But people can accept more than one identity. We see a clear example of this in the EU during its embryonic stage. People are both members of their nation as well as members of this newly expanded community. America provides another clear example. Anyone could be an American because, by definition, it is made up of a various of ethnicities and mixes. When one internalizes one's Americanness, it is the adoption of a set of ideas, principles and culture.

So too must we internalize, over time and generations, our world citizenship. We may not become like the 'green states' of 'Jenoco,' but we can learn to picture ourselves as citizens of the world, with responsibilities to people beyond our kin, ethnicity, religion and nationality. Just as Europeans 'internalized' Monnet's concept of a greater European, so too can we internalize an identity as a world citizen, with all the responsibilities and horizons that it implies.

Our Best Practices: Genocide Prevention, Conflict Prevention, Disease Prevention and Famine Prevention.

In the 2010s, when Fortune 500 companies had problems, they needed to solve, they called the professionals. Organizations like Gallup, the Corporate Executive Board and the Corporate Advisory Board paid large fees per year just so corporations could be members and have access to their databases and staff. When a senior vice president of a division of one of these large successful companies has a problem that is keeping him up at night, his first call when he goes into the office is often to one of these organizations. He/she describes the problem – marketing, layout, rollout, integration, software, labor, downsizing, production and so forth – whatever the problem, usually the 'best practice' staff representative replies 'no problem, we have you covered, I'll call you back soon.'

What happens next is a marvel of modern business. The lead staffer in charge of that client gets his team together and they research comparable situations in their database that other companies went through. Sorting through the specifics, they determine which solution is the industry-best solution and is applicable to their clients' needs. They learn the solution, fly out and teach it to their client. This can save clients millions of dollars and months, even years of headache and chaos. Using the best solutions that someone else has already used and is a proven winner; it is a no-brainer.

I have always hoped that government would function the same way. Why reinvent the wheel? If there is a department, an administration, an urban area, an authority that has brilliantly solved a situation similar to one unfolding elsewhere, shouldn't that database be available? In human rights, conflict prevention, resolution and intervention, there exist best practices too. Much of this intellectual capital, however, is being lost. For example, Ambassador McDonald, about whom much in this chapter is written, died in 2019. He worked every day until his mid-nineties. But when the Ambassador died, there will be incredible institutional memory loss. Organizations that undertake best practices for these norms should be captured so that their lessons learned do not have to be re-learned in the future, and at the cost of thousands or millions of lives.

The Philosophy of Not-Helping.

Which is the Philosophy and Purpose of America: Self Interest or Idealism?

During the five years of the Johnson Administration, the embers of JFK's idealism were visible with the Civil Rights Act, the Voting Rights Act, the Great Society and the War on Poverty. During the following U.S President, Nixon's term, his foreign affairs philosopher, and National Security Advisor, Henry Kissinger espoused and led a realpolitik philosophy based on the self-interest of the U.S. This policy has remained the platform from which almost all U.S. Foreign Policy emanates.

The philosophy of realism was clearly embraced by the ideals of the 1980s-1990s as it was to be known as the 'me' generation. Both liberal and conservative administrations assumed the realpolitik Kissinger concept of 'self-interest', as the guiding principle of the nations' foreign policy, has become elevated and is now perceived as standard and neutral, despite its bias toward one end of the foreign policy political spectrum. Because realism is perceived as neutral, it is difficult to recognize its dangers. But the politics that appeals primarily to self-interest loses the great benefits that come with attempting to improve our world. The joy of a child receiving gifts eventually graduates to a joy of giving to others – usually with your own children. But the benefits of a nations' policies of altruism are geometrically greater. Even today when the U.S State Department considers human rights, it must be considered in the context of our national security interests. The underlying morality of most Americans is not reflected in our foreign policy. While U.S. foreign policy does aid in the service of human rights, it is often done in spite of our moral belief system, not because of them. The undergirding of most of US foreign policy is realpolitik-based. Every recent President's foreign policy has asked the question first 'is engagement there in our self-interest,' when the question of greater value is: 'is human life at stake?'

The world interest is the American interest. Since Kissinger's realism guided U.S of U.S. foreign policy, the viewpoint has held sway ever since. The evidence that realism trumps idealism, regardless of party, can be seen in the failures to act across party lines in Rwanda, Darfur and Nuba, Sudan, D.R. Congo and recently in Syria, C.A.R and Nigeria. None of these areas or nations hold a strategic interest for the United States, but the moral imperative to end the suffering is as compelling as any.

When President Kennedy was assassinated in 1963, hundreds of millions mourned for the loss of a youthful, inspiring leader, but many also mourned the loss of something less tangible; they mourned the loss of idealism. President Kennedy inspired Americans and people throughout the world to dare to dream for a better world.

The elevation of this Kissinger philosophy of self-interest, and its adoption by all presidents who have followed Nixon represents a defeat of Kennedy idealism. Because self-interest is perceived as the cornerstone of foreign policy, it remains unseen, elevated and perceived as neutral. It is not neutral. It has not served my country - the United States, or the world it sometimes protects, well at all.

The idealistic proponents of America argued for better

outreach to teach fledgling democracies the best practices of building a successful democracy. We missed that opportunity when many of the Soviet Republics left the Soviet Union for independence, including Russia itself. Those years of transition from the USSR, to the CIS, to today offered several years of opportunity for the US and the West to play a pivotal role in helping Russia use, and then develop, the training wheels of their democracy. We failed to do this effectively because it was 'not in our strategic interest.' As a result, Russia today is still an authoritarian regime, and remains an active threat in international relations and, ironically, an indirect threat to American interests worldwide.

We failed to reach out throughout the Middle East during the Arab Spring, to aid the cause of democracy. We could have provided aid, advice, training, education, workshops, conflict prevention strategies and the best constitution thinkers and writers from around the world. We should have done that because it was the right thing to do. It also would have been the prudent thing to do in the long-term interests of a peaceful, democratic world. We should help each of these potential countries in transition to help frame these early nations' democratic aspirations in a structure that works, or in one whose principles would give it a good possibility of working, if their people so willed it.

Syria, Nigeria, C.A.R, and D.R. Congo all have human rights failures which would have benefitted from American effort and leadership. After Rwanda's genocide the lesson was clear that early intervention *was* in our self-interest. The fact is, early warning is always in our self-interest because *the world's self-interest is the American self-interest.*

If we do not take on a national responsibility to protect

those in danger, most of these problems will continue, and, more often than not, worsen. The EU is currently taking the lead in much of the preventative and response work in human rights. Russia and China should not be counted on to help and few nations have the resources to be as impactful as the U.S. does.

Is America the nation Kennedy inspired in us when he asked us for selfless sacrifice? Have our policies become too much the product of the realpolitik philosophy of pragmatic leaders who lack the vision and courage to act with urgency to create the world of which we dare dream? That debate is worth having. In the end, by embracing idealistic behavior in US foreign policy, the question becomes moot because promoting democracy and protecting human life is always in our long term self-interest.

Proponents of strict 'self-interest' and realism should concede that in an ever-connected world, the health and welfare of the world community is in our strategic interest. This is not only true because our citizens are from everywhere in the world, nor because we compete for trade partners on the entire world stage, but because the freedom we represent is universal. It is why we are often considered the indispensable nation. The fact that we have failed to act with any discernible urgency in many human rights emergencies does not negate that American ideals are rooted in principals of morality, fairness, freedom and equality. But the greatness of a nation lies in acting on those ideals. The hallmark of freedom is ethical treatment of others. Our Founding Father's assumed the worst in human nature and created a government that attempts to protect against our darker nature, it is a self-evident truth that aiding others in dire need fulfills this.

If the next Century is to see the U.S. continue its role as the world's 'indispensable nation,' it will not be because the U.S is the wealthiest, or the strongest or has the biggest economy. There have been scores of powerful nations, kingdoms and empires which no longer exist. Wealth ebbs, large militaries bankrupt nations and economies crash. Our indispensability is intrinsically tied to our place as the foremost democracy. What is the point of promoting freedom if the freedom we promote is brutal, mean and indifferent? During the Cold War, the U.S. and many of her allies stood for liberty. In the times to come, can the U.S. continue to be a nucleus of democracy-building *and* an indispensable force for human rights, not when it's convenient, not when the world is looking, but as a permanent part of its foreign policy. We should do this in a way that is not paternalistic, materialistic or chest-thumping. It would be fitting for a great nation and a world leader

An Unfinished Recipe – the Missing Ingredient is You

"If we did all the things we are capable of, we would literally astonish ourselves."

Thomas Edison

In January 2010 an earthquake devastated the Caribbean Island nation of Haiti. The first private plane to arrive in Haiti from the west coast of Florida after the January 2010 earthquake was organized by a sixth grader at Out-of-Door Academy in Sarasota. She asked her father if his company plane would transport medical supplies if she organized it and he agreed. There are thousands of examples of young people starting organizations that save lives, help others in need or just make the world a better place to live. Three years ago Jane Evers, former first lady of Bradenton, Florida, established a charity called F.E.L.T – Feeding Empty Little Tummies. She had heard that the number of Manatee County children going hungry had exploded as a result of the recession. The organization grew until children at several elementary and middle schools were supplied with food as well as their families who were also experiencing hunger. Jane died of cancer on New Year's Eve 2014. Three days before she died, she was still running the organization, determined to ensure empty little tummies were filled. They continue to be filled today. The Emperor Augustus said that a leader should die on his feet running his empire and Jane practically did; she died as she helped others. There is not an age, or a place, or a circumstance, where you cannot make a positive impact or your surroundings and, indeed, even the world.

When I was twelve years old my mother gave me a book, *The Autobiography of Malcolm X* and I enjoyed it from the beginning because he wrote the book directly to you, the reader.

This book is written to you, the reader, for you to use. It is written by me, the author, but it is the story of tens of millions of people. *In Case of Genocide – Break Glass* is not just a story of our reaction to the massacre in Sulawesi, Indonesia, it is not just a collection of stories and histories of genocide over the past 100 years. It is *a call to arms* to you. When you hear of genocide, whether close to home or in far off lands, whether its people who are known or unknown to you, do whatever is in your power, and whatever is in your potential to end it. Whenever there is genocide, treat it like the emergency that the lives it is taking deserve. In case of genocide, break glass.

Epilogue

I sat on the porch thinking about the CPG and what we had accomplished. I was proud that the St. Petersburg Holocaust Museum was interested in our archives to possibly tell our story. I pushed past the laziness of the warm Florida day and went back inside, crouching to pull boxes of the CPG archives out of the small gnome-sized closet. After searching through the boxes, I found the two card organizers I had kept from the charity's contacts. I wanted to find out if we had been helpful to the Darfurians. My friends and I had just watched the US Presidential debate the night before and both candidates mentioned their commitment to ending the horror in Darfur, Sudan. Both called it genocide. I did not know with any certainty whether any of the publicity, reports or even the introductions we made for the Darfurians proved to be of any use.

"Hello, is Yusef of the Darfurian Community in Exile there?"

"Yes, yes, Richard, is that you?"

"Yusef, how are you?"

"Much better. Boy, am I glad to hear from you Richard. We tried to contact you to thank you. We emailed you and mailed you but everything just kept coming back."

"Sorry about that Yusef. When we closed, I just wanted to get away from human rights work for a while. I was burnt out."

"Really?"

"Yes," he continued, "you know Richard, we all sat down about three months ago and thought that if you hadn't come out and called it genocide in the months before you left. If you hadn't had that march and brought us together to meet those people – we would never have the gotten coverage we have now. Nobody would be calling it genocide. You know Rich, you really got the ball rolling and we wanted to thank you."

After we hung up the phone, I made the firm decision to write this book. It is not really about the wonderful volunteers we had or the work we undertook, it is really about how the human spirit can overcome indifference, lack of resources and evil conduct through will and perseverance. And that deserves to be shared.

I wish this book could have been solely about life-affirming stories of heroism. Perhaps that will be the next book. But the fact is, today if you live in a country where bad militias, armies or governments dislike you and trouble is coming to your door - run, flee, hide or fight, but do not wait for your rescue – there is no one coming to help. Not until people like you reading this book, and I, change that. This is the reality. There is no international super-structure designed to specifically respond to these areas where the need is greatest but the importance to powerful nations is negligible. This is what need to be corrected. That is the 'call to arms' of this book. Let's demand a system that changes this complete moral blind side of the world community.

My father once wrote about his hope for future generations:

"Thirty generations hence, I hope our golden, god like children look back at us with compassion and generosity, from a vantage point of an enlightened perspective and a profound maturity, and know, that in spite of all our fears, frailties and inadequacies as we beheld the awesome universe, some of us wanted to give them the stars, with love."[62]

In that spirit, let us create a world that is genocide-free. Let that be our gift to the next generation and the generations that come after them.

---

[62] *It's Like This Jim*, 1972.Copyright John J. O'Brien

Author in 1998 in Geneva, Switzerland at 32, where the first chapters of Break Glass were written 25 years ago.

BOOK TWO: GENOCIDE PREVENTION MANUAL.

PART ONE: HOW TO START: ARE YOU SURE? DEFINING AND REFINING YOUR FOCUS.

Are You Sure?

There are a number of variables to determine before you take the plunge into the world of non-profit, human rights of humanitarian endeavor. You should ask yourself whether you are willing to sacrifice your time, hard work, money and resources for little or no pay or, even worse, as was in my case, to assume massive debt incurred by your charity. You will receive little or no credit for the work you do, and some will question your motives for doing it. If you are lucky, your family's criticism of the idea will disappear and become support once they see how worthwhile it is. But do not count on it. Part of your job is also having a handout, becoming, essentially, a professional beggar for a cause you believe in. Whether it is running a Saturday car wash or a black-tie fundraiser, you, as your charity's leader, will have your hand out in some way for most of your professional non-profit life. If these things do not extinguish the ember of your interest to save lives, or do good work, then I recommend taking the plunge. I emerged from the CPG $19,000 in debt to the IRS which was paid off in 18 months. For the lives we saved and the pure joy of getting out of bed every morning knowing that there was the potential to save lives that day – it was absolutely worth it.

As with all things in life, when in doubt, ask a professional. I am not a lawyer, just a former human rights executive trying to open our archives to you to see if they can be of use to you or others interested in human rights endeavor. While I have included dozens of documents from the CPG archives, almost all of them need updating to be useful for your potential organization and should merely serve as a starting point to show you how others have done human rights violation monitoring and advocacy, successfully, before you.

Define Your Focus.

Once you have decided to undertake your human rights or humanitarian NGO (non-government organization), one of the first priorities you will have to grapple with is defining your mission. In business this is a 'mission statement' and it is a good exercise for non-profit human rights or humanitarian organizations as well. The world is so big with so many problems that being as specific as possible can be very useful. However, in your tax status filing you may want to be more general in scope in case your work takes on additional functions. But for your internal mission statement it is important to define exactly what you hope to achieve. The Center for the Prevention of Genocide's mission statement was:

"To take practical measures to anticipate, prevent and report acts of genocide."

Or a longer version:

"to provide early warning of genocide, massacres and massive human rights violations with an aspect of genocide to policymakers, the media and the public to elicit a response to end the human rights violation."

If building a communication network for rape prevention in DR Congo, or a genocide prevention early warning for the Great Lakes region in Western Africa is your mission, then state it. Be clear, so that you can focus your efforts and resources toward your primary goal.

Writing a business plan is an ideal way to lay out your plan for how you will organize your endeavor. A business plan summary can be as brief as one page and a full business plan can be over one-hundred pages in length. What you should have in your mind and committed on paper so you can execute your vision and 'sell' your vision to others better are:

- Your Mission Statement
- Your Potential Board Members
- Your Potential Staff and Volunteer Pool
- What You Want to Accomplish and when in the First Month, First Quarter, Second Quarter, First Year, Second Year.
- Where You Will Set Up Shop.
- How You Envision Your Operation Working – Specifically.
- Projected Budgets and Fundraising.
- Organization and Administration of NGO – How Will It Function Day-to Day.

These are important markers to lay out and keep track of. I strongly recommend 'white boarding' out your ideas and concepts with dry erase markers with your 'brain trust' so that you have talked out some of the ideas and taken some of the not-so-strong ideas out of the plan. For example, unless a foundation has already offered you funding (very unlikely), do not plan on grant money within your first one to four years of your business plan. Most foundations like to see a record of success before they give. Thus the ironic conundrum of most new charities – do you focus on your mission, so that in four years you will be attractive to foundations that give grants and risk going out of business for lack of money? Or do you concentrate on the fundraising while your mission suffers. You would think that there is a happy middle ground, but more often than not, the NGO will scramble for their upcoming rent, utilities and payroll month to month, just like many other businesses starting out, with the drawback that what you are selling does not have many customers.

Well-intended donors and offers of potential grant money sometimes don't materialize and can leave your charity at the edge of insolvency. This happened to the CPG repeatedly including companies that purchased large amounts of PCs which were donated to us and then cancelled the checks. There are some rotten people that will take advantage of your charity's meagre assets, so protect yourself at all times. Ultimately an unfulfilled pledge, a kited check, and debt led us to close our doors in spite of a strong track record.

I do *not* recommend most of the following ways which I tried keep the CPG open the first year.

- Ran it out of my house for three months.
- Spent the first four months writing grant proposals – which were all rejected.
- Used my entire teaching income to subsidize the charity.
- Quit my day job.
- Rented out my house and slept on couch of charity for one year.
- With my dog.
- Borrowed money from family to keep charity going.
- Pinned hopes on 'con man' who promised one million in funding.
- Buddy emptied his bank account to save the charity on Christmas Day.
- Held an Art Show where no one bought art.
- Let car inspection lapse to save money.
- Accepted checks from people who were unknown to the charity.

Refine Your Focus.

The first few weeks, months and probably years, you will not, necessarily, know what you are doing. This doesn't mean you can't be successful. Our first year, we used a rudimentary human rights chart to track abuse. It was crude, but both the Sulawesi, Indonesia massacre and the Nuba Mountain, government-induced famine occurred in our first year and a half with our first crude system. Both were relatively successful. We tracked massive human rights violations at the CPG by using this rudimentary chart. Four years later, we had a much more sophisticated system with emergency crisis procedures, specific strategies and massive contact lists. But first thing first. You have to learn the trade. Pictured here is the actual first early warning chart we used. (We added color). You may want to use something similar to break up your project into regions, countries, types of abuse to create an easy-to-understand graph to determine which areas to focus your organization's attention.

Dress the part and act the part. Whenever I would wonder if I was in over my head, I would put my chin forward, dress well and *act* like a CEO of a major human rights organization. Believe it or not, it works. The projection of confidence and competence even when you don't feel like either is important to those around you depending on your leadership. You are the one person in the room who cannot appear to be in over your head, even though you may be.

Don't reinvent the wheel. If there are organizations, newspapers, blogs, listservs, governments, or media doing a great job in an area you want to cover, do not hesitate to use their research (giving full credit to them when you do) in your early warning assessment. Often their ground staff will be willing to share information with you if you offer to do the same and sometimes even without that offer. By using the work of others, you can your focus on other areas that need attention.

PART TWO: HOW-TO: BUILD YOUR COMMUNICATION NETWORK.

DEVELOPING ON-THE-GROUND RESOURCES.

Once you have researched and exhausted all of the pertinent published media, nonprofit, internet, government and other resources, then you should start to fill in the areas where the information is scarce by reaching out to people and organizations on the ground with personal contact. For example, early during our first year open, abuse in Southern Sudan was hot, Kosovo was cooling down and Colombia, Zimbabwe, D.R. Congo and Indonesia were heating up. We reached out to all of these areas but especially to Indonesia and the Nuba area of Sudan because we felt that there was not enough information coming out of these areas to confirm or deny the charge of human rights violations. We also chased dead ends in Tibet, Angola and elsewhere. Our efforts in reaching out to people and organizations in Nuba and Indonesia particularly paid off with intelligence that played a part in saving lives. Here are some of the ways we reached out to people on the ground in hotspots around the world.

Examples of on-the-ground resources.

i. Human Rights Organizations
ii. Humanitarian Aid Organizations
iii. UN Organizations
iv. Other International Organizations
v. Religious Affiliated Organizations
vi. Media organizations
vii. Individual members of the press on the ground
viii. U.S Embassy Staff

ix. Additional Neutral Embassy Staff
x. Other US and International Staff on the ground
xi. Visiting business people on the ground
xii. Underground organizations
xiii. Indigenous leaders and individuals
xiv. Indigenous press
xv. Indigenous nonprofit, religious and aid organizations
xvi. Other

The conversation with the person on the ground can be something like this:

Here's an Example of what to say on the phone making first contact:

"We are a human rights organization that reports massacres and massive human rights violations. We received reports from Sudanese about massacres in Darfur (Adar, Abu Gidad, Gouz Naim, Krainga,Gondailat), Kutum and Shoba. We want to take further steps to make the information public and influence policy makers to take action but we need to have a confirmation from a non-Sudanese source or a Sudanese worker for international organizations, willing to talk to us. He/She can be from an organization or on a private visit who has witnessed evidence of their occurrence. Could you help us find such a source to prevent further killings?"

Keep track of your conversations and sources and keep their information secure. This is important. Future staffers may need to reach out to confirm a report in the area and your contact may be the one to do it. But their willingness to help is something to note, that too can save your fellow human rights monitors precious time and energy. It is also key when establishing the chain of information that there are credible sources known to you, in the middle of the crisis. The security of their information has everything to do with their safety. Often, the regimes and militias who are persecuting people in the area are more than willing to victimize activists on the ground who are helping to expose human rights crimes. Notes should be taken of the gist of the conversation immediately or within a couple of minutes after the call, as is practical (not in the middle of an emergency crisis action plan). It is important that the institutional memory and chain of communication reflect exactly what was said if it relates to human rights violations. This methodology is important for accuracy and can protect your organization from charges of fabricating information.

Creating excellent on-the-ground contacts, keeping accurate records of those conversations is part of the good housekeeping that can yield results. It also helps to impress the policymakers you advocate to if you have the actual accounts, with names redacted (blacked out); it helps impress the authenticity of the report.

HAVE A STRATEGY: BEGIN WITH THE END IN MIND.

Years ago when playing in chess tournaments, a coach told me to begin the game with the end checkmate of my opponent in mind. The whole purpose of the work you do is to save lives. Always begin the work you do with that end goal in mind. Filing reports and running around is just busy work if it doesn't save or protect lives.

When the day comes that you have an emergency crisis to report, some planning should have taken place beforehand. Before wasting your time reaching out to every member of Congress, all UN departments, all other human rights nonprofit groups and all media of the world, some planning is in order. The best time for this thinking and planning is the quiet time long before the emergency unfolds. If there are six places in the world where human rights violations are likely to occur, then you should have six very specific strategies for how each can be diffused or ended. Who are the people, the policymakers, who can put in motion events to diffuse the danger? Once you have determined who they are you must reach out to them professionally and competently. When the emergency arises, they should already know your name, your organization's name and respect its information and professionalism. When you do your thinking and planning, I recommend white boarding it out with the dry erase markers with your 'brain trust. 'When you identify the phone-call-tree that will help end the abuse, it is up to you to contact as many in that phone tree in advance of any emergency to enlist a commitment for future help if an emergency arises. Your ultimate target may be a Member of the US House of Representatives on the Appropriations Committee, a Presidential Advisor, the head of a governmental or non-profit aid program, a UN agency head or staffer, or even the militia or perpetrators themselves to let them know that the information is out.

On-the-fly strategies *can* work as well, but planning is better. We were caught off-guard (see Introduction Chapter of book) when Sulawesi exploded and Laskar Jihad began killing Christians. We were fortunate that we had reached out to that region of islands months before because of the difficulty of obtaining information after the Moluccas Christian massacre of Muslim two years earlier. Our strategy to confirm the abuse with the US Embassy worked quite by luck. The strategy to target only Australian media in the hope that if they picked it up the western news cycle would pick it up, also worked. We advocated to conservatives in the US House of Representatives that Christians were being massacred in a nation the US was about to give over one-hundred million dollars in military hardware to. Indonesian President Megawati quickly sent troops to stop the massacre in a rare human rights success in the region. She was our target. See our five phone-call-tree target to get to Megawati below.

PHONE-CALL-TREE: FIVE PHONE-CALL EXAMPLE:
1. A call to confirm the firsthand report with a US Embassy official.
2. A visit to a policymaker whose self-interest or sense of humanity and position makes them ideal to get the ball rolling. This was a meeting with the Congressman Cass Ballinger.
3. The policymaker (Congressman) promises to call the White House to express concern for Christians being massacred and to mention the imminent military aid package and encourage the President, or the Vice President or the Secretary of State to call Megawati to encourage a swift response (or she puts in peril the military aid package).
4. The White House calls President Megawati or the appropriate person of influence who is uniquely positioned to exert influence to stop the genocide.
5. Indonesian President, or her equivalent, calls on her generals to dispatch 4,000 troops to Tentena, Sulawesi to chase away Laskar Jihad perpetrators. (She later arrests its leader Umar Thalib).

This strategy was a solid, on-the-fly, solution, in part because of the participation of John Heidenrich the author of *How to Prevent Genocide.*

Two years later when we tracked a massacre in eastern DR Congo, we were better prepared. The UN was considering whether to use force in the mandate for the UN-flagged French troops. With the breaking news of the massacre, we strongly recommended the UN include 'use of force' in the mandate language so the French soldiers could actually do their job to protect civilians. It may seem like a small thing, but success is in the details. The inclusion of use-of-force in the mandate language helped the French bring peace to a region of eastern D. R. Congo that previous missions to 'observe only' failed to bring.

You will need to ask yourself, who or what can stop this potential human rights violation from occurring, how? Once that answer is apparent, your job is to figure the one to five phone calls it will take to put into effect the policy to end the abuse if it starts. Then start reaching out to them. It will, however, take many more than five phone calls to make those connections.

REACHING OUT TO POLICYMAKERS

Your first contact may occur with a staffer to a Congressman or woman on the Foreign Relations committee, Africa sub-committee, or the powerful Appropriations Committee. An initial meeting should include a Power Point or professional-looking presentation where you and your staff present your mission, credentials, methods and desire to cooperate with their office. It should be clear when you have finished that you are enlisting the staff and the Member of Congress to become involved in taking specific steps of urgent action should the crisis explode. Such informational pre-emergency meetings will be crucial if an emergency arises or even if you need to obtain entrée to another influential person; this contact may help open the door for you.

Embassies, UN organizations, US Policymakers and departments, members of the press and other international organizations and nonprofits should also know of your efforts through individual presentations – either in person or remotely.

As with on-the-ground resources, a careful log should be kept of all meetings with all policy makers so that names and willingness of contacts are recorded. These staffs sometimes have high turn-over and it is you and your staff's job to keep apprised of your best contacts who can yield the best results in the best offices.

The following are outdated lists from 2003 of key US and International policymakers and is a good example of the detail needed for effective human rights information dissemination and advocacy. Make sure to add email contact and other pertinent media (Twitter, FB). PLEASE NOTE THESE ARE SAMPLE LISTS WHICH ARE OUTDATED AND YOUR ORGANIZATION MUST UPDATE THEM BEFORE THE LISTS ARE USEFUL. Examples included here are:

- US House of Representatives, U.S. Senate.
- The United Nations and the U.S. State Department.
- Wire, TV and Newspaper. International and Regional.
- The Washington Post staff as a Sample.
- For NGOs, U.N. and government agencies specific departments, appropriate staffers, emergency response personnel and country desk officers are included.
- These lists are all at least 20 years old and are outdated and should be considered examples of the beginning of a policy advocacy list of contacts.

*HOUSE * SENATE * STAFF **

ADVOCACY DIRECTORY 2003
* OUTDATED LIST * SHORTENED FOR SPACE

Name	Position	Phone #	Office
Hon. Henry Hyde	Chairman-Committee on International Relations	202-225-4561	2110 Rayburn HOB
Hon. Lleana Ros-Lehtinen	Chairman-Subcommittee on International Relations Human Rights	202-225-3931	2160 Rayburn HOB
Hon Ben Gilman	Chairman-Subcommittee on Mid-east and South Asia	202-225-3776	2449 Rayburn HOB
Hon. Gary Ackerman	Ranking-Subcommittee on mid-east and South Asia	202-225-2601	2243 Rayburn HOB

Hon. Jim Leach	Chairman-Subcommittee on East Asia and the Pacific	202-225-6576	2186 Rayburn HOB
Hon Eni F.H. Faleomava	Ranking-Subcommittee on East Asia and the Pacific	202-225-8577	2422 Rayburn HOB
Hon. Elton Gallegly	Chairman-Subcommittee on Europe	202-225-5811	2427 Rayburn HOB
Hon. Earl Hilliard	Ranking-Subcommittee on Europe	202-225-2665	1314Rayburn HOB
Hon. Ed Royce	Chairman-Subcommittee on Africa	202-225-4111	2202 Rayburn HOB
Hon. Donald Payne	Ranking-Subcommittee on Africa	202-225-3436	2209 Rayburn HOB
Hon. C.W. "Bill" Young	Chairman-Subcommittee on Appropriations	202-225-5961	2407 Rayburn HOB
Hon. David Obey	Ranking-Appropriations	202-225-3365	2314 Rayburn HOB

Hon. Jim Kolke	Chairman-Subcommittee on Foreign Operations	202-225-2542	2266 Rayburn HOB
Hon. Nita Lowey	Ranking- Foreign Operations	202-225-6506	2329 Rayburn HOB
Hon. Frank Wolf	Chairman-Subcommittee on Commerce, State and Justice	202-225-5136	241 Cannon HOB
Hon Tome Lantos	Ranking-International Relations Committee, Co-Chair, Human Rights Caucus	202-225-3531	2217 Rayburn HOB

Members of the Subcommittee on International Relations and Human Rights

Hon. Christopher Smith	2373 Rayburn HOB	(202) 225-3765
Hon. Ron Paul	203 Cannon HOB	(202) 225-2831
Hon. Cass Ballenger	2182 Rayburn HOB	(202) 225-2576
Hon. Thomas Tancredo	410 Cannon HOB	(202) 225-7882

Hon. Joseph Pitts	204 Cannon HOB	(202) 225-2411
Hon. Cynthia McKinney	124 Cannon HOB	(202) 225-1605
Hon. Robert Menendez	2238 Rayburn HOB	(202) 225-7919
Hon. Grace Napolitano	1609 Longworth HOB	(202) 225-5256
Hon. Adam B. Schiff	437 Cannon HOB	(202) 225-4176

OTHER KEY COMMITTEES
Sub Committee on Foreign Operations

Human Right Caucus

Senate
Key Chairmen and Ranking Members

Subcommittee on International Operations and Terrorism

Subcommittee on Foreign Operations

House International Relations Committee

Regional Sub Committees

Senate Foreign Relations Committee

UNITED NATIONS DEPARTMENTS * US STATE DEPARTMENT *

NOTE: 2003 OUTDATED LIST

Office of the United Nations High Commissioner for Human Rights

Contact: Ms. Elsa Stamatopoulou
Phone: 212-963-2865
Fax:212-963-4097
e-mail: stamatopoulou@un.org

Office of the United Nations High Commissioner for Refugees

Contact: Mr. Arnulv Torbjornsen   NGO Coordinator
Tel: 41-22-739-8290   Fax:41-22-739-7302

Local: Mrs. Guenet Guebre-Christo   Tel: 202-296-5191
                                    Fax:202-296-5660
                                    e-mail: usawa@unhcr.ch

Office for the Coordination of Humanitarian Affairs (OCHA)

Phone: 212-963-1234
Fax: 212-963-1312

Ms. Phyllis Lee   Advocacy and External Relations Unit
Phone: 212-963-4832   Fax: 212-963-9489
e-mail: leep@un.org

United Nations Development Programme (UNDP)

Contact: Ms. Caitlin Wiesen   NGO Section
Phone: 212-906-5906
Fax: 212-906-5313
E-mail: caitlinwiesen@undp.org

World Food Programme (WFP)

Contact: Abigail Spring
Phone: 212-963-5196   Mobile: 917-302-9325
Fax: 212-963-8019
E-mail: springa@un.org

II. US State Department – EXAMPLES - OUTDATED

Operations Center-Emergency Response

Rank	Name	Phone	Office
Director	Laurie Tracy	202-647-2522	7516
Deputy Director Operations	Whitney Baird	202-647-2522	7516
Deputy Director Crisis Management Staff	Ford Hart	202-647-2522	7516
Senior Watch Officer (24 Hours Per Day)		202-647-1512	7516

Editor		202-647-1530	7516	
Crisis Management Staff	Cherrie Daniels	202-647-7640	7516	
Emergency and Evacuations Planning		202-647-7640	7516	
Emergency Relocation		202-647-7640	7516	
Military Representative Col.	Alan C. Ekrem	202-647-6097	7516	

County Departments

Country	Rank	Name	Phone	Office
Burundi	Country Officer	Carolyn Bargeron	202-647-4966	4246
DR Congo	Country Officer	Stefanie Amadeo	202-647-2216	4246
Indonesia	Country Officer	Richard D. Haynes	202-647-2543	5210
	Country Officer	James W. Ellis	202-647-2769	5210

	Country Officer	Karin M. Lang	202-647-2931	5210
Russia	Director	Seth Winnick	202-647-9806	4223
	Deputy	Jonathan Moore	202-647-6743	4223
Rwanda	Country Officer	Amy S. Radetsky	202-647-2973	4246
Sudan	Country Officer	Rob Pyott	202-647-8284	5240
Uganda	Country Officer	Howell Howard	202-647-6453	5240

Regional Secretaries

Region	Name	Phone	Office
African	Walter Kansteiner	202-647-4440	6234A
East Asian	James A. Kelly	202-647-9596	6205
European	Amb. A. Elizabeth Jones	202-647-9626	6226

Near Eastern	William J. Burns	202-647-7209	6242
South Asian	Christina B. Rocca	202-736-4325	6254

Bureau of Population, Refugees and Migration

Title	Name	Phone	Office
Assistant Secretary	Arthur E. Dewey	202-647-7360	5824
Assistance for Africa	Margaret McKelvey	202-663-1027	L505 SA1
Assistance for Asia and the Near East	Joyce Leader	202-663-1063	L505 SA1
Assistance for Europe, NIS and the Americans	Sylvia Bazala	202-663-1024	LA505 SA1

Bureau of Human Rights

Position	Name	Phone	Office

Dir., Ofc of Human Rights and Democracy, DRL	Margot Sullivan	(202) 647-0407	2201 C St., ste. 7802
Asst Sec for Democracy, Human Rights and Labor, DRL	Lorne Craner	(202) 647-2126	2201 C St, ste. 7802

Title	**Name**	**Phone**	**Office**
US Permanent Representative to the UN	John Negroponte	202-736-7555	6317
Deputy	Rosemary DiCarlo	202-736-7555	6317

Secretary of State

Secretary Colin Powell   **202-647-5291**
Personal Assistant Marjorie Jackson   **202-647-7098**

MEDIA OUTREACH.

While it is not practical to reach out to every international, national, regional and local newspaper, TV station and media resource, it is important to have *all* of them at your disposal, especially in the areas where you are monitoring from and reporting to. The following are SAMPLES FROM OUR MEDIA CONTACT LIST OF 2003 AND NEED UPDATING AND NEED MODERN BLOGS & INTERNET MEDIA ADDED. They include:

1. Wire services resources.
2. International newspapers.
3. Regional newspapers.
4. Washington Post and Washington Times beat reporter example.
5. Quick reference regional media sources. A and B.

WIRE * TV * NEWSPAPERS * INTERNATIONAL & REGIONAL *

Contact for all regions (24 hours): NOTE OUTDATED LIST 2003

General International Wire Services

United Press International: focus@upi.com

Human Rights Internet: www.hri.ca/urgent/post.shtml
Associated Press:
- AP International Desk: 212-621-1663
- Press Release e-mail: pr@ap.org
- Headquarters: 212-621-1500
- Washington Number: 202-776-9410
  - Fax: 202-776-9570

Reuters: Please send press releases to:

- New York News Desk
  Tel: +1 646 223 6100
  E-mail: editor@reuters.com
- London News Desk
  E-mail: editor@reuters.com
- Singapore News Desk
  Fax: + 65 870 3820
  Tel: + 65 870 3814
  E-mail: singapore.newsroom@reuters.com
  Please note that we can only accept press releases in electronic format. Press releases are considered for news reports and not passed straight through in the manner of a press release distribution service.

INTERNATIONAL NEWSPAPERS *

Region: International
Country: General

NATO Communiqués, etc. www.nato.int

Amnesty International www.amnesty.org/news

International Herald Tribune
http://www.iht.com/IHT/TODAY/FPAGE

WWW Newslink
http://www.newslink.org/newslink/news.html

One World Daily News Service
http://www.oneworld.org/news.html

Reuters News Media
www.yahoo.com/headlines/current/news.html

Time On Line (not Time Magazine)
www.mandori.com/timeonline

Voice of America's News and English Broadcast Wire
www.voa.gov/11/newswire

US Information Agency: Current News
http://www.usia.gov/products/washfile

ClariNet News http://www.clarinet.com

Global Journalism Links www.uq.oz.au/jrn/world.html

Journalistic Resources Page www.algonet.se

News Index http://www.newindex.com

Newsboy www.newsboy.com

Around-the-World News from *Disciplining a Whole Nation*
www.tecc.co.uk/jesusa/dawnindx.html

Associated Press Newswire http://www.cns.cscns.com

News Link www.neslink.org

Newspapers around the world
www.freenet.mb.ca/community/media.newspapers

WWW Virtual Library www.cais.com/makulow/vlj/html

Global Student Newswire www.jou.ufl.edu/forums/gsn

Region International Organizations
(http://www.newspaperlinks.com)

UN News Centre www.un.org/News

NATO Communiqués, etc. www.nato.int

Human Rights Watch www.hrw.org

Human Rights Internet www.hri.ca

UNHCR www.unhcr.ch

UNHCHR
www.unhchr.ch/hurricane.nsf/NewsRoom?O
penFrameSet

Amnesty International
www.amnesty.org/news

International Newspapers

News Network Africa www.newindex.com

Amnesty International www.amnesty.org/news

SAMPLE: REGIONAL *
NEWSPAPERS *

Region: Americas
Country: United States

(http://www.newspaperlinks.com)

Newspaper - Home Page	City / Country
Boston Globe www.bostonglobe.com/globe/text/	Boston, MA
Chicago Sun-Times www.suntimes.com	Chicago, IL
Chicago Tribune www.chicagotribune.com	Chicago, IL

LA Times http://www.latimes.com	Los Angeles, CA
Christian Science Monitor http://www.csmonitor.com	
USA Today http://www.usatoday.com	
The Wall Street journal Money and Investing Update http://www.update.wsj.com	New York, NY
CNN World News http://www.cnn.com/world/index.html	
NPR News Programs http://www.npr.org	
The Financial Times http://www.ft.com	
ABCNEWS.com www.abcnews.com	
ABC Hourly News Update http://www.prognet.com/contentp/abc/html	
The American Reporter www.newshare.com/reporter/today.html	
New York Times www.nytimes.com	New York, NY
New York Daily News www.mostnewyork.com	New York, NY
New York Post www.nypostonline.com	New York, NY
San Francisco Bay Guardian www.sfbaygaurdian.com	San Francisco, CA

San Francisco Chronical www.sfgate.com — San Francisco, CA

San Francisco Examiner www.examiner.com — San Francisco, CA

Washington Times www.washtimes.com — Washington, D.C.

Washington Post www.washingtonpost.com — Washington, D.C.

(This omitted list is several pages).

SAMPLE: WASHINGTON POST * NEWS * STAFF * OUTDATED – 2003 LIST

Washington Post Key Staff

Beat		e-mail
	Karl Vick	karlvick@AfricaOnline.co.k
Africa, West	Doug Farah	farahd@compuserve.com
Central	Scott Wilson	wilsons@washpost.com
China	Philip P. Pan	panp@washpost.com
China	John Pomfret	jpomfret@compuserve.com
Diplomatic	Nora Boustany	boustanyn@washpost.com
Economics	Sebastian	mallabys@washpost.com

England	T.R. Reid	trreid@twp.com
Europe	Peter Finn	71032.1620@compuserve.c
Foreign	Robert	thomason@washpost.com
foreign	Michael Dobbs	dobbsm@washpost.com
Foreign	Phil Bennett	bennettp@washpost.com
Foreign	Steven Mufson	mufsons@washpost.com
Foreign	David Finkel	finkeld@washpost.com
Foreign,	Andy Mosher	moshera@washpost.com
Indonesia	Rajiv	rajiv@washpost.com
Mexico	Mary Jordan	maryjordan@compuserve.c
Mexico	Kevin Sullivan	kjsullivan@compuserve.co
Military	Vernon Loeb	loebv@washpost.com
Pentagon	Roberto Suro	pentagon@washpost.com
Russia	Peter Baker	bakerp@washpost.com
South	Anthony Faiola	104704.3367@compuserve.
UN	Colum Lynch	lynchc@washpost.com
White	Mike Allen	whitehouse@washpost.com

REACHING OUT TO EMBASSIES.

The same attention to detail should be used in your organization's outreach to foreign ministries or embassies. While it is an honor to speak to a country's Ambassador regarding your mission, it is more likely that your point of entry to the Embassies will be the first political officer, second political officer and that department. Embassies' chains of command are becoming more difficult to navigate because of security issues and firewalls of communication. One thing to keep in mind is that every nation has many Ambassadors and Embassy staffs throughout the world and also at the United Nations. So if your organization needs to navigate a particular nation's chain of command, if stonewalled, you can try the nation's embassy in other nations.

We found that the Scandinavian nations of Norway, Sweden and Denmark have the most pronounced commitment to human rights per capita in the world. Canada and the European Union nations and the E.U itself are also very committed to human rights. At times the United States shows a similar commitment as these nations. There are other natural constituencies that may care and be willing to be active on an issue for regional security reasons, religious and ethnic affiliations. Australia showed a distinct interest in the stability of Indonesia during the turmoil of the 1990s-2000s. Muslim nations were particularly interested in Gujarat and Chechnya where fellow Muslims were being massacred and Albania had a vested interest in the ethnic Albanians when they were in jeopardy in Kosovo in 1999.

There are also other types of Embassies such as NATO and regional organizations like OPEC, ECOWAS, and OAS that yield enormous influence and can also be sources of partnership and funding. By keeping many Embassies informed and impressed with the professionalism and credibility of your information, you are opening doors for allies and partnering advocates with more influence than your organization.

PRESS RELEASES, REPORTS, MICRO REPORTS, BRIEFS, STAFF PREP WORK.

As you are about to lobby Members of Congress, or UN officials or other influential people, you should have your press release and any other pertinent information in your folder. Releasing the information to the media and policymakers in a clear, concise statement accomplishes two things. It focuses your message and informs others, who you will not be personally meeting with, of the situation. A sample of what we included is below. The A, B, Cs of reporting are included in your press release - the who, what, where, when, how and, if possible, why? You should also include one or two sentences describing your organization. Focus on the evidence of the abuse you are reporting and most importantly your organization's specific call to action. If you don't know what the solution is – don't guess. But it is better to have a clear, solid course of action that will end the crisis. A vague notion that someone should do something about this will usually yield little results. But a call to specific policymakers, departments and nations to take specific courses of actions is a realistic starting point to initiate dialogues with the people you want to influence.

The CPG would often also include a one to three page brief with important information about the ground situation such as: history, perpetrators, victims, nature of the abuse, laws being broken and potential solutions. This would be either a Country Fact Sheet, a Micro Report or both. Samples of both are included below. Any policy maker can scan these documents in one to three minutes and have a decent understanding of the situation beyond the press release.

290

Full published reports were usually written in the days and weeks after the emergency unless the report was a warning of an impending danger likely to occur in the future abuse and in later reports recommended courses of action to policy makers and specific international laws which were being broken. In the nature of the abuse section, very clear cut date, location, number of victims and a brief narrative and the source were cited. Some of the CPG reports and templates can be found at https://richardobrien.info/cpg-country-reports .

Reports included: Aceh, Indonesia, Angola, Burma, Burundi, Chechnya, Colombia, Congo Democratic Republic, Ituri Province, Darfur, Sudan, Nuba, Sudan, Gujarat, India, Moluccas, Indonesia, Myanmar, Sulawesi, Indonesia, Uganda, and Zimbabwe.

SAMPLE PRESS RELEASES

Center for the Prevention of Genocide
an affiliate of Improve the World International
1925 N Lynn St., 12th Floor • Arlington, VA 22209
Phone: (703) 528-1002 • Fax: (703) 528-5776

Mission Statement

"To take practical measures to anticipate, prevent and report acts of genocide."

FOR IMMEDIATE RELEASE

Increase in Genocidal Conduct in Northeastern DRC

The CPG warns of the possibility of impending genocide in the Ituri Province of northeastern Democratic Republic of Congo as Hema and Lendu ethnic tensions, manifested in large massacres, escalate.

A large-scale massacre occurred on September 5, 2002, receiving attention briefly from Reuters. The massacre featured ethnic Lendu militias from the Ngiti tribe attacking missionary sites, systematically separating the ethnic Hema members from the others and massacring over 100 in the city of Nyankunde. This was predated by a Hema-led massacre which left approximately 110 Lendu dead near Bunia, also in the province of Ituri, on August 2, 2002. Hema men, women and children were dragged from their houses, and tortured in full public view. One hundred ten were hacked to death with machetes.

292

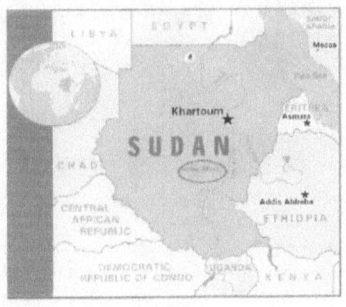

Nature of the Abuse:

A government sponsored campaign to bomb the relief deliveries into the Nuba area resulted in famine conditions. 85,000 Nuba were in jeopardy of starvation in the Summer and Fall of 2001.

Approximately 500 died despite the intervention of USAID and WFP and their ability to negotiate a window of opportunity to fly in emergency relief. If the present cease fire fails the same conditions will likely occur during the Summer and Fall of 2002.

The exterior is simple. A map, a two paragraph description summarizing the who, what, where, when and how of the human rights violations. The cover could serve as a cheat sheet for any policy maker for a sound bite for the news. The interior is very factual, dates, places, victims, perpetrators, key players, and possible solutions.

293

Hotspot Micro-Report

[William Lawson, 13 October 2003
Public Copy]

Center for the Prevention of Genocide
Lynn Street, 12th Floor

1925 N.
Arlington, VA 22209
703-528-1002

Zimbabwe

Summary/Danger

Reports of politically motivated state-organized violence marked the period before the March 2002 presidential elections. However, in the last 2 months, the government has made attempts to allay the worries of the international community by allowing NGOs to distribute aid and food based on their own qualifications, not requiring all aid to go through the central government. The situation, unfortunately, is still very grave with the World Food Program estimating that 5.5 million people need emergency food aid this year. In addition to the starving millions, the government has also moved towards suppressing the independent media on a much larger scale. On 12 September 2003, government soldiers took over the offices of the Daily News, the largest independent newspaper in Zimbabwe, and closed the paper indefinitely. While the reasons given for closing the paper are based on technicalities surrounding the newspaper's national registration, the parent company has challenged its closure in court with no positive results thus far. Finally, it looks as if the closure of the Daily News was just the first step in a renewed campaign against the independent media with several smaller independent newspapers now publicly expressing fears that they are next on the government's list. The situation merits continued attention as international access to independent information is severely restricted and man-induced famine is imminent.

Types of Abuse and Danger

- Man-exacerbated hunger gap (International Crisis Group)
- Torture (Physicians for Human Rights / Denmark)
- State-sponsored violence (IRIN News)
- Suppression of the independent media (Media Institute of South Africa)
- Expulsion of foreign journalists (BBC News)

Field Contacts / Verification

1. Independent Domestic Media
2. Embassies
3. International Human Rights NGOs
4. International Relief NGOs

International Contacts:

UN Office of the High Commissioner for Human Rights

UN Office for the Coordination of Humanitarian Affairs

UN Secretary-General's Office

US Contacts:

State Department

- State emergency task force
- Zimbabwe desk officer
Congress

White House

Foreign Ministries:

US embassy, British embassy, Swedish embassy, Danish embassy, Norwegian embassy, Canadian embassy, South African embassy.

Press:

Washington Post, Reuters, BBC, CNN, Mail & Guardian, SA, AP, UPI, Agence France Presse, Chicago Times, New York Times, Los Angeles Times.

NGOs/Other:

International Crisis Group

Int. Committee for the Red Cross

Amnesty International

Human Rights Watch

Physicians for Human Rights / Denmark

SAMPLE COUNTRY FACT SHEET
NORTH KOREA

Capital:

Pyongyang

Population:

22,466,481

Ethnicities:

Korean, few Chinese and Japanese

Religion:

Buddhism, Confucianism, Christianity

Danger/Nature of Abuse

> Torture
> Exacerbated Famine
> Cannibalism
> Killing of Babies
> Defection
> Public Executions

Monitoring Action

> Fall 2001: Center begins monitoring North Korea
> January 2002: Telephone interview with Dr. Norbert Vollersten, the author of "Inside North Korea"
> Spring 2002: Center publishes North Korean Country Report, "State-encouraged Starvation"
> August 2003: Email contact with the UNICEF in North Korea

Table of Contents

> Fact Sheet
> Micro Report
> Contact List for Verification and Dissemination
> Articles

SAMPLE OF BRIEF ON D.R. CONGO – ALL MILITIAS 2002. 2 OF 7 PAGES. 5 OMITTED.

Group	Leader(s)	Ethnicity/ nationality	Sponsoring State	Present in...	Notes:
APC: *(Armee du people congolais/armee populaire congolais)*					Armed wing of the RCD-K-ML led by Mbusa Nyamwisi.
FAC: *(Forces Armees Congolais)*	Joseph Kabila	Congolese National Army	Kinshasa Government	South & North Kivu and Maniema	
FIPI: *(Front pour l'Integration et la Pacification de l'Ituri)*	Chief Kawa Mandro Panga	Hema	Uganda	Ituri	Formed in 2003 and is composed of UPC members aligned to Uganda.

Group	Leader(s)	Ethnicity/ nationality	Sponsoring State	Present in...	Notes:
					Created (by Uganda) to undermine the UPC when the UPC was working with Rwanda.
Mai Mai	Operational Commander Lambert Konga Kanape (for Mai-Mai Maniema)	Traditional tribal warriors	Loosely allied to the Kinshasa government	Spread through out eastern Congo.	

PREP WORK SAMPLE:
SUMMARY NOTES AMONG STAFF

As your organization grows, so will your need for internal communications and collaboration among past, present and future staff and volunteers. Here are two real life examples of such communications about human rights networks on the ground which are essential to getting information about massacres confirmed and out.

Short summary of the massacres and the names of surrounding towns:

████████ is the Sudanese person who first came to us and is helping find third party sources. Call him, ████████ or the other Sudanese sources to clarify names of towns and their locations.

In the massacre in Darfur, we heard about from ████ and the one which we originally started investigating happened on the 28th, 29th of July, with more than 80 people killed, not many women. We have information about massacres in Adar, Abu Gidad, Gouz Naim, Krainga and Gondailat. Our Sudanese sources say that men are targeted and that is why they make the bigger part of the victims. Bigger cities in the areas are Miski, Kutum, 200 miles north-west from Al Fashir. Kutum is a town and the region where the villages are. Refer to them when you contact new sources that have not been contacted. Thus they will more easily identify the exact place you refer to.

The two days earlier massacre in Shoba (the one you can obtain information about from ████████), involves 51 killed, we have their names but no details. ████████████ from

███████████████ seems to know that it did happen. As her Sudanese sources say, the attack was conducted by Arab militias and government soldiers. The day before, attacks were conducted in other villages and that maybe a reason for women to have fled Shoba and an explanation for the majority of male victims. However, ██████████ does not have their own people on the ground. Other attacks have been made in Baghdai (land attack) and Kutum and Tina – bombing. All the information that comes to ██████████ and other international organizations at this point is international organizations is through Sudanese people. Relief Sudanese workers are under pressure not to share what they have seen. ██████████ told me one relief Sudanese worker was shot in Khartoum.

Most promising contacts concerning Darfur:

1. ██████████ from ████████████████ Sudan knows somebody from ████████ who was in Al Fashir. He could say only that government is arming militias but no specific incidents were given to mescal him to follow up on finding the contact of this woman he knows.
2. Call Spanish ██████████ (ask for ████████; he has not been contacted yet). They have the same number as the Sudanese ████████████████████. Ask for their office in Al Fashir. Now nobody is answering in the Khartoum office.
3. Follow up on ████████████████████. They will have an investigation group next month.
4. ██████████████ can be a good source.
5. Consult Rich on the massacre ██████████████ saw in the East Upper Nile in a place called Longa Chack. This is SPLM controlled area though and an oil region. According to him 59 people were killed, 3 boys were taken hostages and killed, 6 women and 7 girls were taken for forced labor. That was a land attack, Christians were supposedly

300

targeted (we need to get a proof from him why he thinks so). Most of his sources seemed to be Sudanese he interviewed right after the massacre. The Monitoring Team (CPMT, check the State Dept. web site for updates on their activities) has been there and blamed the SPLA for the massacre.
Other bigger cities in the area (helps when you contact people) – ██████, ██████.

6. Pressure ██████████. He should know more than he says although he is unwilling to talk but seems to be a good source.

7. ████████ (has been contacted) or ████ from ██ Air Services (not contacted on Darfur) can have more pilots' contact information.

8. Call ██████ to obtain the report they have on the Shoba massacre (which is in the same area where the one we were investigating) and to obtain the telephone numbers of international organizations on the ground.

PREP WORK SAMPLE: NOTES BETWEEN STAFF F'OR KEEPING ON-THE-GROUND-CONTACTS IN HOTSPOTS

We had high turnover between semesters as some students would leave and others would replace them. As a result, writing notes between 'generations' of staffs was common. Here's an example.

Uganda

* On the ground contacts were hard to find by emailing straight into the country. The people are very weary and most of the internet and email access is controlled by the government. What worked best was to find a person either here in the US or Europe, create a connection with that person, and ask them to pass the information along to their contacts in the country.

* You should email the contacts on the ground that I have made to make sure the CPG stays fresh in their minds, and they know who to contact in case of an emergency.

* The Uganda report, written by my predecessor was very complete. However, I felt as though it was lacking a complete historical analysis of the situation, as well as an in-depth research on what violations the government is committing. It is in these areas where I think further research is necessary.

Helpful websites:

http://irinnews.org/
http://news.bbc.co.uk/2/hi/africa/
http://allafrica.com/   www.afp.com
http://www.acholipeace.org/

Search mechanisms:

Lexis-Nexis

Local newspapers (often biased):

The Monitor http://www.monitor.co.ug/   New Vision http://www.newvision.co.ug/   Uganda Globe http://www.ugandaglobe.com/

Other sources (to make sure you keep updated with):

www.amnesty.org

www.hrw.org

www.state.gov/p/af

PART THREE: HOW-TO: ADVOCATE AFFECTIVELY.

There is a concept of 'seven degrees of separation,' that holds that any two people in the world are connected through seven people. The key is figuring out who those people are. In human rights it's simpler and action can probably be effected within five degrees of separation, within five contacts. When the massacre began in Sulawesi, Indonesia, I needed Congressman Ballinger or someone else who had President Bush's ear, call President Bush, convince him to call President Megawati of Indonesia and convince her to convince her nearest General to deploy his forces to intervene, that's four degrees of separation to a human rights intervention that could save lives. As best I can tell, that is what happened that stopped the Poso and Tentena massacres.

Let's say you have some potentially lifesaving, time-sensitive information. You need this one particular policy maker to listen and act because he or she is one of the few people on the planet in a position to save those lives. You need to convince that person in front of you to do the right thing. You are armed with the facts and something else they don't have, the knowledge that today they can do the thing they wanted to do when they were elected to Congress or joined the UN to do – to help. No matter how cynical or different politically the person is from your personal political views, you must treat them with respect to convey the urgency of the issue. This is no place or forum for your personal political views; stay focused on the mission at hand. This is a clear opportunity for that person to do something relatively simple to help save these lives and receive credit for it. It is truly a win-win for the policymaker sitting across from you – if you can impress them and break their indifference. Stay professional, but absolutely make sure to impart the urgency and importance of the role they are playing and be specific in your request for action. Be prepared to answer any and all questions that can come up, even the simple ones like 'how many people live there?' 'How many are people are in danger?' 'Who are the perpetrators?' 'What's their religion?' 'What's the US interest in this?' 'How does this affect the people of my district? 'If at all possible, ask the policy maker to place the phone call(s) necessary, in front of you. Have the numbers ready.

Read the short book by Milo Frank *How to get your Point Across in 30 Second or Less*. It taken an hour to read. Also very helpful for these situations is Mark McCormack's *What They Don't Teach You at Harvard Business School*. It will help you focus your message, listen aggressively, get what you want and leave when you have it.

I was once standing in front of a young man who was a top portfolio executive at a commercial real estate company. His folio included two buildings that were next to each other and slated to be demolished within two years. The 4000 square foot penthouse of the larger building was vacant and had been so for many years. I knew from the building maintenance staff who let me view the penthouse that there were roof leaks and issue with the gigantic Trane air conditioner that heated and cooled the space. I had a Trane repairman and a roofer give me estimates (the Trane was actually fine and just needed fluids). When I finally convinced the real estate executive to walk around with me, he was very hesitant to lease the space because of the 'issues.' When he finally agreed to the idea of my taking responsibility for any repairs to the space, it came to the money. We had practically none. I said:

"You know John, you're whole life you listen to your parents, go to school and go to church to learn the moral lessons of your life in the hope that when you are confronted with a decision that you can make that will save lives, that you make the right decision. After all that time, this, today, right now, is that occasion in your life." (By the way - less than 30 Seconds).

"What exactly are you asking me for?"

"Donate the space to our charity."

"I can't, I just can't, and I would lose my job."

At the end, he charged us $1 per square foot per month, which was by far the cheapest rent anyone paid on the Potomac River overlooking Georgetown. The space allowed us to expand our efforts, house donated computers in the basketball court and house three other charities. It was a lifesaver, figuratively and literally.

Advocacy can take many forms. You can personally advocate to a policymaker. You can advocate over the phone. You can send an email, or a letter, or a fax or all three with a press release with an encouragement to action like the example on the following page.

In the summer of 2003, the CPG began a report on the effects of the use of nuclear weapons on the populations of India and Pakistan in different scenarios of an exchange between the two. We had top experts led by a Congressman contribute to the report so it had credibility. We maneuvered to have the reports placed on the negotiation table of the first face-to-face negotiations between the two nations since they almost went to war in 2002. Attached to the report was a letter encouraging both sides to consider the perilous danger that the situation presented because there was: no military protocol, no hotline and no confidence building measures between the two regarding nuclear dangers This was more dangerous than almost any time during the Cold War between the US and the USSR who had all of these safeguards in place to protect against accidental nuclear war and unbridled escalation. While they did not agree on anything substantive during this first meeting, they did agree on the agenda for the *next* meeting. The second meeting would focus on increasing cooperation in military protocol, hotline communication capability and confidence building measures between the two regarding nuclear dangers.

Having a credible report in the right hands at the right moment is also an effective way to advocate without being in the room.

PART FOUR: EARLY WARNING SYSTEM&METHODOLOGY.

FIRST GENERATION 2000 – 2002.

There were three generations of early warning systems at the CPG: 2000-2002, 2002-2003 and 2003-2004. The first from 2000 – early 2002 was essentially a sign which told staff how to respond if a massacre occurred and a chart hung in the main office to track ongoing massive human rights violations around the world. It was crude and rudimentary but, nonetheless, effective for both unfolding emergencies and sorting through a world of human rights violations for the most heinous ones. The first sign for the Emergency Crisis Procedure are on the following pages. The original sign read 'In Case of genocide – Break Glass,' from which this book is named. Years ago many fire alarms in buildings would have a glass partition to prevent false alarms and read: 'In Case of Fire, Break Glass.' Same idea.

STEPS FOR COMBATTING UNFOLDING GENOCIDE

I. CONFIRM IT

  1. Attempt to confirm the massive human rights abuse with ground asset.
  2. Attempt to confirm via embassies, NGOs and on-site corporate assets.
  3. Attempt to confirm via media and wire service sources in the area.

II. USE SATELLITE IMAGING FOR CONFIRMATION

  1. Obtain coordinates of massive abuse by on ground asset.
  2. Give coordinates for human rights violation to Stephanie Provost to contract out to commercial satellite company.
  3. Analyze images in-house.
  4. Confirm analysis with outside imaging expert(s).

III. CONTACT ALL MEDIA FOR IMAGE PUBLICATION

  1. Give image to several national and international media outlets.
  2. Follow-up with availability to media.

IV. PRESENT IMAGES TO UN SECURITY COUNCIL

  1. Determine best conduit to UN Security Council (member state, NGO, Multilateral) and prepare it for UN presentation.
  2. Present UN Security Council with evidence of Genocide.

V. DISPLAY BLACK FLAG OF GENOCIDE OUTSIDE OFFICE

2002 Emergency Steps:

1. **Contact Board and Staff**
   A. **Contact Rich**
   B. **Contact Board Members**
   C. **Contact Early Warning Supervisor**
   D. **Contact Regional Staff**
2. **Confirm It**
   A. **Check Online Sources**
      i. **Wire Services**
      ii. **News Sources**
      iii. **Regional News Sources**
   B. **Confirm with Neutral Third Party Observers**
      i. **UN-Based Groups**
      ii. **US Contacts**
      iii. **Other Governments**
      iv. **Relief/Human Rights Organizations**
      v. **Indigenous Neutral Sources**
      vi. **Journalists in the Field**
3. **Release It**
   A. **Note: How to Write A Press Release**
   B. **Contact Media in Each Venue/Time Zone**
4. **Contact Key Agencies/Policymakers**
   A. **US Government, UN, etc.**
   B. **Regional Offices**
5. **Follow-Up**
   A. **UN, etc.**
   B. **Embassies**
   C. **Other**

SECOND GENERATION METHODOLOGY 2002 – 2003.

The second generation of early warning system and emergency crisis response was used from 2002 – 2003. It was formalized into a manual with more standardized procedures to target responses and capture valuable 'process' information so to improve the methodology over time. This version, written in 2002, is identifiable by the long rectangular boxes with headings to the right of each sub-heading. Like this one

This manual is divided into five sections: administration, criteria and standards, country reports, quarterly journal, emergency crisis procedure and the appendices with charts and samples. It is a more fully developed system encompassing everything from on-the-ground contacts, lobbying and report writing to standard office procedures. It was our first standardized methodology.

The next several pages are direct copies of the CPG Methodology from 2002 – 2003, and then the most advanced methodology was developed by our fourth year just as we ran out of money to stay open.

The EWS Mission 2002 – 2003

The EW department monitors international hotspots for indicators of genocide and develops resources – people and organizations – that can report and/or confirm massive human rights violations. It is the responsibility of the EW department to facilitate acquired evidence to the appropriate governmental, international, and national non-governmental organizations, as well as to the media. It is essential that the EW department maintain a neutral, non-political, and non-religious approach. Please keep this in mind when researching international news sources.

The following manual is intended to guide you through the methods and procedures of the Early Warning Department. Please use it as your reference guide.

Good Luck this semester!

EWS – Table of Contents…Everything you ever wanted to know about the Early Warning Department

2nd Generation Phone Etiquette

1. Please keep in mind that each time you answer the telephone you are representing this   organization, our mission, and our ideals.
2. Approach each call with professionalism and politeness.
3.   Basic script for answering CPG phone calls:

> "CPG. This is _____. How may I help you?" "Hi, is Rich there?"
> "May I ask who is calling?" (ALWAYS ASK WHO IS CALLING!!)
> "This is Mr. Z."
> "Hold on one second please."
> TELL RICH WHO IS CALLING….PLEASE DO NOT YELL IT DOWN THE HALLWAY!!!
>
> If Rich is unavailable. "I'm sorry, Mr. O'Brien is in a meeting right now. Could I please take a message?" "Please let him know that Mr. Z called from XX organization. He has my number."   "Why don't you give me your number, just in case? I will have him call you back as soon as possible.   Thank you."(ALWAYS GET A NAME AND NUMBER. IF YOU ARE UNSURE OF THE NAME, PLEASE ASK THE CALLER TO SPELL IT FOR YOU).

THE CPG CRITERIA FOR GENOCIDE

The CPG adheres to a strict definition of genocide. This definition is based solely on articles (A) and (C) of the UN Convention on Genocide. This was done to differentiate between loss of life due to a military conflict which was incidental to the conflict and not intentional, as well as differentiating between the less violent types of genocide which include language, culture and displacement.

FIRST STANDARD – DOES IT MEET THE UN DEFINITION?

The Center recognizes a restricted version 1948 UN Convention on Genocide definition of genocide: any of the noted acts with the intent to destroy, in whole or in part, a national, ethnic, racial or religious group. These standards represent articles A and C of the Convention.

SECOND STANDARD – IS IT HABITUAL?

The Center must find the occurrence of massacre of an unarmed civilian group to have occurred several times to confirm a pattern of activity.

THIRD STANDARD – IS IT INTENTIONAL?

The Center distinguishes between massive human rights violations that have an aspect of manslaughter (unintentional) versus murder (intentional). Corroborating evidence of premeditation need not be provided. De facto intention can be assigned to the perpetrators by ongoing criminal negligence.

FOURTH STANDARD – IS IT PRIMARY CHARACTERISTICS OF THE ABUSE?

No magic number exists that makes the killing of people genocide. When there are several repeated human rights violations, killing of an UN-recognized group becomes the primary nature or characteristic above all other abuse, then this final genocide standard has been met.

CPG PRECURSORS TO GENOCIDE

THE GENOCIDE PREVENTION OFFICE
HUMAN RIGHTS VIOLATION PRECURSORS TO GENOCIDE

Civil Rights Violations — Physical/Destructive Actions or Precursors of Genocide

INSTRUCTIONS FOR THE HUMAN RIGHTS VIOLATIONS CHART & WEBPAGE.

Please refer to the Appendix for the starting points for how to update the online human rights violations chart. The authors of this manual did not feel comfortable writing updated instructions since they never saw this online chart. However, these are important guidelines for the future of the website.

Good luck. ☺

How to use this chart:

This chart is a convenient way to monitor human rights violations – possible warning signs of future genocide. The chart is easy to use. On the right side, running from top to bottom, is a list of countries. These are states with human rights abuse on their records. They are organized alphabetically. A fire icon next to one of these states indicates the danger is happening now. You may click on the country names for a brief report on the problems within these states.

The chart's upper row, running across, is a list of various human rights abuses. The further to the right you look, the more extreme the abuse. The red cells indicate a precursor of genocide. Each of these abuses may be clicked on for a brief definition of the abuse.

The rows and columns intersect in the middle part of the chart. You will find that certain points are marked with an "X" An X signifies a violation of rights. Go directly up from the X to see which violation has been committed and to the extreme left of the X to see where this violation has been committed.

Conveniently, you may click on the Xs to view articles from unbiased sources giving proof of that particular human rights violation.

Weekly Genocide Chart Update Format

1. Highlight the current events (shortly, precisely, and neutrally). This should be done in one sentence.

   E.g., Ethnic cleansing of oil concession areas continues in the South of Sudan.

2. Summary (historical inquiry) of the present situation (2 sentences). *E.g., The 17 years civil war has produced nearly two million causalities and largely pits the militarized Islamic North against the poorly armed Christian and animist of the South. The Northern forces are pushing the Nuer and Nuba from their South Central lands to gain access to the untapped oil fields there.*

3. List the indicators or precursors to genocide and human rights violations occurring in the area.

   E.g., Indicators of genocide present include massacring unarmed populations as the primary characteristic of the abuse, habitual and intentional targeting of the Nuer, Nuba, and Dinka ethnicities. Precursors of genocide include frequent one-sided casualties, frequent physician brutality, ethnic cleansing, and restricted transportation.

4. List informational sources used in report.

E.g., This brief was compiled from BBC, IRIN, UN press and first-hand accounts.

COUNTRY REPORTS

The mission of the CPG features myriad projects designed to raise awareness of modern genocide. These include a lecture series, a television show, a journal, and country reports. Often, country reports are at the heart of any EWS intern's experience.

Included are the formats for preliminary reports and country reports. However, although the Center attempts to standardize its documents as much as possible, different reports have done things to different degrees, whether it is in the length, the format of explaining the nature of abuses, and in the application of international law other than the Genocide Convention. We recommend that you look over a few reports to get a feel for what exactly is necessary in yours.

PHASE I

Research and Contact.

The first days on staff, you will read the prior reports and folio information on your assigned country/countries. You will be quizzed on the key players, events, locations when you are ready. You will then reach out to neutral third parties on the ground in the hot spots you are monitoring to introduce yourself and make sure the line of communication is open and they know what to do to get you real time

317

information if trouble begins. **You will also reach out to your key policymakers and reporters who cover this area and introduce yourself to them and reaffirm your and their expectations if an emergency unfolds. Your country hot spot folder will have your lists of these contacts. Below is an example of a script you can use when reaching out to these contacts.**

Making Contacts

Example Cold-Call Script

Contact: "Hello?"

CPG: "Hi, my name is ___ with the Center for the Prevention of Genocide. Mr. X gave me your name and number as a possible reference. We recently received some information regarding possible genocidal incidents in Southern Sudan and because Mr. X told us that you were just in that region I was wondering if you would be willing to answer some question."

Contact: "Sure, I'd be happy to help, but tell me who you are with again?"

CPG: "The Center for the Prevention of Genocide. We are a non-profit, non-political, non-governmental organization that monitors hot spots, gathers evidence, and facilitates the information to the UN Security Council, the EU, and the media. We rely heavily upon the information from contacts who have been on the ground and are familiar with the area. That is why we wanted to contact you."

Contact: "Oh, I see."

CPG: "What areas were you in while in Southern Sudan?"

Contact: "Well, I was in Tanj for a month with the WFP and in the Nuba Mountains for about six weeks."

CPG: "Those are two areas on which we are keeping a close eye. Did you see any types of human rights violations or destruction from military forces?"

** Continue to extract precise information from the contact **

Contact: Yes, I was in there with John Doe. He's with Reuters, but I think he's back in the US now."

CPG: "DO you think he would mind if we contacted him?"

Contact: "No, I don't think he would mind. Let me email him and give him a heads-up about what you are calling about, but I'm sure he'd be happy to talk with you."

CPG: "Wonderful. Do you have John's contact information?"

Contact: "Sure, it's . .blah blah blah."

CPG: "Thank you so much for that information. It's extremely useful. DO you mind if I contacted you again should we come up with any more question?"

Contact: "Not at all. Let me know if I can be of any more assistance."

CPG: "Sure. Let me give you my contact information if you think of anything else. The number is 703-528-1002 and you can email me at info@improvetheworld.org. Again, my name is ___. If I'm not in you can talk to Richard O'Brien, our Director."

Reminder: By signing the non-disclosure form, you are not permitted to keep, tell, or discuss the contacts' information or whereabouts. This is extremely important because people could be in danger if their contact information is disclosed to the wrong people.

PHASE II PRELIMINARY REPORT

ELEMENTS OF A PRELIMINARY REPORT:

- 2-3 Pages
- Include title page and synopsis
- Brief history (past 5-10 years)
- Identify Key Players
- Identify Nature of the Abuse
- Identify if this is genocide (Why/Why not?Who's definition of genocide?)
- Does the situation warrant a full report/analysis?

Preliminary Reports – suggested format

    I.   **Introduction**

        This should be a short introduction to the general conflict. Your purpose in the report is not to analyze the conflict in detail so keep it short. Just put in the important information that will show how the conflict came about and who is involved. Keep this section limited to at most one page.

    II.   **Information on the Parties Involved**

This section should be divided into two, one in which you introduce the background of the groups involved and another citing the current goals of these groups. Focus on the groups at which you are pointing the finger for possible genocidal activities. Include groups and organizations that collaborate on such efforts. Since many of these conflicts have been around for a long time, the goals of these groups may and usually have changed since their initial formation. You should detail these changes especially with regards to current activities and reasons for the change in goals.

III. **Nature of the Violence**

This is the biggest section of the report. Your argument involves the nature of the human rights abuses, violence, and killings, so this analysis should be very thorough. Be sure to cite as many specific examples of incidents that are genocidal in nature. These should be in as much detail as you have available. This includes how many people were killed, how they were killed, who was targeted, why they were targeted, etc.

IV. **Is this Genocide?**

This is where you get into the "nitty-gritty" about whether or not what is currently going on could be considered genocide. Take the four standards of genocide that this organization uses and compare the abuses to these four standards. Be very specific on why or why not the violence fits each of these standards.

V. **Complicating Factors**

This section is your chance to express your concern about how you expect people in the international community to react to the situation on which you are reporting. Whether it is genocide or just human rights violations, you should include the complicating factors in getting involved in this country/situation. Examples are things like a *time factor*. Some of these conflicts have been going on for decades, whereas others have just really started to escalate. Outside countries and organizations are usually less likely to get involved when the violence has been going on forever. Another example is any complications with *resources* such as drugs in Colombia, oil in Sudan, and diamonds in Sierra Leone. Other possible resources that are fought over include land and water. If these resources play a part in the conflict, this is where you need to mention it. Other complicating factors are *aid programs* from other countries that are already in place.

VI.   **Conclusion**
This somewhat speaks for itself. But this is also a chance to suggest possible action that this organization can/should do regarding the situation. This does not necessarily have to include a public declaration of genocide, but could also include the possibility of helping in some other way to alleviate or reduce the killings that are going on. For the purposes of this report, these suggestions should just be a brief overview of further action. If the situation warrants action, a separate report should address those specific possibilities for involvement.

NOTE: The CPG Country Reports ultimately included these five sections: History, key players (perpetrators and victims), nature of the abuse, genocide or other legal determination, potential strategies for resolution.

- o **For an example of a preliminary report, please refer to the Appendix for the Kurdistan report (Spring 2002)**

Phase III FULL COUNTRY REPORT

Country reports follow the same guidelines as the preliminary reports but include more details and more in-depth research. Please refer to the Appendix for the North Korea and Sulawesi report.

BASIC ELEMENTS OF THE FULL COUNTRY REPORT

I.   Table of Contents (please refer to Appendix for style formats)

II.   Introduction
- including history of conflict, and often the present situation

III.   Present Situation & Key Players
- For example:
  - o government
  - o Rebel groups
  - o Relief organizations
  - o Civilian victims
  - o Rumors of crimes, if relevant and substantial

IV.   What is the nature of the abuse?

- Overview of the violence…can be outlined under broad descriptions of abuse, "**Food Aid and Food Diversion**" (see Appendix for North Korea report), or specific incidents.
- Example:

> **Date:** October 1, 2001
>
> **Place:** Tomata, Sulawesi
>
> **Victims:** Three Christians
>
> A large number of buildings were burned in the central Sulawesi town of Tomata, following attack by Jihad troops. Among the destroyed buildings were a church, a school and teachers' quarters, as well as over 60 homes, among them the house of the preacher at the church. Three people were killed (ICC).

V. Application of Genocide
- Does the conflict meet the refined UN definition (articles (a) and (c))?
- Is it habitual?
- Is it intentional?
- Is killing the primary characteristic of the abuse?

VI. Legal Section – provide an overview of any other international laws being broken in the conflict

VII. Conclusion

VIII. Appendix (optional)…for example, eyewitness accounts

EARLY WARNING CRISIS PROCEDURES

Imagine that you are staying late at the CPG, working on a term paper and monitoring the news in case of emergency. You get an email saying that there has been a massacre in Sulawesi. What do you do? What..do..you…do?

The right answer is that there is a procedure in place for such emergencies. In the Sulawesi example, there was a late night scramble to try and get the word out about the massacre and prevent further death. Luckily, President Megawati of Indonesia actually bowed to international pressure. From now on, though, we won't be flying by the seat of our pants.

The Early Warning Crisis Procedures manual was intended to be an idiot-proof step-by-step guide on what to do in case of a humanitarian emergency. The first main step is to notify Richard O'Brien and the board members of the situation. As you are trying to get a hold of them, however, it is necessary to begin confirming the facts and then getting the word out to key policymakers. Therefore, in addition to calling the board, you should also call your department head and any fellow intern working on the relevant region of the world to help you out, even if from home.

Here are the basic steps:

1. **Contact Board and Staff**
   D. Contact Rich
   E. Contact Board Members
   F. Contact Early Warning Supervisor
   G. Contact Regional Staff
1. **Confirm It**
   a. Check Online Sources
      i. Wire Services

        ii. News Sources

        iii. Regional News Sources

    b. Confirm with Neutral Third Party Observers

        i. UN-Based Groups

        ii. US Contacts

        iii. Other Governments

        iv. Relief/Human Rights Organizations

        v. Indigenous Neutral Sources

        vi. Journalists in the Field

2. **Release It**

    a. Note: How to Write A Press Release

    b. Contact Media in Each Venue/Time Zone

3. **Contact Key Agencies/Policymakers**

    a. US Government, UN, etc.

    b. Regional Offices

4. **Follow-Up**

    a. UN, etc.

    b. Embassies

    c. Other

The Crisis Procedures manual should be located along with the other ITWI binders in the front PR office. There should be one intern working heavily on this project. The skeleton of the binder is done, but there are things that need to be completed and updated.

Step ONE:

First, the board of directors list needs to be prettified ☺ so does the actual index tabs of the binder itself – I like the Avery 8-tab clear index tabs, but I ran out so I had to improvise. Please make it look better.

Second, the entire list of executive staff and interns to be contacted needs to be changed as of course we have complete turnover this semester.

Step TWO:

This part actually is pretty well done, but of course it needs to be constantly revised and updated.

STEP THREE:

This part is partially done. It needs to be constantly updated, and also, regions such as South Asia are completely blank.

STEPS FOUR AND FIVE:

This is your main job. It is necessary to find key policymakers to contact both in the first night and in the following days. Here are some guidelines.

Night ONE: contact the **Emergency Task Force** for both the **State Department** and the **Congress**.

For the rest, you will have to decide what is night ONE and what can be done in the following days. Here are places to look.

    A. Stateside:
1. Emergency task force
2. Secretary of State's office (this has been begun)
3. Appropriate Assistant Secretary of State
4. Deputy Assistant Secretary of State
5. Ambassador at large for War Crimes

6. other ambassadors at large NOT connected to countries (ex: UN)
7. Key policymakers for each region
8. American ambassador on the ground. Ambassadors of other governments here with strategic interests there.

B. USAID (Natsio's office), etc.
C. Congress
   1. Emergency task force
   2. Caucus on Human Rights – Senate and HoR
   3. IR committee
   4. Friends of HR violation monitors caucus (defunct at the moment) – ex: Bob Zachritz
   5. Lead Staffers who can disseminate info

D. UN
1. Find our "dream budget" – that lists key players
2. also look in PR binder for contacts
3. Secretary's office
4. OCHA
5. UNHCHR – Mary Robinson's office
6. Dr. Clark – Early Warning System
7. WFP
8. UNHCR

E. Other Human Rights and Relief Organizations
   1. Save the Children
   2. Feed the Children
   3. Oxfam
   4. Human Rights Watch
   5. Amnesty International

6. Genocide Watch
7. Medecins Sans Frontieres
8. etc, etc.

Good luck! The electronic version of the manual, that needs to be updated and reconciled, is in three places: 1. The disk in the binder 2. A backup disk entitled Early Warning System 3. In the backup computer under ITWI backup files, Early Warning, Early Warning System.

SUPPORT MATERIALS TO 2002 – 2003 MANUAL: THREE DAY PLAN

First night

1. The first, and most important thing, is to verify. Use the sources listed in the Regional Neutral Sources section. Try to choose neutral sources who are not related to the original source (i.e. don't accept reports from two members of the same organization. Try sources on our indigenous list or, worse comes to worse, UN offices. UNHCR has many people at in the field at any given moment in lots of our Hot Spot countries).
NOTE: When you are making these calls it is important to remember that these might be contacts which either haven't been contacted in over a year or were never contacted by us (especially in the case of Embassy staff) but merely were put on a list. Identify yourself as a part of CPG and attempt to give a VERY

brief synopsis of the situation, but with the pertinent location information and the groups affected.

Example Conversation:

Contact: Yes?

CPG: Hello, my name is Bob Smith. I'm with the Center for the Prevention of Genocide in Washington, DC. We have received a report from a USAID worker of widespread targeting of Muslim villagers in the districts of Chandinagar and the Northeast suburbs of Ahmnabad. Wire reports haven't picked up the story yet, I was hoping you could provide confirmation on this fact.

DO NOT release the contact's information to your neutral source. If in doubt DON'T say anything, it is often dangerous. Instead use general terms like "an AID worker" or "a stringer."

If you are put off be sure to leave your contact info in case they do come up with something.

If they give you info try to be as precise as possible, you want village names, means, background stuff (like a sudden increase in hate speeches etc.). Anything that will look official when Rich has to go talk to Congress folk the next day.

Also, ask if they know of anyone else in the area that may have relevant information and obtain their contact info.

2. Assuming confirmation, you need to do a press release. There is a template included in the guide, make sure to follow the formatting guidelines.

To distribute the press release go in this order: 1. Wire services (all numbers listed)

2. Big Three: Washington Post, NY Times and LA Times

3. Regional sources: there should be at least one newspaper for each region, try to fax or e-mail the release

3. Government officials need to be alerted. If you haven't spoken to the US Embassy in the country, do so now, giving them a detailed report. Contact the closest UNHCR and UNHCHR office. Follow the guide, e-mailing, calling or faxing everyone listed on the crisis sheet. MAKE SURE to get in touch with the desk officer at the State Department.

Second Day

1. A fact sheet with more info than the press release needs to be prepared with talking points for Rich and whoever else will be talking to officials. People should be calling and e-mailing heavily now to try and pinpoint the information.

2. Contact broadcast media in the region to establish if there is any footage (video OR audio) of the incident in question. If so, arrange for a courier and offer footage to Western media outlets.

3. Follow up with major media to establish who will be running the story. Offer to help them with contacting

sources, etc. If they *aren't* running the story be sure to find out why. (No access, no one on the ground, not "gripping" enough?)

Record these reasons for future reference and don't be shy about countering if the reason seems superficial.

First, Second and Third Day

1. Target specific policymakers who are in positions to resolve or influence the situation and make appointments, in phone or in person, to discuss specific course of action recommended to resolve the crisis.
2. Prepare presentations complete with notecards and practice with a colleague your presentation, your recommendations and fielding questions on the crisis.

SUMMARY OF STAFF NOTES ON DARFUR MASSACRE – EWS COMMUNICATION

Short summary of the massacres and the names of surrounding towns:

███████████ is the Sudanese person who first came to us and is helping find third party sources. Call him, ████████ or the other Sudanese sources to clarify names of towns and their locations.

In the massacre in Darfur, we heard about from ████ and the one which we originally started investigating happened on the 28th, 29th of July, with more than 80 people killed, not many women. We have information about massacres in Adar, Abu

Gidad, Gouz Naim, Krainga and Gondailat. Our Sudanese sources say that men are targeted and that is why they make the bigger part of the victims. Bigger cities in the areas are Miski, Kutum, 200 miles north-west from Al Fashir. Kutum is a town and the region where the villages are. Refer to them when you contact new sources that have not been contacted. Thus they will more easily identify the exact place you refer to.

The two days earlier massacre in Shoba (the one you can obtain information about from ████████), involves 51 killed, we have their names but no details ██████████████ from ████████████████ seems to know that it did happen. As her Sudanese sources say, the attack was conducted by Arab militias and government soldiers. The day before, attacks were conducted in other villages and that maybe a reason for women to have fled Shoba and an explanation for the majority of male victims. However ███████████ does not have their own people on the ground. Other attacks have been made in Baghdai (land attack) and Kutum and Tina – bombing. All the information that comes to ████████ and other international organizations at this point is international organizations is through Sudanese people. Relief Sudanese workers are under pressure not to share what they have seen. ████████ told me one relief Sudanese worker was shot in Khartoum.

Most promising contacts concerning Darfur:

6. ████████ from ██████████████████ knows somebody from ██████ who was in Al Fashir. He could say only that government is arming militias but no specific incidents were given to mescal him to follow up on finding the contact of this woman he knows.

7. Call Spanish ▮▮▮▮▮ (ask for ▮▮▮▮▮; he has not been contacted yet). They have the same number as the Sudanese Red Crescent in Khartoum. Ask for their office in Al Fashir. Now nobody is answering in the Khartoum office.
8. Follow up ▮▮▮▮▮▮▮▮▮▮▮. They will have an investigation group next month.
9. The Irish Goal can be a good source.
10. Consult Rich on the massacre ▮▮▮▮▮▮▮ saw in the East Upper Nile in a place called Longa Chack. This is SPLM controlled area though and an oil region. According to him 59 people were killed, 3 boys were taken hostages and killed, 6 women and 7 girls were taken for forced labor. That was a land attack, Christians were supposedly targeted (we need to get a proof from him why he thinks so). Most of his sources seemed to be Sudanese he interviewed right after the massacre. The Monitoring Team (CPMT, check the State Dept. web site for updates on their activities) has been there and blamed the SPLA for the massacre.
    Other bigger cities in the area (helps when you contact people) ▮▮▮▮▮, ▮▮▮▮▮.

6. Pressure ▮▮▮▮▮▮. He should know more than he says although he is unwilling to talk but seems to be a good source.

7. ▮▮▮▮▮ (has been contacted) or ▮▮▮ from ▮▮ Air Services (not contacted on Darfur) can have more pilots' contact information.

8. Call ▮▮▮▮▮ to obtain the report they have on the Shoba massacre (which is in the same area where the one we were investigating) and to obtain the telephone numbers of international organizations on the ground.

A list of the Darfur sources follows on the next page.

What to say on the phone making first contact:

We are a human rights .... We received reports from Sudanese about massacres in Darfur (Adar, Abu Gidad, Gouz Naim, Krainga,Gondailat), Kutum and Shoba. We want to take further steps to make the information public and influence policy makers to take action but we need to have a confirmation from a non-Sudanese source or a Sudanese worker for international organizations, willing to talk to us. He/She can be from an organization or on a private visit and maybe happened to see massacres or a strong enough evidence of their occurrence. Could you help us find such a source to prevent further killings?

CRISIS WARNING DOCUMENTATION: AFTER THE FACT

CRISIS WARNING DOCUMENTATION

Date: August 9th, 2002

Place: ***Bunia, Ituri Province, The Democratic Republic of Congo***

Crisis Issue: Massacre of non-Hema civilians by the Hema militia, aided by the Ugandan army, in the city of Bunia. As of August 5, 2002, Hema group backed by Ugandan army kidnapped and executed civilians in Ndoromo military camp, Bunia. They threatened to kill more people (those who are not originally from Ituri).

Crisis Brief Description: On August 8th, 2002, at about 1:00p.m. Interns Corynne Harvey and Mayuko Shimakage received e-mail regarding the city of Bunia, in the Northeastern Ituri district of the DRC. The e-mail claimed that the Ugandan Army was aiding a militia composed of the Hema ethnic group in surrounding non-Hema neighborhoods to rape and kill the inhabitants. After receiving confirmation from the Associated Press and the BBC wire reports, the Center for the Prevention of Genocide contacted the embassies of Uganda and The DRC, along with OCHA and UNHCHR. A press release and copy of the original e-mail was e-mailed or faxed to media outlets and those we had spoken to in the UN and foreign governments. According to Suliman Baldo with Human Rights Watch, pressure was brought to bear on the UN by media outlets to go in and, as per the mandate of the peacekeeping force in the region, protect the civilian population. There is a difficulty in tracing the paper trail to determine how extensive CPG's influence was in this outcome.

Center's Action:

10:30 am: Receive e-mail in French from ████████████████, member of ████████, an ███████████████████████████ in east DRC. The e-mail is composed of three reports from local sources in Bunia, which describes killing of civilians and surrounding of the city of Bunia by Hema militia groups and the Ugandan army.

11:00 am: The e-mail is sent to ███████████████, a French speaker, to translate the text while John Kruger and Roy Harrison do a rough translation.

11:00 am: An intelligence source was contacted by Corynne to confirm the information. They had not received any word on the situation. Corynne forwarded them the e-mail from ████████ ██████.

Extensive search conducted online to find confirmation of e-mail. ████████████, head of DRC research for Human Rights Watch, and ████████████, epidemiologist and DRC researcher with International Rescue Committee are contacted. A message is left for ████████. A desk worker at IRC says

338

they've been hearing the same information.

1:34 PM: MISNA issues a report bylined in Bunia which claims at least 37 dead and many more injured. Also confirms the complicity of the Ugandan army in the act.

1:36 PM: AP issues a report bylined from Kigali; which claims at least 48 people, mostly civilians, have been killdeer in Bunia in the fighting. This report also highlights the close ties between the Hema and the Ugandans.

1:40 PM: Corynne informs Rich that the situation required attention. EWS heads, PR head and the Great Lakes researchers meet to discuss options. It is decided to issue a press release and to call up key policy makers (non-Congressional, Congress is out of session) to promote a public statement on the situations.

1:46 PM: BBC issues a report confirming the fighting including information included in the regular e-mail.

2:00 PM: Intelligence source calls back to confirm much of the information in the e-mail.

2:15 PM: Talking points on the conflict are prepared for Rich, along with a quick, two sentence synopsis of the situation.

3:00: PM: Two groups are formed. John, Roy and Anam work in the conference rooms to get a rough draft of the press release. Rich begins to call UN and government officials. Corynne assists in the release writing and stays near Rich in case he needs information.

List of those called by Rich:

1. E. Bwomono Olobo, officer, the Ugandan Embassy. Mr. Olobo was contacted to inform the Ugandan government that our organization would be releasing negative info to the

government and to give them an opportunity to respond to the accusations.

2. Mr. Mokende, Charge D'Affaires, the DRC Embassy. Mr. Mokende was contacted to establish whether the DRC government was aware of the situation in the east. Mr. Mokende was not, and so all pertinent information was faxed to his office.

3. Kathy (?), at the State Department Emergency Task Force, is contacted. Kathy was not aware of the situation and took down all relevant background information.

4. Karen (?), OCHA. The Africa desk at OCHA was contacted to ensure they were aware of the situation. There were not, so all pertinent information was faxed to their office. Yvonne Rademacher, UNHCHR. UNHCHR was contacted to ensure they were aware of the

situation. All pertinent information was faxed to their office.

4:45 PM: The press release was approved by Rich and transferred on to company letterhead. Copies were e-mailed or faxed to all major media outlets and to the officials whom we had communicated with.

6:00 PM: A call is received from the office of UN Special Rapporteur, Bacre N'Diaye to please forward all information so that he could investigate the matter further.

Outcome: Pressure was placed on the UN by internal sources and the media to send in MONUC forces. MONUC did enter the region and, except for the most severely affected areas, there is calm in the city now. Uganda has been diplomatically pressured to remove their troops and to ensure that they do not favor the Hema over other groups.

Mistakes/Problems: No effort made to contact the authors of the AP, MISNA, or BBC reports nor to contact the US embassies in Kigali, Kampala or Kinshasa.

SAMPLE OF A SMALLER EMERGENCY CRISIS PROCEDURE RESPONSE.

Chechen Refugee Crisis

Contact: Deborah Parkinson, Roy Harrison

3 December 2002 – Wednesday

The *New York Times* runs a story claiming that Russian officials had begun the process of repatriating Chechen refugees in the adjacent Russian Republic of Ingushetia.

Deborah Parkinson receives information from *Prague Watchdog*, a human rights organization that monitors Chechnya, concerning the exact methods used by Russian officials in returning the refugees to Chechnya. (See attached press release). This information had not yet been published or broadcast by the major media.

Richard O'Brien and Deborah Parkinson call Roy Harrison and request a general course of action. In his response Roy states that because the UN and NGOs are all familiar with the present situation, the best plan would be a media blitz in an attempt to heighten common awareness of the movements. Specifically, it is suggested that a letter to the editor be written and submitted to the *Times*.

Richard O'Brien wants a focused response directed toward embassies of Muslim countries, including Saudi Arabia and Turkey.

4 December 2002 – Thursday

8:00am-9:30am – Deborah Parkinson and Roy Harrison create draft press release and letter to the editor.

11:00am-4:00pm – Gather contact information for embassies and media organizations.

Faxed press release to:

Amnesty International	12126271451
Arab League	12025740331
Denmark Embassy	12023281470
HRW	12026124333
ICG	12027851630
Indonesian Embassy	12027755365
Norwegian Embassy	12023370870
Pakistani Embassy	12023870484
Saudi Arabian Embassy	12029445983
Swedish Embassy	12024672699
Turkish Embassy	12026126744

World Org. v. Torture		12022965704

5 December 2002 – Friday

Began media blitz by ascertaining contacts within organizations through Deborah's remaining contacts at a previous PR firm.

Contacted and pitched story idea to:

CNN – Atlanta News Desk		14048273134
BBC – Eurasian/Russian Desk	Elizabeth	44-2073790346
	Meagan	12122457560
	Stephanie	12023938333
CBS – Foreign Desk	Allison	(tel)12129753019
ABC – World News Tonight – Assignment Desk		(tel)12124562700 London bureau: Kelly Rockwell (kelly.rockwell@abc.com)

NBC – World Nightly News – Int'l News Desk	Christina	12015835222
FOXNews	Amy Burknolder, Sr. Producer	12123015436 (amy.burkholder@foxnews. com)
Al Jazeera	Stephanie	(tel)12023931333 (fax)12023938333 Thomas@aljazeerausa.com
Washington Post	Peter Baker – Moscow Correspondent	foreign@washpost.com
Washington Post	Phil Bennet – Asst Managing Editor, Foreign News	bennetp@washpost.com
New York Times	Foreign Correspondents	foreign@nytimes.com

| Washington Times | David Jones, Editor | (tel)12026363244 |
| | | (fax)12028327278 |

Postmortem

One major problem was the lack of contacts within media organizations. Media outlets have near-impregnable firewalls. ITWI Public Relations needs to do a better job of making contacts with upper management in media organizations.

CPG needs to expand its goals in making on the ground contacts. CPG needs to develop the necessary rapport with OTG correspondents to allow for the direct forwarding of information. Having this ability – instead of calling regional bureaus and dealing with telephone trees – would shave time off of response times.

EXAMPLES OF NOTES AMONG STAFF – UGANDA.

* On the ground contacts were hard to find by emailing straight into the country. The people are very weary and most of the internet and email access is controlled by the government. What worked best was to find a person either here in the US or Europe, create a connection with that person, and ask them to pass the information along to their contacts in the country.

* You should email the contacts on the ground that I have made to make sure the CPG stays fresh in their minds, and they know who to contact in case of an emergency.

* The Uganda report, written by my predecessor was very complete. However, I felt as though it was lacking a complete historical analysis of the situation, as well as an in-depth research on what violations the government is committing... It is in these areas where I think further research is necessary.

Helpful websites:

> http://irinnews.org/
> http://news.bbc.co.uk/2/hi/africa/
> http://allafrica.com/   www.afp.com
> http://www.acholipeace.org/

Search mechanisms:

> Lexis-Nexis

Local newspapers (often biased):

> The Monitor http://www.monitor.co.ug/   New Vision http://www.newvision.co.ug/   Uganda   Globe http://www.ugandaglobe.com/

Other sources (to make sure you keep updated with):

> www.amnesty.org   www.hrw.org
> www.state.gov/p/af

THIRD (FINAL) GENERATION EARLY WARNING METHODOLOGY MANUAL 2003 – 2004.

The following is the final generation of early warning system at the CPG. It is the result of four years of genocide-prevention experience of approximately two hundred people. It concentrates on the early warning methodology and the early warning crisis procedures.

From those who went before..."

THE CENTER FOR THE PREVENTION OF GENOCIDE
EARLY WARNING SYSTEM METHODOLOGY 2003

Introduction

The Center for the Prevention of Genocide was established in October of 2000 with the mission of anticipating and preventing acts of genocide in remote locations around the world. Since then it has developed a practical early warning system designed to bring first-hand accounts of abuse from the areas it monitors to policy makers reliably and quickly. It has served as a responsible channel for information from the field to policy makers at the UN, in the US, several foreign ministries and the media.

The Center has published twenty-two reports as well as a journal and it has hosted lecture and TV series on the subject of genocide and genocide prevention. It is through its early warning work that the Center fulfills its most valuable role in warning specific offices designed to respond to these exact kinds of humanitarian emergencies. Through the use of qualified volunteer researchers several lines of communication have been developed in remote hotspots around the world. Neutral third party observers are used as sources in the field to report or verify massive human rights violations or ominous signs of abuse to come. The Center uses a variety of reliable and trustworthy sources including, but not limited to, members of the media, Embassy staff, UN agencies, Relief organizations, other human rights organizations, missionaries as well as international business persons doing work in the area.

The Early Warning System concentrates on emergency situations which are genocidal or pre-genocidal, or areas where a crisis with potential trigger mechanisms poses a credible threat to a vulnerable minority. The narrow scope of this mission has enabled the Center to concentrate its resources on areas where people are most endangered but have been largely overlooked.

History

The Center has monitored over twenty-five hotspots during its existence. Similar to a fire engine company, whenever a crisis arises in one of the areas, the Center responds with an emergency crisis procedure. This includes neutral third party verification of the abuse or dangerous pre-genocidal indicator and then a release of the confirmed information to the appropriate officers at the UN, the US State Department, the media and several foreign ministries. There have been twelve emergency crisis procedure in the past two years with several of them being false alarms. Below is a breakdown of five situations that were not false alarms, but where early warning is likely to have played a direct role in the cessation of violence.

- Nuba Mountain Range, Sudan Summer 2001: A Man-Induced Famine which would have claimed approximately 85,000 lives due to government and government sponsored militia bombing of humanitarian relief flights was averted due to USAID airlift of 2800 metric tons of sorghum to the area. The week before the initiative was announced, the Center put on a presentation at USAID with comprehensive evidence of (article 2, section c: 1948 genocide Convention) man-induced famine, this may have sealed Director Natsios' findings and furthered the decision to intervene.

- Sulawesi, Indonesia, December 2, 2001: Muslim on Christian violence, originally initiated by Christians in the Moluccas Islands, sparked anew in Sulawesi. Over 45,000 Christians became trapped by members of Laskar Jihad which had vowed to massacre them by Christmas. The Center received the information before the wire services carried it, verified it through a credible ground contact, released it to the wire and forwarded the information to the US House of Representatives Subcommittee on Human Rights members and staffs. Unlike the Moluccas where there was no intervention and where word of massacres did not reach the West for several months, the Sulawesi violence was instantly reported and President Megawati subsequently send

351

4,000 troops within 48 hours and secured the safety of the population.

- Gujarat, India Summer/fall 2002: Further Hindu on Muslim violence, initiated originally by Muslims angered by the destruction of a Mosque, was averted by swift action on the part of the Indian government. Hindu Ultra-Nationalists were poised to continue the systematic rape and attacks on the Muslim minority community during a controversial festival when the Indian government intervened with 500 Sikh police officers to neutrally guard the peace. The Center issues two reports on the nature of the violence though the crisis.

- Chechnya, Russia December 2002: The Russian government had indicated an intention to liquidate the Chechen refugee camps in Ingushetia during the winter months. Such an action would likely result in the deaths of some of the elderly and infirm in the Chechen population. After the striking of the first camp of 1500 the transfers were halted in part due to the vigilance of the UN and NGOs like the Center who helped apprise policy makers of the dangerous exposure to the elements that the population was being subjected to.

- Ituri and South Kivu Province, DR Congo, August 2002 – May 2003: Ituri: Hema and Lendu militia reprisal killing of each other's vulnerable populations largely escaped notice due to the larger civil war issues in DR Congo. The Center has issued three separate press releases and undertaken four emergency crisis procedures to inform policy makers of this unfolding danger. At present the UN has stationed 750 peacekeepers and is seeking to expand its mandate to include more. South Kivu: RCD Goma rebels were responsible for the massacre of unarmed civilians in a rival rebel area. The UN has dispatched a fact finding mission to the area.

Methodology

The Early Warning System has four components beginning with:

A.   Narrowing the research focus to a manageable number of likely locations where genocidal or pre-genocidal activities are likely to flare.

B.   Intensive monitoring of this narrow sector of the human rights field.

C.   Monitoring outreach to standard sources and the building of new field networks.

D.   When necessary, the emergency crisis procedure   which includes:

I. Verification

II. Dissemination to policy makers

III. Follow up to check results

IV. Documentation of crisis response

353

A. Narrowing the Research Focus

It is during this first step of narrowing the focus that several factors are weighed. It is important that the Center narrow the scope of the large part of its research on between 8-15 hotspots. The Center does not have the resources of an Amnesty International nor does it need them with the scope being narrowed to the few hotspots that show strong pre-genocidal indicators. A preponderance of evidence of pre-genocidal abuse or indicators is the criteria for considering a remote area for concentrated research. There are four sets of indicators that are weighed. The presence of the first three set of indicators make the argument, in order of weighed importance, for assigning the area as an area of concentrated research and monitoring. The last set of indicators detracts from the argument that the area should become or remain an area of concentration. These sets of indicators are:

I. Genocidal or pre-genocidal indicators or abuse (all lists on following page)

II. Triggers, significant historical, neutral, economic, social or other factors

III. Human rights violations that contribute to pre-genocidal conditions

IV. Mitigating circumstances

B. Genocidal or pre-genocidal indicators or abuse

I. INDICATORS

Any perpetration of the following, but not limited to the following acts toward a religious, ethnic, national or racial group by government, militia, religious or other organized group will be seriously considered for the concentrated monitoring of a remote area.

-intentional massacre of unarmed civilians (Article 2, Section A, 1948 Convention on Genocide)

-civilian targeting during military campaigns (Art. 2 Sec. C)
-one-sided   physical   brutality   (Art.2   Sec.   Etc.)
-torture
-mutilation
-bringing about conditions in order for a group to perish
-man-induced famine
-near man-induced famine
-man-exacerbated* famine
-near man-exacerbated famine
-murder of children of the minority
-removal of the children of the minority
-denial of water or emergency medical attention
-systematic rape of women
-media or government vilification of a minority

---

* Center for the Prevention of Genocide Terminology

355

-internment, peace or concentration camps for a minority.
-ethnic cleansing or forcible movement of a people
-ideological cleansing*
-public call for expendability of a population
-presence of death or target lists
-ID that specifically identifies ethnicity, religion or race
-destruction of cattle or subsistence food supply
-destruction of religious temple or site of historical importance
-disarmament of a minority only
-forced labor/overwork
-human biological testing/medical experiments
-abduction
-forced marriage
-forced labor
-unconfirmed but credible reports of any of these abuses or indicators

II. Triggers, significant historical, neutral, economic, social or other factors

Triggers

-assassination or forcible government change with ethnic, religious or racial implications

---

* Center for the Prevention of Genocide Terminology

-a power vacuum left by the withdrawal or stabilizing armed forces, collapse of a government, etc.

-uneasy power transfer

-controversial treaty implementation

-maneuvering or serious negotiating phase of peace talks

-controversial/violence prone celebration, anniversary or event approaching

-transfer of resource from one group to another

-a written or verbal order to destroy a group/ a call to arms

-a written or verbal encouragement to target/have vengeance on a minority

-justice denied

-revenge or reprisal killing over personal strife between individuals from different groups

-initiation of warfare

-perceived alliance with enemy during warfare

-a rapidly deteriorating military situation

-a plebiscite, independence vote or other significant democratic exercise with serious implications

-an act of terrorism attributed to members of the minority

Historical

-a history of massacres of minority

-a history of repression by one group over another

-a history of pogroms

-a history of vilification or dehumanization of a minority

-use of inflammatory symbols, flags or markings that conjure previous abuse

-celebration of instances of perceived or actual abuse of minority

-an attempt to redraw borders or regional or local boundaries according to historical claims

-no history of democracy or accountability

Military

-troop movements surrounding unarmed populations

-brokering of weapons

-increasing military and paramilitary training camps

-mass destruction of property

-forcible displacement

-targeting of civilian pop centers

-scorched-earth (i.e. government practices such as destruction of property, including agricultural land, population, etc.)

-displacement

-stockpiling tools of violence (assault rifles, machetes, torture artifacts, especially in conjunction with "death lists" or vilification of a group]

-increasing military and paramilitary training [especially in conjunction with "death lists" or vilification of a group]

Neutral Contributing Factors

-remote geographic location

-lack of internet, phone or radio

-lack of press coverage

-lack of transportation to and from the area

-natural disaster

-famine

Economic

-severe downturn in the economy

-traditional cash crop fails or bottoms out

-ethnic, religious or racial competition of limited resources and or jobs

-minority group had possession, lives on or near or has legitimate claim to valuable national resource

-presence of valuable national resource in area unprotected by the central government

-removal of resources from one group to benefit another

-hold and/or transfer of resources

-redirecting aid supplies for sale

-poor infrastructure/lack of access (physical, informational) to remote hot spots

-looting of minority

-political marginalization of minority

-off-limits to humanitarian relief

-exclusion of foreigners in conflict zones

-slavery

-attacks on relief workers

-domestic resistance to relief operations

-prediction of "hunger gap"

-lack of food, drought, physical insecurity

Social

-misunderstood/misrepresented social customs that lead to raise in tension

-conflicting religious sites

-jealousy of minority success

-marginalized group lives outside norms of social construct

III. Human rights violations that contribute to pre-genocidal conditions

-lack of freedom of speech
-lack of freedom of press
-lack of right to gather/assembly   -
lack of freedom of religion
-presence of second class citizens
-restricted right to habeas corpus
-disarmament of a minority
-restricted right of movement
-press controlled by government
-laws specific to a minority
-laws designed to disempower a minority
-party membership for food allocation

-higher taxes for a minority
-persecution of political party (state and/or non- state)
-outlawing of political parties
-lack of clear mandate (national and/or international)
-diluted political will (national and/or international)
-denial of education
-exclusion of minority from governmental positions
-arbitrary detention/political prison
-reconciliation breakage
-segregation of minority
-restricted religious service
-restricted intermarriage
-2nd class citizen status
- unilateral abrogation of a treaty
-restriction of cultural education
-restriction of higher education use
-restricted cultural mobility
-public identification of minority members
-poor attention to conflict due to no strategic interest of western countries
-lack of funding for assistance miss
-political movement demonstrations as targets
-delay of substantive negotiations/peace talks
-racist/ultra-nationalist controlling an authoritarian regime

IV. Mitigating circumstances

The following are circumstances which may mitigate or decrease the need for a concentrated level of research and monitoring in an area.

-to reported or observed continuation of massive human rights violations which could be construed as pre-genocidal

-very few incidents which could be construed as pre-genocidal

-a recent effective peace accord

-a recent effective cease fire

-cessation of hostilities

-the presence of UN or Internationally recognized or invited third party forces

-the presence of UN or Internationally recognized or invited third party observers

-the presence of a significant amount of human rights organizations

-the presence of a significant amount of relief organizations

-the presence of press coverage on the area

-the active work of the UN Security Council on the resolution of the issue

-the active work of regional players to resolve the issue

-the active work of the national government to resolve the issue

-the active work of conflict resolution, intervention and prevention NGOs

-the re-establishment of essential services or a relatively stable economy

-the resolution of the trigger and or the issue behind the trigger for the instability

-the presence of reconciliation or truth commissions supported by the general population of both groups in question

-the establishment of rule of law

-the prosecution and punishment of heinous acts, crimes against humanity, acts of genocide or other abuse under the domestic, regional or ICC law

-the establishment of a form of democracy

C. Outreach to standard sources and building new field networks

Researchers read all Center paperwork, press releases, files and reports on the area to be monitored as well as received instruction and direction from executive staff and mentors or senior fellows at the Center. After immersing themselves in the background history, key players, nature of abuse, indicators of abuse and the present situation, the fellow or researcher will then familiarize themselves with the wire, list serve, media, UN and international resources available and begin monitoring these standard areas for indications of a worsening of the ground situation. Every day, whether at the Center or not, the researcher will check their list serves, messages and standard information sources online to verify the ground status of their area of concentration. Each researcher is assigned a secondary area of concentration to serve as backup in case the primary researcher in that area is unavailable for an emergency in their area. This secondary area of concentration requires a somewhat less stringent but still thorough knowledge of the on the ground situation and the resources available for the emergency crisis procedure.

The Center must rely on individuals in or near these hotspots for verification of abuse or disturbance and for informing the Center when an emergency is unfolding. Neutral third party observers are used as sources in the field to report or verify massive human rights violations or ominous signs of abuse to come. The Center uses a variety of reliable and trustworthy sources including but not limited to, members of the media, Embassy staff, UN agencies, Relief organizations, other human rights organizations, missionaries as well as international business persons doing work in the area.

It is the responsibility of the Primary Human Rights Violation Monitor to contact the Center's field sources, continue to develop a relationship with them, assess the level of information that may be available and to expand the Center's contacts on the ground through the internet, phone and fax. The utmost care must be taken not to compromise the identity of any of these sources to anyone outside of the Center.

D. The emergency crisis procedure

Occasionally a situation will heat up to a point where the Human Rights Violation Monitor will indicate a crisis may be brewing or unfolding. These crises usually take the form of a massacre or similar act of calamity beginning to unfold or being warned locally. Because of our sources close to the heart of the matter we are able to get a good feel for the situation sometimes days before it explodes and sometimes weeks before the policy makers are aware of it. This makes the service we provide unique and invaluable. If there appears to be a situation that may result in a precursor to genocidal conduct becoming genocidal or a clear deterioration in an area we are monitoring, the Human Rights Violation Monitor is required to inform the Director of the Center, or in his absence, a Board member or an appointed executive staff member. A decision will be made whether to invoke the emergency crisis procedure. The analogy of a fire engine company responding to almost every call is apt here as there are more false alarms than not, however, once invoked, the procedure should be followed through to its conclusion. The steps of the procedure (protocol) are:

     I. Verification

     II. Dissemination to policy makers

     III. Follow up to check results

     IV. Documentation of crisis response

I. Verification.

The human rights violation monitors, supervised by the Director or a board member will lead a team in ascertaining whether the wire services are carrying word of the abuse or unfolding calamity. If the wire is not carrying it then the primary business of the Center is independent verification of the event using neutral third party sources. Using largely telephone and email, the Center will reach out to already established contacts in the area to verify reports of ongoing events. If verification cannot be obtained through already established contacts, a concerted effort will be made to verify the events through reliable neutral third parties on the ground including but not limited to embassy staff, international reporters, and qualified NGOs in the field. After confirming the report of abuse or danger, the Center will undertake to consider the reliability and quality of the source and information before releasing it to the public. While two neutral third party sources are ideal for verification, depending on the source, a single confirmation of information from the field may be sufficient if the source is reliable.

II. Dissemination.

Prior to publishing a press release or contacting policy makers a strategy session will be held to assess the most efficient use of the Center's resources and the specific policy makers who are most likely to be able to effect the ground situation. Once that list is complete, two things will happen simultaneously. A press release will be drafted for distribution to the wire, press, UN, US State Department, specific foreign ministries and other policy making or human rights entities. Concurrently the Director and one or two monitors and possibly a senior fellow will begin to call policy makers according to the strategic plan. After the press release has been drafted it will be edited and then released via fax and internet to the remaining policy makers. Offices should be contacted in an effort to follow up the receipt of the fax and the disposition of the information. It is appropriate to ask staff what course of action in response to the information is being taken. It is very important to receive and record the individuals and the organizations who are verbally contacted and who indicate that the information is being reviewed.

III. Follow Up.

As the information is disseminated it is important that a series of phone calls and email go out to confirm that the information has gotten into the right hands. Without harassing, follow up phone calls should be made at the time, during the course of the day and over the next few days until the information sought is ascertained. The strategy session group will meet again to assess the productivity of the news release and determine if a change in strategy is necessary or if the crisis procedure has fulfilled its goals.

IV. Documentation.

All contacts, information receipt, wire reports, confirmation, procedure, response and information dissemination will be documented on an Early Warning Crisis Response Sheet.

Emergency Crisis Procedures 2001 – 2003

1. Nuba Mountain Range, Sudan, Summer **2001**: Gave comprehensive information to USAID regarding man-induced famine: USAID intervened.

2. Sulawesi, Indonesia, December 2001: Released info of massacres to wire, press, and Congress: Indonesian President sent 4,000 troops.

3. Zimbabwe, Mtebeleland, Spring **2002**: Monitored use of man-exacerbated famine as an election tool prepared for press campaign. Stood down.

4. Gujarat, India, Summer 2002: Hindu Nationalists prepare for further attacks on Muslim minority: Neutral Sikh police intervene. Stood down.

5. Southern Sudan, Summer 2002: Issued first genocide warning along with many human rights organizations.

6. Ituri Province, D.R.Congo, August 2002: Released Hema on Lendu massacre info to wire, press, UN & US: UN asks for more observers for Ituri.

7. Ituri Province, D.R.Congo, September 2002: Lendu on Hema reprisal killings at a hospital was vastly under reported info forwarded to UN & US.

8. Nuba Mountain Range, Sudan, September 2002: Give detailed information of the smuggling of arms to the US monitoring agency.

9. Chechnya, Russia, December 2002: Center's warning re: the liquidation of Chechen camps in Ingushetia occurs. Backdoor approaches works.

10. Ituri Province, D.R.Congo, March **2003**: Center following reports of massacres and releasing info to UN.

11. South Kivu, D.R.Congo, April 2003: Released info to press, UN & US of RCDGoma rebel attack on civilians. UN sends fact-finding mission.

12 Ituri Province, D.R.Congo, May 2003: Center following reports of instability in area released info to UN & US. UN Security Council weighs in.

PART FIVE: ADMINISTRATION AND PERSONNEL.

    a. Space
    b. Company handbook
    c. Hiring
    d. Training
    e. Filings

Your new organization will need a few essentials to get started including a location, a staff, training materials, a company handbook and the knowledge of which paperwork to file and when.

OFFICE SPACE

There are many alternatives to running the charity out of your own home during your first months and years. If inexpensive commercial space is unavailable, other charities sometimes have space they are willing to donate or lease at bargain rates to other charities with similar focuses. Buildings which are slated to be demolished in a few years often have low occupancy and very inexpensive rents as well. Today there are alternatives to these out-of-the-box ideas. There is flexible shared space just for small businesses and just for non-profit organizations. Sometimes the space is simply shared board room and general space. But the upside is to have ready office equipment and a good internet signal available in a stable environment. The cafes around town are suitable for interviews, individual workspaces, group projects and even meetings if the space and management allow it. I once found inexpensive office space in a building where I wanted the office by looking for second floor windows that looked unoccupied. The entire second floor needed renovation. The owner was thinking of renovating it and now he had a customer that would defray some of his costs. There are also owners who will consider work in lieu of rent.

At the end of the day, most of your work can be done via computer and phone, so permanent space can sometimes be optional during your initial months. However, if you have a budget for it, nothing encourages real work like a real space where individuals need to show up to on a regular basis. Telecommuting is a popular alternative to traditional office work, but it does have its downside and is definitely not for everyone. I have found that there is a considerable amount of the workforce who's work suffers when they are not required to be in an office. I noticed that deadlines begin to be missed, office meetings are missed and the quality of the work decreases. Then there were the authors of our North Korea and India-Pakistan reports. None of them ever set foot inside our offices and these were among our best reports. You must ultimately judge for yourself the person and the best space for their productivity.

COMPANY HANDBOOK

After the first six months of your existence, it is probably time to put together some of the rules, expectations, job descriptions and other important information in a handbook. This helps clarify expectations, gives your organization a more professional demeanor and helps with training. Much of the information can be found online except of course the specific policies and knowhow that you and your organization want to impart to incoming staff and volunteers. It is also important to outline appropriate codes of conduct here in order to define what a safe, clean and happy workplace is. However, you must be ready, yourself, to live within the confines of the rules laid out in your manual. As the leader of your organization, you are held, rightfully, to a higher standard than the rest of the staff and volunteers. The expression 'it is lonely at the top' is correct.

The Director, President or Administrator can be friendly and professional, but workplace friendships have to fall within a code of conduct that keeps a certain amount of arm's length. At the end of the day, you are the main trainer, the main supervisor, performance evaluator, and the person who chastises, suspends or even fires staff and volunteers when performance and professionalism are substandard. While it is good to foster open lines of communication, friendliness and professionalism be sure to observe that you hold yourself to the highest standards of professionalism. Also, if problems do arise later during employment, keep notes of performance reviews and have the employee sign the review so a clear pattern emerges from the paperwork that you have worked with and warned the employee to change the behavior, in case dismissal is the only resolution.

SAMPLE: Non-Disclosure Agreement.

For good consideration, and in consideration of being employed by and/or volunteering at The center for the Prevention of Genocide and its affiliate organizations (herein referred to as the Organization), I the undersigned hereby agree and acknowledge:

1) That during the course of my employment/volunteerism, there may be disclosed to me certain confidential and proprietary information of the Organizations, consisting of but not limited to:
    a) Technical information – methods, processes, formulae, compositions, systems, techniques, inventions, machines, computer programs, and research projects.
    b) Business information – donor/customer lists, prospect research, pricing data, sources of

supply, financial data and marketing, production, and fundraising systems and plans.

2) I agree that I shall not during the time of employment/volunteerism with the Organization or at any time after use for myself or others or disclose or divulge to others, including future employees, any trade secrets, confidential information, or any other proprietary data of the Organization in violation of this agreement.

3) That upon the termination of my employment/volunteerism from the Organization:

a) I shall return to the Organization all documents and property of the Organization including but not limited to curriculum materials, reports, manuals, correspondence, customer lists, computer programs, rolodexes, and all other materials or copies thereof relating in any way to the Organization's business or in any way obtained by me during the course of my employment/volunteerism.

b) The Organization may notify any future or prospective employer or third party of the existence of this agreement and shall be entitled to full injunctive relief for any breach.

c) This agreement shall be binding upon me and my personal representatives and successors in interest, and shall inure to the benefit of the Organization, its successors and assigns.

Signed this _____ day of _____, 20_____.

_____

_____

Supervisor

Employee/Volunteer

SAMPLE: PERSONNEL POLICIES.

Personal Appearance

Personal appearance as an employee has an influence upon the impressions formed by the visitors to our facilities and offices. In general, attire should be neat and casual. During business meetings in the office and outside of the office, a standard type of business attire must be adhered to. When involved in meetings, or important internal gatherings (e.g. Board Meetings), it may not be appropriate to dress more casually.

CPG practices casual dress to enhance an enjoyable and productive workplace, unless management advises staff that on a particular day, they must adhere to business rather than casual dress for operational reasons. Examples of inappropriate clothing items that should not be worn in the office include: any clothing with obscene and/or inappropriate language and/or pictures, work-out clothing, halter/tube tops, muscle shirts, lycra wear; extremely short dresses and skirts, shorts, tight fitting or inappropriately revealing clothing, and clothing with holes or tears. It is important to use good judgment and talk to the supervisor regarding questions about dress code.

Appropriate business attire for women consists of suit coats with matching skirts or slacks, dresses, women's sport coats/blazers with a skirt or slacks, and for men: suits, sport coats, jackets, ties, dress socks, long-sleeved dress shirts, short-sleeved dress shirts, dress pants, and dress shoes.

Heavy perfumes and colognes are sometimes irritating to persons with certain allergies or chemical sensitivities. Please use them in moderation.

Political activities

Although CPG supports the private participation by employees in the elective process, federal tax law requires that CPG prohibit the use of its resources for partisan political activity. The following guidelines apply:

1) Employees may not use CPG phones, stationery, supplies, equipment or any other CPG resource to support any political candidate or for any other partisan political objective;
2) Employees may not, in privately supporting or opposing any political candidate or partisan political objective, identify themselves with CPG or attempt to use their position with the organization to gain credibility for political purposes;
3) Employees may not, while on the job, engage in any type of partisan political activity, including wearing buttons or other insignia.

Confidentiality of Information

Each employee must observe strict confidentiality in the safeguarding of all confidential business information as well as personal information pertaining to clients, clients' families and other employees. Such material may be made available to CPG and staff members that have a valid need for the material but may not be released to others without the written approval of the client or employee. Client and personnel files are kept locked when not under the direct supervision of the staff charged with their maintenance.

Employees who by position description are exposed to confidential information are required to sign a non-disclosure agreement as a condition to employment. Employees who improperly use or disclose trade secrets or confidential business information will be subject to disciplinary action, up to and including termination of employment and legal action, even if they do not actually benefit from the disclosed information.

Employees are responsible for safeguarding information when using computer equipment. Employees must use caution when using passwords and are not permitted to release such information to unauthorized staff.

When in doubt regarding the status of information, please refer to your immediate supervisor.

Organizational Communications

CPG's management staff is committed to maintaining open communications. It encourages and provides the opportunity to talk with one another openly and without restraint. If there are questions or problems, they should first be discussed with the immediate supervisor; if he or she does not satisfactorily respond to the problem or concern, the employee should then contact the person to whom his/her supervisor reports. If he or she does not respond satisfactorily to the problem, the employee should then contact the President & CEO depending on the reporting structure of their specific division.

Attendance and Punctuality

To maintain a safe and productive work environment, CPG expects employees to be reliable and punctual in reporting to work as scheduled. Absenteeism and tardiness place a burden on other employees and compromise CPGs' ability to provide quality services. In the rare instance when an employee cannot avoid being late to work or is unable to work as scheduled, he or she must notify the Office Manager and his or her supervisor directly as soon as possible in advance of the anticipated tardiness or absence.

The employee must call his or her immediate supervisor each day of his or her absence, until a date of return has been established. An employee who fails to contact the immediate supervisor may be considered as having voluntarily resigned. In the event an employee is absent due to illness and/or injury, CPG reserves the right to request a doctor's statement. Poor attendance (other than approved leave) and excessive tardiness are disruptive and unproductive. Either may lead to corrective action, including termination of employment.

Each full-time employee is allowed 15 paid days of combined sick leave, vacation and/or personal leave during one contracted year. Any long periods of absence whether paid or unpaid must be approved by the employee's immediate supervisor, and arrangements must be made to delegate responsibilities to a third party for the duration of the leave.

Dating and Fraternization

Although CPG attempts to respect employees' privacy, some off-duty conduct potentially impacts the organization. Romantic and dating relationships between employees in supervisor-subordinate relationships are inappropriate, and such relationships should be avoided because they may be destructive to effective employment relations and could create conflicts of interest and morale problems. Should a romantic or dating relationship occur, both employees must communicate the relationship to the Director of Human Resources or the CEO, who will make attempts to treat the information confidentially, so that a transfer, reassignment, or other appropriate action may be taken.

Furthermore, employees traveling on CPG business or attending CPG-sponsored events are expected to conduct themselves at all times with decorum during and after hours.

Sexual Harassment and Other Unlawful Harassment

CPG is committed to providing a work environment that is free of discrimination and unlawful harassment. CPG prohibits harassment in the workplace, whether committed by supervisory or non-supervisory personnel or by third parties including vendors, members, contractors, volunteers and interns. No supervisor may threaten or insinuate, either explicitly or implicitly, that an employee's submission to, or rejection of, sexual advances will in any way influence any personnel decisions regarding that employee's employment, wages, advancement, assigned duties or any other condition of employment or career development.

Other harassing conduct in the workplace that may create an offensive and hostile work environment, whether it is in the form of physical or verbal harassment, and regardless of whether committed by supervisory or non-supervisory personnel, is also prohibited. This includes, but is not limited to, repeated offensive language or conduct, unwelcome sexual flirtations, advances, propositions, continued or repeated verbal abuse of a sexual nature, graphic verbal commentaries about an individual's body, sexually degrading words used to describe an individual and the display in the workplace of sexually suggestive or other offensive objects or pictures.

Any employee who has experienced or who is aware of an incident of sexual or other unlawful harassment must promptly report the matter to his or her immediate supervisor. If the supervisor is unavailable or if the employee believes it would be inappropriate to contact the supervisor, the employee should immediately contact the Office Manager. Such internal complaints will be investigated promptly, and prompt action will be taken. Any employee with questions about the internal process or concerns about possible harassment or discriminatory treatment is urged to seek appropriate consultation with a suitable senior administrator.

No employee will suffer retaliation, reprisal or intimidation as a result of reporting an incident in good faith. CPG maintains confidentiality in these investigations to the extent feasible and consistent with an effective investigation and resolution, and enforcement of this policy.

Discriminatory treatment, which is found to be based upon an individual employee's race, ethnicity, age, religion, sex, or other legally protected characteristics, is also strictly prohibited. The same disciplinary and investigative standards applicable to sexual harassment will be applicable to other forms of unlawful harassment to the same extent.

Harassment can occur with a single incident or through a pattern of behavior. Harassment can result from a broad range of actions, which may include but are not limited to physical or mental abuse, racial insults, derogatory ethnic jokes, unwelcome verbal or physical conduct regarding race, color, religion, national origin, sex, age or disability.

It is the responsibility of the management staff and all employees to ensure that harassment does not occur.

This statement against harassment extends to prohibiting the acts of non-employees that result in harassment in the workplace.

Drug-Free Workplace

It is CPGs desire to provide a drug-free, healthy, and safe workplace and to comply with all applicable laws. To promote this goal, employees are required to report to work in appropriate mental and physical condition to perform their jobs in a satisfactory manner.

While on CPG premises and while conducting business-related activities off CPG premises, no employee may use, possess, distribute, sell, or be under the influence of alcohol or illegal drugs. Employees may use physician-prescribed medications provided that the use of such medications does not adversely affect job performance or the safety of the client, employee or other individuals in the workplace.

Employees are urged to immediately report any incidents or suspected incidents of illegal drug or alcohol activity, including use or impairment, to their immediate supervisor. To the extent feasible and consistent with handling the problem, an employee's report of suspected drug activity would be handled in a confidential manner.

Persons who are taking prescription medication with side effects that may pose a risk to their safety and to the safety of others or that inhibits the individual's ability to perform their job duties should report side effects to their immediate supervisor. Medical information will be kept confidential and when appropriate, reasonable accommodations will be made.

Consistent with this policy, CPG reserves the right to conduct such tests as it deems prudent, appropriate and scientifically sound in order to monitor, verify or prevent the use of alcohol or controlled substances by CPG employees. Furthermore, CPG reserves the right to implement a screening program for applicants and/or transferees for identified job categories where the use/abuse of controlled substances and/or alcohol would be of concern given the nature and duties of the identified job categories.

Employees with questions or concerns about substance dependency or abuse are encouraged to discuss options with their immediate supervisor.

CPG's offices are smoke-free.

Internet and Electronic Mail Policy

As part of CPGs business, employees increasingly use and exploit electronic forms of communication and information exchange. Employees have access to one or more forms of electronic media and services (computer, e-mail, telephones, voice mail, fax machines, external electronic bulletin boards, wire services, on-line services, and the internet).

CPG encourages the use of these media and associated services because they make communication more efficient and effective, and because they are valuable sources of information (e.g. about members, new laws and regulations). However, electronic media and services provided by CPG are CPGs property, and their purpose is to facilitate CPGs business.

Knowingly transmitting, retrieving, or storage of any communications of a discriminatory or harassing nature, which are derogatory to any individual or group, which are obscene or X-rated communications, are of a defamatory or threatening nature, for "chain letters", or for any other purpose which is illegal or against CPG policy or contrary to CPGs interest.

Electronic media and services are primarily for CPG business use. Limited, occasional, or incidental use of electronic media is understandable and acceptable – as is the case with personal phone calls. However, the employees need to demonstrate a sense of responsibility and may not abuse the privilege.

Electronic information created and/or communicated by an employee using e-mail, word processing, utility programs, spreadsheets, voice mail, telephones, internet/BBS access, etc. will generally be monitored by CPG, and we respect our employees' wish to work without CPG constantly monitoring their actions. However, the following conditions should be noted:

1) CPG reserves the right to routinely monitor usage patterns for both voice and data communications (e.g. number called or site accessed, call length, times of day calls). Reasons for this include cost analysis and allocation and the management of our gateway to the Internet.

2) CPG also reserves the right, in its discretion, to review any employee's electronic files and messages and usage to the extent necessary to ensure that electronic media and services are

being used in compliance with the law and with this and other CPG policies.

Employees should therefore not assume electronic and other forms of communication are totally private and confidential and should transmit highly sensitive information in other ways. In other words, employees have no reasonable expectation of privacy on CPGs electronic systems.

Employees must respect the confidentiality of other people's electronic communications and my not attempt to read their communications, hack into other systems or other people's logins, crack passwords, breach computer or network security measures, or monitor electronic files or communications of other employees or third parties except by explicit direction of CPG management.

Electronic media and services should not be used in a manner that is likely to cause network congestion or significantly hamper the ability of other people to access and use the system.

Any messages or information sent by an employee to one or more individuals via an electronic network (e.g. bulletin board, on-line service, or internet) are statements identifiable and attributable to CPG. While some users include personal disclaimers in electronic messages, it should be noted that there would still be a connection with CPG, and the statement might still be associated with CPG. All communications sent by employees via a network must comply with this and other CPG policies and may not disclose any confidential or proprietary information.

Any employee found to be abusing the privilege of CPG-facilitated access to electronic media or services will be subject to corrective action and/or risk having the privilege removed for him/herself and possibly other employees.

With the rapidly changing nature of electronic media, and the proper etiquette for use on the Internet, which is developing among users of external on-line services and the Internet, this policy cannot lay down rules to cover every possible situation. Instead, it expresses CPGs philosophy and sets forth general principles to be applied to use of electronic media and services.

NOTE:

If you have any questions pertaining to the above policies, please address them with your immediate supervisor.

HIRING

The hiring and training of your employees and volunteers are, perhaps, the most important aspect of your job. A well screened and well trained crew is invaluable to the execution of your charities mission. Don't save time by not screening, interviewing and training well. It will come back to haunt you.

There are many places to recruit staff and volunteers. I usually focused on College campus career centers because the recruits were eager to learn and do well and very trainable. During the interview process make sure to have set questions to ask and specific questions derived from the contents of their resume. Also make sure to ask what they applicant is hoping to gain from their experience working at your charity. This helps in setting proper expectations. Knowing what they perceive as their strengths and weaknesses is a helpful way to know what to work on if they come to work for you and also any potential weaknesses that may be deal breakers for you.

Note their professionalism, 'fringe' times of the meeting, the competency with which they write their letter, resume, present themselves and communicate. Be honest about your expectations and what they can expect. Being fair to your potential staff and volunteers will be appreciated. Let them decide if they want to be part of a 'start up' NGO. You must also be prepared to answer questions about your organization, its mission, resources, successes and failures. Prior to the meeting, you and your staff should have reviewed their resume to screen them for an interview. If possible, have a second person in the interview. Sometimes a second pair of eyes will pick up a talent or worrisome quality that you may miss.

I once interviewed a young lady who dropped the 'S' bomb in the interview. By the second 'S' bomb, I knew I would not hire her. At the end I asked her how her interviews were going so far. She said, 'To be honest, not so good. I am not getting any callbacks and I can't figure why.' So I asked her if she wanted some unsolicited advice. She readily agreed. 'First of all, you are not getting the position and I wanted to tell you why.' I told her that swearing in an interview was the third rail of interviews and a look of realization came over her face. She had been so busy trying to be herself and not be nervous that she was unaware she was dropping inappropriate words in every interview. 'Also,' I said, 'No one really wants to meet the *real* you. They want to meet your Ambassador. The best you there is. Be yourself, but the best version of you.' That applies to interviewers as well as interviewees.

Interns

Ideally the Intern Coordinator will handle the interviewing process, but it often gets mandated to PR. You will obtain intern applications/resumes via email inquiries, and career fairs at Georgetown, American University, George Mason University, and George Washington University. We usually receive information about the upcoming fairs, but it is a good idea to contact the schools to make sure none slips through the cracks.

385

Reviewing resumes:

1. Look for education level curriculum/major
2. Note any human rights experience
3. Note any non-profit history
4. Note fluency or proficiency in languages other than English
5. Look for experience abroad

Contacting candidates:

1. Create a log sheet of who you contact and when
2. See below for sample form letter for requesting an interview
3. Make sure to note something personal in their background when you make the initial contact
4. For those you do not contact place their resume in a separate file
5. Keep a separate sheet to note when they will come in for an interview and don't forget to check first with the master schedule
6. Make a note on the master schedule of the interview time
7. Be sure to mark off if they show up or not

Accepting Interns:

1. During the interview make sure the interviewing committee makes a note of what is the best to get a hold of the candidate
2. If you determine email is the most efficient see form below for sample of acceptance letter
3. Make sure you indicate the exact position the candidate is being offered (interviewers will note this)
4. Create two files: Accept offer and Decline Offer

5. As candidates get back to you about whether they accept or decline place them in the appropriate folder also make note of when they can begin and how many days they are committing to work (days and times)
6. Keep a master schedule of incoming interns
7. Be sure to email accepted interns about training daytime and date

SAMPLE: Email Forms

Contact Form for Interviews

Dear _____,

Thank you for expressing an interest in our organization. We are currently in the process of interviewing prospective interns for the Fall (Summer/Winter/Spring) semester. We have reviewed your resume and believe your experience in _____ makes you a good candidate for a position at the Center.

We would like to bring you in for an interview. Please indicate when you will be available so we can arrange time that is suitable (or suggest a specific time or times we have available to interview).

We look forward to hearing from you.

Sincerely,

Your Name

Your Position Title

Center for the Prevention of Genocide

Sample Contact form for Offering a Position.

Dear _____,

Thank you for coming in to interview last _____.
After reviewing your resume and notes from your interview
we are pleased to offer you a position as _____ in
our _____ Department. We feel as though you have
the skills and experience, we are looking for in an intern.

Please indicate within a week or so whether you will be
accepting or declining our offer. If you do accept, please let
us know which days you will be available to work during
the semester. You may respond by email or telephone 703-
528-1002. We will be getting in touch with you about the
start date/training day.

Looking forward to having you on staff,

Sample Contact form for Rejecting a Candidate.

Dear _____,

Thank you for coming in to interview last _____.
After reviewing your resume and notes from your interview

we are unfortunately unable to offer you a position at this time.

Please feel free to contact us in the future concerning possible internship opportunities.

Sincerely,

Your Name

Your Position Title/Center for the Prevention of Genocide

TRAINING

In the first several years of your organization, I believe it is important for you or the best expert and teacher you have on staff to thoroughly train each staff member and volunteer who joins your organization. A nice professional PowerPoint to go over the highlights of your organization and what is expected from each position will be helpful. Encourage your new hire to take notes. After the video, personally go through every section of the handbook with the new hire, taking the time to answer any questions. If your employee is to receive a country book regarding the area they are to monitor, it is important that this book remain in the office at all times. Copies of sections can be made or emailed to themselves, but you don't want to lose institutional memory of notes and reports held within each book. Go over every aspect of the position with the new hire. How to research their area. How to make phone calls and emails professionally. How to reach out to on the ground contacts and build relationships, how to track their country in the news, blogs, listservs and through other organizations. How to build rapport and put on presentations for policymakers. How to draft a press release, a brief, write a complete report, edit a report, serve as a secondary human rights monitor for another country and how to enact an emergency crisis procedure and build a strategy to save lives in their area.

If you treat the training for the position with respect and importance, your new staffer is more likely to respect the position and its requirements.

FILINGS.

When you begin your organization, if you are to remain a nonprofit (recommended) you will file a 501C 3 for nonprofit status. Years ago this was relatively straight forward and would take a few days to complete. Usually it would be rejected once or twice until you had the paperwork exactly as the IRS wanted and then it was approved. Today it is a more complex and detailed form. Often people hire a professional to fill it out. Otherwise, expect to take 2 – 4 weeks to complete the paperwork and 2-3 months before it is approved, at a minimum.

It is also key that you file for and receive your EIN and file your W2s I9s and W4s and other appropriate state, payroll, federal withholding for your paid staff. For me, hiring an accountant was the best and easiest way to make sure everything was filed on time and we knew how much was owed and what to do and when. I strongly recommend this unless you are good with numbers and forms and need to save money. If you use all volunteers, there may still be a requirement to file taxes for payroll with a zero written in.

PART SIX: TECHNOLOGY, FUNDING AND TEMPLATES.

TECHNOLOGY.

As technology has proliferated everything we do, it should also make your job easier. As text messages and instant photographs and videos of abuse can be instantly uploaded and produced, it has the potential to make the world a much more transparent place regarding massive human rights violations. There are so many different types of social media that can be used to provide a website, a gathering place for discussion, a blog to disseminate information, that getting word out to the world can be as easy as receiving information on your computer alone in your home, confirming it on the phone with a first-hand source and uploading photos, videos and a press release to the world. Jemera Rone was a one woman army of information about abuse in Southern Sudan for Human Rights Watch. Her blog/listserv gave daily updates from throughout the regions and was the best source of breaking news for the world on this region. She was one woman and her reports ended in 2006, before much of the today's technology appeared.

Twitter, Facebook, YouTube, TikTok, LinkedIn and other emerging media are excellent resources for fundraising and awareness building. If your tech person does not have the time to set these up and if you are not particularly tech savvy, then find the person on staff who uses the medium the most and ask if they would be interested in helping develop and build that media. You might be surprised at the information and access these media can build.

FUNDING.

Most charities and businesses fail. It is a fact of life. Mine did. The CPG went out of business after four years of human rights reporting. But during that time, it saved lives. I categorically, do not regret doing it. With the exception of my wonderful children, it is the thing in my life of which I am most proud. Even my father was proud of it. We failed because of a lack of funding. A genocide-prevention early warning system is not as attractive a charity as cute kittens, or sympathetic as homeless vets or as easily recognizable as local scholarships. It is a difficult sell – even to people who have seen it work or who have suffered the abuse themselves.

There are many cautionary stories of non-profit organizations and new businesses closing quickly because of a lack of funding. This is a natural hazard of the terrain of business and charity. Grant money is scarce, your friends and family resources soon run out and the mad scramble is on to find the donor(s) who will fund your mission. There is another recent development that has changed how some non-profits and other startups canvass for support before they launch. Crowd funding is a relatively new internet-driven fundraising vehicle that allow people throughout the world to see and hear your vision and decide if they will support it. It allows you to test market essentially if the idea is viable or resonates with enough potential investors or donors.

Build your donor base, plan events, and, in time, try for grant money. Try the newer internet based donation concepts - the more fundraising tools in your tool bag, the better.

There are foundations and other sources of grant but they usually require a track record, which, to be honest, after the three or four years of doing the mission, when they will finally look at your organization, you may be out of business by then.

But there are generous individuals who will surprise you. There are car washes, computer sales and a host of other ways to keep the lights on. We sold computers that DC areas companies donated to us over a three year period. We had art shows (unsuccessful) and performances (semi-successful). Early on, we had decided that we would focus on the mission and not as much on the money so that for however long we were open, we would be doing the job we set out to do.

We never had more than a $300,000 budget during any given year, which is very small. We had four to six employees and the rest were interns, volunteers and fellows. Our rent was mostly donated to us by a generous company. For most of the months we were open, I had no idea where the next month's rent was coming from, but it always somehow appeared until the very end. My point here is the same I would say about running a business. If you can look yourself in the eye and say, 'I am' willing to take this chance, even if I lose this much money, time and effort.' For me it was two classic cars, several thousand dollars and more than two years unpaid. If you can say that and know that it is likely only to exist for a short while, but the mission is still important enough to do – do it.

Sometimes the funding finds you. If not, the lives saved or the effort made, though difficult, will leave your soul far richer than you anticipated.

MORE TEMPLATES.

This section includes some templates that may be helpful to you when starting out. You will have to tweak them to suit your organization and specific needs. They can all be found online for free at https://richardobrien.info/cpg-country-reports . Templates included are:

A Crisis Action Plan Worksheet

A Staff Meeting Log

A Press Release

Press Release Formatting

Several Press Release Examples

A Country Fact Sheet

A Country Report Cover

Human Rights Legal Matrix

Example of Full Legal Section – Burundi

CRISIS ACTION PLAN WORKSHEET

Please fill out *every* field as you go. See the example if there are any questions. If additional space is needed, please continue on to a separate sheet.

I. Initial Contact:

Location of event: _____

Source: _____

Time/Manner of contact: _____

II. Contact Board and Staff

Please include time each was contacted and if it was successful (i.e. were they home)

Board Members: _____

_____

_____

_____

Region Staff: _____

_____

III. Confirmation

Wire Services Checked:

_____

_____
_____

_____

News Sources Checked:

_____

_____
_____

_____

Neutral Sources:

IV. Press Release

V. Contact Agencies and Policy Makers

Please list the person contacted, the manner of contact (e-mail, voice mail etc.), the time of contact and the response received. Thanks.

State Department:

Emergency Task Force:

24 Hot Line:

_____

Director/Deputy:

_____

Emergency Coordinator:

_____

Country Desk Officer:

_____

Regional Secretary:

_____

Bureau of Refugees, etc.:

_____

Bureau of Human Rights:

_____

Undersecretary for

Political affairs:

_____

US Mission to UN:

_____

Secretary of State:

_____

Congress

House Foreign Relations Committee

Chairman:

_____

Ranking Member:

_____

Regional sub-committee

Chairman:

_____

Ranking Member:

_____

Senate Foreign Relations Committee

Chairman:

_____

Ranking Member:

_____

Regional Subcommittee

Chairman:

_____

Ranking Member:

_____

Key Staff members for

Region:

_____

TEMPLATE: STAFF MEETING LOG

10/22/03
12:30 PM

Meeting called by:	Type of meeting:
Facilitator:	Note taker:
Timekeeper:	

Attendees:

Please read:

Please bring:

Agenda

Weekly Executive Staff Meeting

*PRESS * RELEASE * TEMPLATE*

FOR IMMEDIATE RELEASE

Contact:

>

> } 4 spaces

>

(Title)

>

> } 2 spaces

"ARLINGTON, VA. - 10/16/2003   (in Bold)(3 spaces)(One sentence title)"

>

> } 2 spaces

(1st paragraph)

>

> } 2 spaces

(2nd paragraph)

>

}

\>   2 spaces

"For more information on the Center for the Prevention of Genocide, please contact us by phone or visit our website at www.genocideprevention.org."

FORMATING AND CONTENT

Use 8 ½ x 11 paper
If e-mail be sure to include a subject line (ex: Massacre in Rwanda)
Use a minimum of one-inch margins on each side of the page
Use **bold** for the headline
Try to keep it to 5 paragraphs of two to three sentences each
If continuing onto the next page use: -more-
After all the last paragraph type: ###
Include all contact info at the top and bottom of the release
Do NOT use excessive adjectives or include opinion
Use inverted pyramid format, the most important information all listed in the first two paragraphs, then supporting information
Make SURE to answer the Who, What, When, Where, Why, How
Include the date in the header
Have at least two other people proof before it is sent off

Headline (In Bold, Meat of the Story)

City, State, Country, Date- Who, What, When, Where, Why, How. Answer without any political spin, but do include quick analysis

Example: Armed Hutu nationalists targeted the minority Tutsi ethnic group in Rwanda's capital city Kigali last night in an apparent reaction to the assassination of Rwandan President Juvenal Habyarimana.

Do not say: Crazed Hutu extremists began to slaughter innocent Tutsi women and children after President Juvenal Habyarimana was assassinated last night.

The next paragraph can include more supporting facts. Try to be specific. Include region, specific villages, towns cities, group names, manner of rights abuse, and any rough estimates

DO NOT overestimate or guess in an effort to get it published. It will only discredit you later.

However, verified parameter figures are acceptable, even if they are sizeable (i.e. between 400 and 900 killed). Include a quote from one of the sources, but do not name them personally, remember, this is the information age, you never know who is reading the Post.

At bottom include any pertinent information or extra sources.

Contact information.

EXAMPLE: FOR IMMEDIATE RELEASE

Contact: Richard O'Brien (703) 528-1002

info@improvetheworld.org

Thousands of Sudanese Refugees Streaming into Chad

Raises Suspicion of Human Rights Violations

ARLINGTON, VA, September 24, 2003 — Increased military activity and unconfirmed massacres have forced an estimated 70,000 refugees from the Darfur states of western Sudan to flee to Chad last week.

The international organization Médecins Sans Frontiéres reports that thousands of Sudanese refugees from western Sudan's Darfur states have sought refuge in Chad to escape fighting between the Sudanese government and the rebels. In the small villages of Tiné and Birak alone, there are some 11,000 Sudanese refugees, 75% of whom are women and children. There are still more refugees in the surrounding villages, and there are more coming from Sudan.

Although the Sudanese government and the Sudan Liberation Movement/Army (SLM/A), the rebel group which operates in Darfur, signed a 45-day ceasefire agreement effective September 6, the SLM/A has accused the government of continuing to target civilians. According to the SLM/A, the government has deliberately attacked civilians by helicopter, gunship, and militia groups almost daily since the agreement went into effect. The government denies these allegations.

Human Rights Watch reported that these alleged attacks have caused thousands of Sudanese refugees to flee Darfur in order to "escape government and militia persecution." The United Nations reports that the conflict has claimed 3,000 lives and displaced 400,000 persons since February 2003.

Confirmations of alleged massacres near Misla and Kutumtowns in Darfur have been difficult to obtain because there are no independent observers on the ground.

EXAMPLE: Russian Government Coerces Chechens to Leave Refugee Camps

Ingushetia, Russia, December 5, 2002 - The Russian government has begun coercively returning Chechen refugees to war-torn Chechnya, several on the ground sources indicate. Up to 20,000 displaced people are at risk of humanitarian abandonment in the height of winter, and the United Nations High Commissioner for Refugees has expressed alarm that the refugees may be left without shelter in the freezing temperatures.

The Russian Human Rights Ombudsman stated last spring that this type of liquidation could result in one of the worst human rights crises in recent Russian history.

According to on the ground sources, the Center for the Prevention of Genocide has learned that the Russian government is using various intimidation tactics to pursue a policy of Chechen refugee repatriation. Gas and electricity have been turned off in certain camps. It has also been reported that migration officials persistently press refugees, asking individuals up to 10 times a day why they have not yet left the camps. It was also reported that refugees have left their tents and returned to find them dismantled by Russian officials. The Los Angeles Times today reported that refugees were offered food, contingent upon indicating that the repatriation was voluntary.

The Russian government has promised to provide adequate shelter in Chechnya, but this is questionable in light of the fact that the facilities to which they have been brought are reported to be missing windows. Some are without heat and are otherwise unlivable. Chechnya still remains consumed by war and is therefore an inhospitable environment for civilians. There have been cases reported of repatriated refugees who have found the conditions in Chechnya undesirable and have since returned to Ingushetia.

The first camps to be liquidated were in Aki-Yurt town. The Russian government promised to complete the process by 20 December, putting in jeopardy up to 18,500 people.

Since 1999, as many as 150,000 Chechen civilians have sought refuge in the neighboring Russian Republic of Ingushetia. Food and shelter have been provided by international humanitarian organizations. At present, no international human rights organizations are permitted to witness the dismantling of camps.

For more information, contact: Richard O'Brien 703-528-1002 http://www.genocideprevention.org/chechnya.htm>.

TEMPLATE: COUNTRY FACT SHEET

[Country Name]

Summary/Danger

[Short summary of the reasons why this particular country is under observation; noting the particular dangers that threaten the area]

Types of Abuse and Danger

[Evidence of the abuses and breaches of human rights, and possibly acts of genocide; include sources]

Field Contacts Verification

*[For public copy, include NGOs, embassies, etc. **DO NOT** mention individual network contacts, especially if it could compromise their anonymity and safety. In the private version, all field contacts should be mentioned, including those barred from the public copy.]*

Dissemination

[All contacts used to disseminate information to policy makers, including politicians on Capitol Hill, the media and perhaps even foreign governments (such as those within the EU).]

Collaborating Human Rights Organizations

[Include here all those in collaboration with the Center for the Prevention of Genocide, such as NGOs or experts.]

REPORT NAME

Organization Name

SUBTITLE

Author

Name

Findings

A paragraph that summarizes the most important information from the report and possible recommendations.

Editorial Board

Names

Board of Directors

Names

407

Law Applicable to Internal Tensions and Armed Conflicts:

	Internal Tensions not = Armed Conflict.	Internal Armed Conflict (Armed conflict between state government and domestic non-governmental armed forces)	International Armed Conflict (Entire body of international law only applies in armed conflict between two or more states)	Internationalized Armed Conflict (Armed conflict between state government and non-governmental armed forces, with foreign government troops intervening on side of domestic dissidents)
Applicable Law	*International Human Rights Law* applies to state parties. Some HR norms also apply to individuals.	*Core Principles of Customary International Law* apply also to internal conflicts. Examples: Principles of Civilian Immunity and Proportionality.	*Customary International Law*	1- Between Domestic Government and Domestic Non-government forces: *Rules of Internal Armed Conflict.*
Applicable Law	In addition, *Domestic Law* applies.	*Article 3* common to the four Geneva Conventions of 1949 applies to all parties (gvmt/non-gvmt) regardless of ratification.	*Four Geneva Conventions of 1949 and Protocol I.* Applicability contingent on ratification.	2- Between Domestic Government troops and Foreign Government forces intervening on side of Domestic Dissidents: *Rules of International Armed Conflict.*
Applicable Law		*Protocol II*, if ratified by state party.	*Non-Derogable International Human Rights Law* applies to state parties. Some HR norms also apply to individuals.	3- Between Domestic Government troops and Foreign Non-Government forces intervening on side of Domestic Dissidents: *Same Rules as Internal Armed Conflict*
Applicable Law		*Non-Derogable International Human Rights Law* applies to state parties. Some HR norms also apply to individuals.	*Domestic Law* usually continues to apply, at least in part.	4- Between any Non-Government forces in any armed conflict in own or third country: *Same Rules as Internal Armed Conflict*
Applicable Law		*Domestic Law* usually continues to apply, at least in part.		*Non-Derogable International Human Rights Law* applies to state parties. Some HR

SAMPLE: BURUNDI LEGAL SECTION

The civil war in Burundi is considered a non-international armed conflict, despite the clearly internationalized aspects of the conflict through the involvement of other countries in the Great Lakes Region. The Democratic Republic of Congo is allowing Burundian Hutu rebel groups to attack locations inside Burundi from Congolese soil. The Democratic Republic of Congo has allowed Burundian rebel groups to stay within its borders in exchange for help in fighting Congolese rebels who are supported by Rwanda. Burundian rebel groups have also established relations with Tanzania and have set up camps on its territory. Rebels are known to take prisoners to locations in Tanzania. The parties to the civil war are the Tutsi minority and the Hutu majority; the Tutsis representing the Burundian army and the Hutus comprising the rebel groups.

Although Burundi currently operates under a transitional constitution that calls for the sharing of power between Hutus and Tutsis, the civil war continues. Despite the power sharing agreement, many Hutus are still fearful of what their fate may become with continued domination of the army by the Tutsi ethnic group (afrol.com). A peace Agreement signed by the major Hutu rebel group and the Burundian government, and which will take effect on December 31, 2002, contained a clause to eventually disarm both the rebels and the army, however, analysts feel that this may not be realistic (UN OCHA). Although one Hutu group has become a party to the cease-fire agreement, and smaller group, the FNL has refused to sit at the table. On December 4 the FNL raided a military position near the capital city of Bujumbura, and close to 3,000 civilians fled their homes upon the arrival of the rebel group (Agence France-Presse). According to UN reports, however, the civilians returned to their homes the next day. Another incident on December 9 was reported when the FNL accused the army of firing on rebel positions (Agence France Presse). The civil war is continuing on a smaller scale than it was prior to the signing of the peace agreement, but Burundi is still not seeing complete peace. However, the African Union is going to continue to try to eventually bring all parties to the conflict into the cease-fire agreement (UN OCHA).

In this crisis, both sides have been guilty of massive human rights violations; the Burundian armed forces have forced many Tutsi into camps and arbitrarily shot people if found outside of the camps, and both Hutu and Tutsi have raided villages and also killed conscientious objectors and other actual or supposed opponents of the own group.

International Humanitarian Law (Law of Warfare)

Geneva Conventions and Additional Protocol II

Burundi became a party to the Geneva conventions in 1971 and acceded to both Additional Protocols in 1993. As indicated in the following paragraphs, the Burundian government has violated many of the protections of civilians in internal armed conflicts provided by Protocol II. Article 4 of Protocol II strengthens and crystallizes Article 3 common to the four Geneva Conventions.

<u>Displacement</u>: One of the most publicized occurrences of this civil war has been the forced displacement of civilians into relocation camps.

> Article 5:1 (b) [Persons deprived of their liberty] shall, to the same extent as the local civilian population, be provided with food and drinking water and be afforded safeguards as regards health and hygiene and protection against the rigors of the climate and the dangers of the armed conflict

The refugee camps do not have adequate shelter, sanitation or resources, and have essentially become breeding grounds for disease (Amnesty International, USCR). People are not permitted to leave the camps let alone return to their agricultural land to maintain it. At times, those who request permission to tend to their lands are forced to pay camp guards to leave but must return to the camp or risk being killed (GlobalSecurity.org). Those who are unable to pay, or who cannot maintain their lands adequately become dependent on food provided by relief organizations, which is seldom sufficient.

> Article 17:1 The displacement of the civilian population shall not be ordered for reasons related to the conflict unless the security of the civilians involved or imperative military reasons so demand. Should such displacements have to be carried out, all possible measure shall be

411

taken in order that the civilian population may be received under satisfactory conditions of shelter, hygiene, health, safety and nutrition.

Article 17:2 Civilians shall not be compelled to leave their own territory for reasons connected with the conflict.

In other words, Article 17 provides protection against any forced movement based on political motives including gaining control over opposition forces. The government of Burundi states that the mass movement of up to 550,000 people since 1993 into these camps has been for the purpose of protecting them against rebel factions. However, as reported by human rights groups, many of the people who are displaced are Hutus and much of the displacement is taking place to maintain control over Hutus, and/or any person thought to be siding with the rebels. The rationale of the army is that if Hutus are placed in camps, the popular support for the rebels will diminish. Additionally, reports state that Burundian officials relocated a group of Hutus from the capital city of Bujumbura in order to exercise greater control over them—clearly, political motives instigated the forced movement (Human Rights Watch).

<u>Murder and Torture including Rape</u>:

Additional Protocol II

Article 4:1　All persons who do not take a direct part or who have ceased to take part

in hostilities, whether or not their liberty has been restricted, are entitled to respect for their person, honor and convictions and religious practices. They shall in all circumstances be treated humanely, without any adverse distinction. It is prohibited to order that there shall be no survivors.

Article 4:2　Without prejudice to the generality of the forgoing, the following acts against the persons referred to in paragraph I are and shall remain prohibited at any time and in any place whatsoever:

(a)　Violence to the life, health and physical or mental well-being of

persons, in particular murder as well as cruel treatment such as torture, mutilation or any form of corporal punishment;

(e)　Outrages upon personal dignity, in particular humiliating and degrading treatment, rape,

413

enforced prostitution and any form of indecent assault;

(f)   Slavery and the slave trade in all forms

The Burundian army is guilty of wide scale violations of this article. Groups known as the Guardians of Peace are groups of men commissioned by the army and forced to serve as part of a para-military cadre to protect civilian communities from rebel attacks and to ensure that people do not escape from the camps. Many reports state that the Guardians have turned against the people they are protecting whether they are from the same ethnic group or not. Because they are not paid the Guardians have stolen from and threatened the lives of people in order to exercise power over them and force people to give them food and money. Their exercise of power also includes acts of rape, which are seldom reported because women fear retribution. The Guardians further diverge from their mission when they follow military orders to kill anyone who refuses to go into the relocation camps or who is found off the grounds of the camp without permission. People not in camps are suspected of supporting the rebels and face death without trial or judgment. If the Guardians refuse to follow military orders, they are subject to beating and/or death.

Acts of aggression against women, including rape and forced servitude also violate this portion of Protocol II. In the government sponsored camps women are often being raped but are too afraid to speak about it. Rebels have been reported to abduct women for sexual and domestic servitude in their camps. (Human Rights Watch)

Child Soldiers:

Article 4:3   Children shall be provided with the care and aid they require, and in particular:

(c)   Children who have not attained the age of fifteen years shall neither be recruited in the armed forces or groups nor allowed to take part in hostilities

Many Guardians of Peace and many army recruits are children under the age of 15. Government as well as rebel groups are guilty of recruiting young children, or forcibly taking them to join their ranks. The army has been reported to recruit children from relocation camps, and rebel groups have been reported to kidnap school age children from grades four to six and forcibly inducting them to be part of the rebel forces. Both the army and Rebels send children into combat in front of themselves so that the children are killed first. As part of army induction ceremonies, officials force children to kill other children who have refused to join. Usually the killings are conducted with machetes or other such tools. If a child refuses to participate in the induction he faces death or severe beating.

The United States Committee for Refugees reported that the Tutsi leader of the 1996 coup, Pierre Buyoya, encouraged youths to take up arms to help defend Burundi, and made public announcements to give weapons to young Tutsis (www.africaaction.org).

Rome ICC Statute

Burundi has signed, but not ratified the *Rome Statute of the International Criminal Court (ICC),* the first permanent tribunal established to end impunity for war crimes, genocide and crimes against humanity. It is noteworthy that Burundi has

415

signed the *ICC Statute*, because signing an international treaty constitutes a general endorsement of the instrument. Although signature does not commit a country to proceed to ratification, it does create an obligation to refrain from conduct that would defeat or undermine the treaty's objectives.

Moreover, genocide, crimes against humanity, war crimes and many other crimes covered by the ICC Statute are crimes under Customary International Law, regardless of treaty obligations. For serious international crimes, no immunity is afforded.

The definition of Genocide in Article 6 of the ICC Statute closely resembles that of the *Genocide Convention*.

Articles 7:1   For the purpose of [the ICC] Statute, "crime against humanity" means any of the following acts when committed as part of a widespread or systematic attack directed against any civilian population, with knowledge of the attack:

(a)   Murder;

(b)   Extermination;

(c)   Enslavement;

(d)   Deportation or forcible transfer of population;

(e)   Imprisonment or other severe deprivation of physical liberty in violation of fundamental rules of international law;

(f)   Torture;

(g) Rape, sexual slavery, enforced prostitution, forced pregnancy, enforced sterilization, or any other form of sexual violence of comparable gravity;

(h) Persecution against any identifiable group or collectivity on political, racial, national, ethnic, cultural, religious, gender as defined in paragraph 3, or other grounds that are universally recognized as impermissible under international law, in connection with any act referred to in this paragraph or any crime within the jurisdiction of the Court;

(i) Enforced disappearance of persons;

(j) The crime of apartheid;

(k) Other inhumane acts of a similar character intentionally causing great suffering, or serious injury to body or to mental or physical health.

Article 8:2   For the purpose of [the ICC] Statute, "war crimes" means:

(a) Grave breaches of the Geneva Conventions of 12 August 1949, namely, any of the following acts against persons or property protected under the provisions of the relevant Geneva Convention:

i. Willful killing;

ii. Torture or inhuman treatment, including biological experiments;

417

iii. Willfully causing great suffering, or serious injury to body or health;

iv. Extensive destruction and appropriation of property, not justified by military necessity and carried out unlawfully and wantonly;

v. Compelling a prisoner of war or other protected person to serve in the forces of a hostile Power;

vi. Willfully depriving a prisoner of war or other protected person of the rights of fair and regular trial;

vii. Unlawful deportation or transfer or unlawful confinement;

viii. Taking of hostages.

The Burundian army's wide scale murder; forcible transfer of population; torture; persecution against an identifiable group; pillage; rape; mutilation; and its practice of forcibly recruiting children under age 15 to participate actively in hostilities are all violations of the customary law provisions listed above.

The rebel forces in Burundi are also guilty of some of these crimes including wide scale murder; torture; persecution of an identifiable group; rape; pillage; subjecting persons to forced physical labor; mutilation; and forcibly recruiting children under age 15 to participate actively in hostilities. Each of these actions are examples of crimes against humanity under the ICC Statute, and most are crimes under international law as well.

Human Rights Law

International Convention on the Elimination of All Forms of Racial Discrimination
Burundi ratified this convention in 1977. Article 2, 1(a) of the Convention states, "Each State Party undertakes not to sponsor, defend or support racial discrimination by any persons or organizations…" However, the Burundian Tutsi dominated army is guilty of participating in racially discriminatory practices against the Hutu majority and against Tutsis who are thought to support or assist Hutu rebels. Similarly, Hutu rebels are guilty of targeting and killing members of the Tutsi group, and of their own group for similar reasons. The government is attempting to rectify the divide between Hutus and Tutsi under the new power-sharing agreement. However, killings and persecution against both ethnic groups are still occurring.

International Covenant on Civil and Political Rights (ICCPR)
Burundi acceded to the ICCPR in 1990. Provisions of this Covenant that have been violated include:

Article 7   No one shall be subjected to torture or to cruel, inhuman or degrading treatment or punishment.

Article 10:1   All persons deprived of their liberty shall be treated with humanity and with respect for the inherent dignity of the human person.

Article 14:1   All persons shall be equal before the courts and tribunals.

Article 20:1   Any propaganda for war shall be prohibited by law.
Article 20:2   Any advocacy of national, racial or religious hatred that constitutes incitement to discrimination, hostility or violence shall be prohibited by law.

Article 26   All persons are equal before the law and are entitled without any discrimination to the equal protection of the law.

Convention against Torture and Other Cruel, Inhuman or Degrading Treatment or Punishment

Burundi acceded to this treaty in 1993. As described above, torture at the hands of the army against people in relocation camps, against rebels and against people hiding in bush areas, has become a commonly reported practice.

Article 1:   For the purposes of this Convention, torture means any act by which severe pain or suffering, whether physical or mental, is intentionally inflicted on a person for such purposes as obtaining from him or a third person information or a confession, punishing him for an act he or a third person has committed or is suspected of having committed, or intimidating or coercing him or a third person, or for any reason based on discrimination of any kind, when such pain or suffering is inflicted by or at the instigation of or with the consent or acquiescence of a public official or other person acting in an official capacity.

Article 4:1   Each State Party shall ensure that all acts of torture are offences under its criminal law. The same shall apply to an attempt to commit torture and to an act by any person which constitutes complicity or participation in torture.

Article 10:1   Each State Party shall ensure that….the prohibition against torture [is] fully included in the training of law enforcement personnel, civil or military, medical personnel, public officials and other persons who may be involved in the custody, interrogation or treatment of any individual subjected to any form of arrest, detention or imprisonment.

Convention on the Rights of the Child

Burundi ratified this convention in 1990. The practice of government as well as rebel groups of forcibly recruiting children to join their ranks violate the Convention.

Article 19:1   States Parties shall take all appropriate legislative, administrative, social and educational measures to protect the child from all forms of physical or mental violence..."

Article 37 :a   No child shall be subjected to torture or other cruel, inhuman or degrading treatment or punishment.

The manner in which children are recruited, forcibly taken, and treated by both the army and the rebel groups in Burundi is a clear violation of Article 37.

Article 38   States Parties shall take all feasible measures to ensure that persons who have not attained the age of fifteen years do not take a direct part in hostilities. In accordance with their obligations under international humanitarian law to protect the civilian population in armed conflicts, States Parties shall take all feasible measures to ensure protection and care of children who are affected by an armed conflict.

African [Banjul] Charter on Human and Peoples' Rights

Burundi acceded to this Charter in 1989. The Banjul Charter endorses the principles of the treaties mentioned in the foregoing. The Banjul Charter includes:

Article 4   Human beings are inviolable. Every human being shall be entitled to respect for his life and the integrity of his person. No one may be arbitrarily deprived of this right.

Article 5   Every individual shall have the right to the respect of the dignity inherent in a human being and to the recognition of his legal status. All forms of exploitation and degradation of man particularly slavery, slave trade, torture, cruel, inhuman or degrading punishment and treatment shall be prohibited.

Article 18:3   The State shall ensure the elimination of every discrimination against women and also ensure the protection of the rights of the woman and the child as stipulated in international declarations and conventions.

Article 28   Every individual shall have the duty to respect and consider his fellow beings without discrimination, and to maintain relations aimed at promoting, safeguarding and reinforcing mutual respect and tolerance.

Sources:

- Africaaction.org, "Burundi: USCR Statement/VOA Report; Coup in Burundi: Initial Recommendations and Analysis," July 30, 1996, http://www.africaaction.org/docs96/uscr9608.htm
- Afrolnews.com, "Still no Peace Agreement for Burundi," November 8, 2002, http://www.afrol.com/News2002/bur015_peace_agreement.htm

- Agence France-Presse, "3,000 Civilians flee fighting near Burundi capital: governor," December 4, 2002, http://wwww.reliefweb.int/w/rwb.nsf/6686f45896f15dbc8 52567ae00530132/a781d96cdb3fba5149256c86001c0d27? OpenDocument

- Agence France-Presse, "Burundi rebels accuse army of breaching cease-fire," December 9, 2002, http://wwww.reliefweb.int/w/rwb.nsf/6686f45896f15dbc8 52567ae00530132/d47a8943e90b042849256c8b001b3ea5 ?OpenDocument

- Amnesty International, "Burundi: Forced relocation; new patterns of human rights abuses," July 15, 1997, http://www.web.amnesty.org/ai.nsf/index/AFR160191997

- Global Security.org, "Burundi Civil War," July 15, 2002, http://www.globalsecurity.org/military/world/war/burundi. htm

- Human Rights Watch, "Emptying the Hills: Regroupment Camps in Burundi," July 2000, http://www.hrw.org/reports/2000/burundi2/

- Human Rights Watch, "World Report 2002: Africa: Burundi," 2002, http://www.hrw.org/wr2k2/africa2.html

- U.S. Committee for Refugees, "Country Report: Burundi," 2002, http://www.refugees.org/world/countryrpt/africa/2000/bur undi.htm

- UN OCHA, Integrated Regional Information Network, " Burundi: Interview with Mamdou Bah, AU representative," December 12, 2002, http://wwww.reliefweb.int/w/rwb.nsf/6686f45896f15dbc8

52567ae00530132/4b12e281e4da5148c1256c8d003e003f?
OpenDocument

- UN OCHA, Integrated Regional Information Network,
  "Burundi: Government, main rebel group sign cease fire
  deal," December 3, 2002,
  http://wwww.reliefweb.int/w/rwb.nsf/6686f45896f15dbc8
  52567ae00530132/a06e4169d6084c22c1256c840041aa2d
  ?OpenDocument

Author on a Creative Loafing magazine cover for the CPG's work on Sulawesi, Indonesia.

ABOUT THE AUTHOR

Richard O'Brien was raised in Toronto, Canada and Sarasota, Florida. He is a product of Culver Academies, American University and Georgetown University and wrote much of this manuscript in 2014 as a visiting scholar at (S-CAR) now the Carter School, at George Mason University. As a teacher, he instructed classes in *International Human Rights*, *Conflict in the Modern World* and *World Ideologies* at the University of

South Florida and *World History, Women's Issues, American History, Geography and U.S Government* at the Duke Ellington School of the Arts in DC. A writer and human rights activist, he founded The Center for the Prevention of Genocide (CPG) from 2000 – 2004. The CPG actively worked to intervene and prevent genocide, massacres, human rights violations and starvation in in the following areas: Sulawesi, Indonesia, Nuba, Sudan, Darfur, Sudan, Chechnya, Colombia, Ituri and N. & S. Kivu, D. R. Congo, Uganda, Burundi, Zimbabwe, and Gujarat, India. During its existence the CPG also fielded a lecture series, a TV series, a yearly journal, more than twenty human rights reports and an India-Pakistan Nuclear Conflict Warning paper. By the time of its closing, the CPG had an office staff of 25 employees, interns, fellows and volunteers and a network of more than 700 individuals in hotspots worldwide.

His human rights work has been featured in Business Insider and on the cover of Creative Loafing, he has been published in the Washington post and the New York Times, interviewed on National TV and NPR and has given testimony in Congressional Sub-Committee and at the U.N. Subsequently, he has authored *Women Presidents and Prime Ministers*, 2017, 2018 and 2024 editions and has a TED X lecture on the same subject. He calls the DMV and Florida his home, and is the proud father of twins, Annalise and John A.C. O'Brien.

JENOCO PUBLISHING www.jenoco.org
Jenoco Publishing publishes works in human rights, women's issues, fiction and non-fiction and the twenty plus unpublished manuscripts of the O'Brien family.

Experience the most harrowing stories of 100 years of genocide and a group of students who prevent it. $19.99 Abridged. 258 pages.

The Unabridged version features 200 additional pages, a 'how to' manual on how to create a human rights early warning system. $34.99

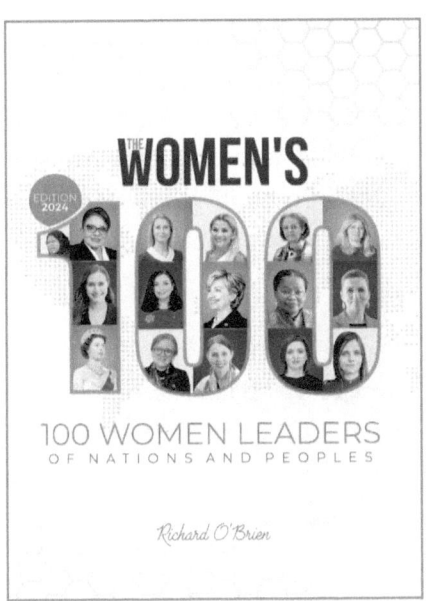

The Women's 100: 100 Women Leaders of Nations and Peoples

By Richard O'Brien

Meet the more than 100 women who have served as President or Prime Minister of their respective countries around the world and learn the stories of their adventures, struggles and accomplishments.

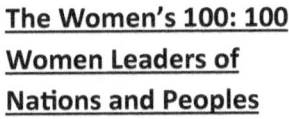

It's Like This

By Jack O'Brien

Ecclesiastic muralist and President of the Canadian's Writer's Guild John (Jack) O'Brien lived his life to the fullest, a lifelong deep love, the horrors and camaraderie of war and his art. He has taken his artist's pallet to put you on the battlefield, in the bedroom and in his mind. $14.99 Poetry. Vivid imagery.

Touretters. This rare collection of 30 autobiographical stories written by parents and individuals who are living with TS. This book helps demystify the condition and touch your heart.

Non-Fiction. $19.99 Vivid imagery and language.

A Long Road Home By Dennis Mitch Maley.

After losing her mother to cancer, 22-year old aspiring singer Jenny Harris couldn't be more alone. Enter T.K. Connolly, a debauched recluse of a writer who is revealed as her biological father. Thet share a journey of self-discovery in the South. Fiction. $19.99

Matthew Mejia's TheFEEL marks his first book of poetry and is raw, powerful and vulnerable. Featured in Southern California College literature classes as an emerging talent.
Poetry. $14.99

www.ingramcontent.com/pod-product-compliance
Lightning Source LLC
Chambersburg PA
CBHW020429130626
46549CB00001B/46